DON'T FORGET YOUR LUNCH

Diapers to Diploma Parenting Wisdom

Kelli Wheeler

**Author of
Momservations®: The Fine Print of
Parenting**

Hawthorne Street Press

DON'T FORGET YOUR LUNCH: Diapers to Diploma Parenting
Wisdom

Copyright © 2020 by Kelli Wheeler

Photos by Kelli Wheeler, Ron Silveira,
Whitney Wheeler, and Wendy Finnecy

ISBN: 978-1-7357465-0-0

Library of Congress Control Number: 2020918165.

Hawthorne Street Press
P.O. Box 60502
Sacramento, CA 95860

Printed in the United States of America

Momservations.com
Twitter.com/Momservations
Facebook.com/Momservations
Instagram.com/Momservations

Dedicated to Logan and Whitney,

my heart walking around outside my body.

Contents

CHAPTER 1: In the Beginning There Was Chaos

CHAPTER 2: School Daze

CHAPTER 3: Preteen Testing Ground

CHAPTER 4: Rule Book for Parenting in the Digital Age

CHAPTER 5: Teenager Tales

CHAPTER 6: Operation Independence

The decision to have a child is momentous. It is to forever have your heart go walking around outside your body.

~ Elizabeth Stone

INTRODUCTION

Parenting: The Endless Conversation

Momservation: Parenting—the collection of wonderful life stories you live out simply because one day you rolled across the cozy, comfy castle and said to Hubby, "Let's make this more interesting…"

☺   ☺   ☺

It still amazes me when people write or stop me to say how much they enjoy reading my Momservations® column and blog. It's always a great relief to know I haven't just been amusing myself all this time.

Over the years, friends and readers I've met frequently ask me if I ever run out of things to talk about. Let me put it this way: In addition to a monthly parenting column that was published for 15 years by Sacramento's Inside Publications, publishing my first book, MOMSERVATIONS®: THE FINE PRINT OF PARENTING, continuing to write a weekly blog, speaking to groups about parenting, producing freelance articles for parenting publications, and now culminating with this "greatest hits" collection in your hands...If that is not proof enough the topic of parenting provides endless fodder for me, my husband (he of tired ears) can attest I *always* have something to say.

In fact, I have a harder time narrowing down what to talk about. There's potty training nightmares, cute kid quotables, education anxiety, family dynamics, discipline issues, baby's firsts, bullies and friends, heartwarming milestones, health scares, holiday traditions, teenager troubles, sleepless nights, crazy schedules, fun family memories—name any topic and I can tie it back into a parenting experience that is universal.

It's fascinating to me that as soon as you have a kid, you instantly have a connection and topic of conversation with anyone else who's ever had a child. It's a fraternity of about a three billion people. The world's biggest community chat room.

The very nature of parenting puts you in proximity with other parents eager for commiseration, validation and bragging rights. For example, when I'm waiting to pick up my kids from school, I'm talking with other moms. We gossip about teachers, compare homework hassles, bemoan the rigors of after school activities, worry about our children's academic progress, brag about our kids without making it sound like we are, wonder what we're going to make for dinner, coordinate playdates, and share news about friends.

When I'm visiting with other parents at sports practice we gossip about coaches, compare scheduling hassles, bemoan the rigors of getting each child to their respective practices, worry about our kids' athletic abilities and confidence, wonder what we should pick up at the store for dinner, brag about our kids without making it sound like we are, coordinate carpool schedules, and share inside information about skills of kids on other teams.

When I'm hanging out with my mom's group friends we gossip about our babysitters, compare husband hassles, bemoan the rigors of consistent discipline, worry about balancing work and family, brag about our kids without making it sound like we are, wonder what to do with all the leftovers in the fridge, coordinate girls' night out, and share parenting horror stories we've heard.

When I'm catching up with my childhood friends we gossip about classmates who have turned into surprisingly good parents, compare housework hassles, bemoan the rigors of trying to still look like the teenagers we used to be, worry about our parenting techniques, brag about our kids without making it sound like we are, wonder if we can get our husband's to take us out to dinner, and share new news about old friends.

When I'm making small talk with parents I've just met, we gossip about local schools, compare our children's stats (age, grade, school, teacher, etc.), bemoan the rigors of trying to find more time to fit it all in, worry about our kids making the right friends, brag about our kids without making it sound like we are, wonder if we already did pizza night this week, and share our connection to mutual acquaintances.

The point is, there is always someone, somewhere I can yack at about parenting. Whether I'm in a grocery line, a Target aisle, a Costco food court, a PetSmart check-out, at a local park, at sign-ups, waiting at a restaurant, filling up my car, picking up the dry cleaning, ordering a pizza, or buying Girl Scout cookies, I can find another parent mirroring my experience at that very moment and we can instantly find something to talk about and connect on.

By writing Momservations® for the last decade and a half, I like to think I tapped into a rich vein of conversation that's been around since the birth of Cain and Abel with Adam and Eve lamenting about how to handle sibling rivalry. I've been lucky enough to have the publisher and editors of Inside Arden believe in me and give me free reign to subject people to what I think. I've been blessed with children who provide me endless material. I'm grateful that anyone cares to read what I might have to say.

And I'm giddy that with each new birth of a child two more members are initiated into this parenting chat room— potentially giving me another set of ears to tug on.

PROLOGUE

I always knew I wanted a family one day. When I pictured my perfect 2.5 kids plus dog to go along with my perfect husband and house with white picket fence, I saw us frolicking on our impossibly green front lawn, or splashing in the pool together, or laughing and singing as we rode our bikes down the tree-lined driveway.

Yeah, about that. Turns out kids don't usually arrive into a family school-age and ready for recreation as I pictured them, let alone able to wipe their own butts and buckle their own seatbelts.

Let's just say, infancy wasn't my best genre. By the time I had my two kids, a boy and a girl seventeen months apart, I was nearly done in by the sleepless nights, what-are-you-trying-to-tell-me? crying, and the Groundhog Day movie-like daily routine of sleep, eat, poop, pump, nap, bath, play, eat, poop, pump, repeat.

When my kids became old enough to say, "Mommy, my ear hurts," now we were getting somewhere.

Thank goodness the joys of parenting start early with the reward of firsts: smiles, giggles, roll-overs, crawling, talking, walking, and slobbery open-mouth kisses and pudgy-wristed waves hello. And this crazy urge to wrap your babies in bubble-wrap to protect your heart that now lives outside your body.

Besides the tremendous amount of heavy lifting that goes into being a parent (Mom and Dad, you made it look too easy), what I could have never anticipated about my perfect vision of parenthood was the take your breath away, heart-constricting, all-consuming love that instantly turns you from a "me" to a "we" person the instant your babies are born. Attach to that an equally debilitating fear for your new, young charges' safety…and parenthood isn't for the faint of heart.

So you vow to do your best, gain new respect for your parents (along with offering an apology), and dig in trying to reward the universe for blessing you with, obviously, the most beautiful, smart, talented, wonderful children ever to walk the earth. With a prayer of "Please, Lord, don't let me screw this up," you roll up your sleeves and get to work trying to launch some amazing people out into the world.

When I emerged from the fog of two kids under two, fairly confident that we could finally take the mommy training wheels off, I began writing my Momservations® family column. I never claimed to know what I was doing, but merely invited everyone along for the ride of figuring it out together—new parents, experienced parents, grandparents.

It was a journey that began so agonizingly slow during the dependency of infancy that I would hiss at parents who told me to savor these moments because they go so fast, "Then how about you come and breast feed from sore nipples at three in the morning?"

A journey that suddenly swept me up in nightly baths and bedtime books, sack lunches and reading logs, field trips and carpools, spelling bees and talent shows, soccer, swimming, baseball, ballet, softball, band, theater, water polo, basketball, volleyball, football, volunteering and sideline cheering, hosting and coaching…a calendar more color-coded than a Girl Scout cookie order form.

By the time my kids started high school, I was cursing myself for not taking seriously the mother who warned me in Target with my crying toddler and infant, "The days are long but the years are short." I was starting to have panic attacks after every home game, speech tournament, Homecoming rally and spring formal. Who hit the fast-forward button? The countdown to an empty nest ticked loudest in a house left empty by driving teens off to meet friends.

As 18 years flew by, I hoped that at the end of documenting the child-rearing years I would finally be able to say, "HA! See? I didn't screw it up and the kids turned out more than okay—they turned out amazing!"

But then, if I was being honest with myself I'd have to admit: These two little people who were randomly/cosmically assigned to call me "Mom" and my husband, Trey, "Dad" really came out already who they were going to be. We just happened to be along for the ride. And to make sure they didn't get diaper rash or forget their permission slip.

It's been one hell of a ride. Not perfect, but better than I could have ever imagined for my imaginary 2.5 kids and dog.

Join me now in taking a look back to see what worked, what didn't work, and when that trip with the kids actually becomes a real vacation.

CHAPTER 1

In the Beginning There Was Chaos

Momservations®
Thank Heaven for Little Boys and Girls

- It's too bad the closest a man will ever feel to the miracle of life kicking inside him is on chili cheese dog night.
- Giving birth is relief in knowing your child will never be a bigger literal pain in the ass than the day they were born.
- Holding your child for the first time is confirmation that you did indeed do something amazing with your life.
- A baby's first smile is to know you are loved for just being you.
- Babies are God's way of reminding us that change can be a good thing.
- Nothing beats new car smell like new baby smell.
- If we knew how quickly our children would outgrow us, we'd never set them down as babies.
- It is impossible to know how fiercely you can love someone with the personality of a turnip until you've held your newborn baby in your arms.
- To snuggle a baby on your chest is to know in that moment everything is right in the world.
- If you want to know what trust looks like, gaze into the eyes of a baby.
- Every time a baby cries in the night and someone gets up from a dead sleep, a mother earns her wings.
- Baby giggles instantly changes sacrifice into joy.
- You don't know what you're capable of until faced with the variety of fluids that can come out of a baby.
- The true gift of your children is realizing you weren't really living until they came along.

Every Day is Mother's Day

Momservation: It's hard to be a "me" person when a "we" is involved.

☺ ☺ ☺

Before I had kids one of my favorite things to do was sleep in on Sunday morning, read the paper in bed, and if it was football season, transfer from bed to couch to take in a few games. I guess I did the same if it wasn't football season too.

I distinctly remember when I gave that all up—Friday, October 24, 1999, 7:31 p.m. As I stared into the blue eyes of my newborn son wondering what he must be thinking, I detected an answer.

"It's all about me now, Mom."

And how.

On that fateful day my life was turned upside down forever. And if that wasn't enough, I doubled the fun 17 months later with a girl. It is impossible to be a "me" person when a "we" is involved. Especially when the "we" is a helpless infant who needs constant love and attention.

I remember rolling over at 5 a.m. to the wails of a hungry newborn on the first Sunday after becoming Mom and saying to my husband, "I won't be sleeping in again for another 18 years am I?"

Make that 18 years and 17 months.

Now when Mother's Day rolls around, my husband and kids know exactly what Mommy wants for her special day. They let me sleep in as late as I want, and when I wake up, the Sunday paper is at the foot of the bed. And since Mother's Day is not during football season, they offer me my next favorite indulgence, going to the movies—by myself. The gift of "me" time for a mother is priceless.

Seriously though, Mother's Day to me is every day of the year. It is a perpetual gift that I feel so blessed to receive. Some days I wish I could wrap up each little giggle and look of wonderment in tiny packages to save forever. I would re-gift them to myself when my babies' voices turn deep with age and I've heard for the hundredth time, "Yeah Mom, I know."

Every day brings new adventure, whether challenging or rewarding. Some days I sit back and envelop myself in their innocence and freedom of responsibility, becoming a kid again myself. Other days when the work of motherhood threatens to bring me down, I try to remind myself to enjoy the journey. Even the worst days will make the joyous ones seem that much brighter and will become part of our family history.

I believe children are little reminders of heaven to bring with us on our journey. They make us see past ourselves and help us reap the benefits of investing in someone else's happiness. How can it not be a gift from God when you realize someone else's happiness can become your own?

Momservations®
Survival Tips for New Parents

1. **Sleep when the baby sleeps.** Or, what are you doing awake right now? If you're lucky, newborns will give you 3-4 hour stretches of being asleep. While they're sleeping if you're trying to catch up on all the things that fall to the wayside when caring for an infant you will soon become a zombie. Zombies don't make good parents. Maybe take that shower you've been needing, but then get some sleep—you're going to need it for this job.

2. **Create a routine.** Welcome to the movie *Ground Hog Day*—mind-numbing repetition is now your life. The baby wakes up, you change it, you feed it, you have some awake time together, rinse, repeat. Yes, you will do this over and over aching for that first smile or roll-over to change things up, but this will also be your saving grace. Babies like routine and cry less when you meet their needs. When their needs are met, then you can meet yours—as long as it fits with the schedule.

3. **Get a good diaper bag.** Because it is now an extension of your body. Like a good Boy Scout you need to always be prepared. Make it functional, not cute. I actually got a backpack from REI because

    A) Then Hubby would carry it without protest of it was too girly (key)

  B) You could wear it on both shoulders distributing the weight more evenly of all the crap you need to keep a baby happy

  C) A backpack has more pockets, compartments, and functionality than standard cutesy diaper bags.

4. **Invest in a good stroller and car seat.** These babies are in it for the long haul (both the equipment and the kid). Your infant will turn into a baby, then a toddler, then a kid who needs to be transported everywhere. Try to find strollers and car seats that will transition through the stages safely and then buy a good one that will last and take the abuse of daily use. It will save you money in the long run and your kid is worth it despite the ill will you harbor them at 3 a.m.

5. **Buy in bulk.** Diapers, baby wipes, formula, baby food, Diaper Genie refills, onsies, burp cloths, and Shout stain remover. Those things you use on nearly an hourly basis go quickly and you will need for many, many moons. Stock up on them when they're on sale, buy them at Costco or Sam's Club, and buy them when you think you have enough and don't need more. You always need more.

6. **Get out of the house.** Despite the little old lady in Target who's giving you the stink-eye for taking a fresh newborn out of the house already, continue to do it. For your sanity and for your baby's immunity. Studies have shown sheltering your baby for fear of germs actually makes them more sensitive and more susceptible without exposure to the outside world. Plus, you will go crazy if

you don't get adult interaction. Join a playgroup, go for a walk, stroll the mall, take Gymboree classes, find excuses to get out and be social.

7. **Splurge on gadgets.** Necessity is the mother of invention and mothers are creating lots of new products to make parenting easier. When my kids were little it was the Diaper Genie, the Baby Bjorn, and the multi-serving formula dispenser. Now there's the mamaRoo bouncer, video monitors, wipe warmers, and hi-tech high chairs. If it keeps you from dissolving into a fit of frustrated tears, it's worth every penny.

8. **Change your perspective.** When the seasoned mother in the grocery store tells your sleep-deprived, sanity-by-a-thread self to enjoy this time because it's fleeting—try not to flip her off and tell her, "Yeah, time really flies at 2 a.m. with a screaming baby!" Trust her. Infancy was not my best genre, but now I wish I had kissed their little toes one more time, snuggled them a little longer instead of getting to the laundry, and could feel again my cheek lying on their impossibly silky soft heads.

9. **Parent on your terms.** Take the advice you need and ignore the advice you don't. If you and your baby are happier with a halo of pacifiers around their head to soothe themselves, who cares about the naysayers? I've yet to see a kid walk a graduation procession with a binkie in their mouth. Don't want to breastfeed, want to go back to work, believe in a family bed? Everyone's got an opinion, but the only one that matters is your own. You're

raising this kid not them and I haven't met a perfect parent yet.

10. **Ask for help.** If you try to be super-mom the only thing you'll succeed in is being super stressed, super sleep-deprived, super cranky, and super emotional. Let your husband feed the baby too much. Let your mother-in-law put the wrong outfit on. Let your neighbor bring you their horrible chicken casserole. Call your dad to come awkwardly hold the baby so you can shower. Call your best friend to sing off-key to the baby just so you can get a moment alone. Let people who want to help you, help. Ask for help when you need it without judgment if they're doing it right. Parenting is hard and you can take any help you can get. That's what makes you a better parent.

Who's Having Thanksgiving?

Momservation: That new baby smell seals the deal every time.

☺   ☺   ☺

Whoever has the new baby wins.

That's what it comes down to during the holiday season and the fight for who gets to host Thanksgiving, who doesn't have to travel, or who can get families to compromise and finally come up with a solution to the age old question: Who's having Thanksgiving?

So all you new parents out there who are having a hard time wading through your exhaustion to find the bright side of sleepless nights, stinky diapers, incessant crying, and no time to fulfill your own needs, here is a great perk to your infant until they start rewarding you with smiles: family will do anything to see them.

For the first three years of being married, it was never even a consideration that coming to our home with the shower curtain closet doors and mismatched furniture could be a solution to which side of the family we spent Thanksgiving with. We either went to the Bay Area or we went to Monterey and one time we tried bringing the Bay Area family to Monterey. It was a precarious juggle of trying to keep everyone happy and not making one family feel like their grown baby was being stolen away by the new family.

Enter Logan Gene Wheeler, 7 pounds, 6 ounces, 19 inches long, one month before Thanksgiving.

When I told my mom (who lived in Palm Springs and had been shafted the previous three Thanksgivings due to distance) that I couldn't imagine traveling with an infant so soon, she quickly hatched a plan.

"Then we'll come to you!"

"What about Jeff and his kids? Doesn't he have them this Thanksgiving?" I asked not wanting to create a problem for my mom's husband.

"We'll just bring the boys. We'll get a hotel room!" Problem was solved for Mom even though I wasn't sure how two teenagers were going to enjoy being dragged to Sacramento or how two other sides of families would take being out of the running for Baby's First Thanksgiving.

I soon had answers. Dad didn't even consider going to Monterey to be with his family as we had for my entire life. He and his dog were taking the office with the loveseat hide-a-bed. My aunt Sandie and Gramma, the two reigning hostesses of Monterey Thanksgivings quickly broke tradition too, recruiting Auntie Chris and snapping up a hotel room. My in-laws, once they were comfortable that my sister-in-law's family had plans in the Bay Area, jumped on the idea, waving off the inconvenience of round-trip driving on Thanksgiving.

"I got ol' Shirl to keep me company," my father-in-law chuckled in his deep baritone referring to his wife.

Even my brother, stationed in Washington and who I had spent a rare holiday with since he joined the Navy at 18, was driving fifteen hours with his family and taking the guest room.

I harbored little delusion that everyone was turning tradition on its ear just to see me and Trey. Traveling long distances, giving up comfort, and squeezing themselves into our home around a Thanksgiving table that only a few years before had been a picnic table (that had hosted more games of Quarters than china plate dinners), was all for the new baby.

Logan, he who mainly slept, ate, and pooped (though quite adorably) was the Thanksgiving whisperer; he was bringing everyone together. Because when you have four generations of family bridging the generation gap, three divorced individuals agreeing to play nice, and two different sides of families eager to come together—all to see one little baby—it brings home the meaning of the holidays.

Family.

Of course, once everyone got their fill of holding the baby, snuggling the baby, smelling the baby, gushing over the baby, and putting stickers on the baby (Logan would get you back one day, Cousin Jake), we were back to jostling over who was going to have Thanksgiving the next year.

Mom won. All the passengers on the airplane lost because Logan had an undiagnosed ear infection.

Make a Note of It

Momservation: In the craziness of raising kids, of course you're going to forget some things. But you won't forget the truly important things.

☺   ☺   ☺

If you were to look at my children's baby books it would look like my kids stopped aging somewhere around the time the first molars came in (about two years for those of you who didn't even get that far).

That's alright though. I know I'm in good company. Show me a mother who has religiously kept *all* her children's baby books up to date and I'll show you a woman desperate to cross something off her bucket list.

Like most moms, I came out of the gates strong. I have little lima bean ultrasound photos in both my children's baby books. I also have the updated ultrasound photos where they're finally starting to resemble babies and you swear they already have your nose and daddy's lips.

Both kids have their hospital bracelets and birth announcements in the book, but my first born, Logan, has his neatly taped to the corresponding page with loving notations written underneath. My second born, Whitney, just has hers thrown in the baby book box.

I did fill out the family tree for both (easy), and what the pop culture was the year they were born (fun). In Logan's book I completed pages in great detail titled *Sweet Preparations, Nesting,* and *The Great Day.* Experiencing my first pregnancy, the novelty of it so wondrous and exciting, I eagerly wrote out answers to prompts like *My appearance during pregnancy* and *How I felt about being pregnant.* Here's one of my notations: "…in the end it got uncomfortable and it was hard to sleep, but I couldn't wait to meet my first baby!"

I never got around to those pages in Whitney's book. If I had it probably would've said, "Get this baby out of here and off my bladder already! Isn't it enough that I won't get any sleep when he/she arrives?"

I did fill out the pages of "firsts" for both, because no matter how many babies you have those never get old or too tedious to make a note of. Those delightful milestones of first smile, first tooth, crawling, walking; first word, first peepee in the potty easily make the book. Over the years I've also hastily stuffed in things like first haircut, first tooth, and first drawing. Plus, all over the house in drawers and closets are mementos from other firsts that never made it into the book.

In fact, I have a drawer filled with slips of paper marking important milestones, funny quotes or cute observations I thought I would one day add to the kids' baby books. Even if I never do, I'm just happy to have these back-up aids to my memory because I know I'm going to blink and my children will be grown. I would be devastated if I couldn't recall that funny thing my son said when he was two or how old my daughter was when she sang for the first time, "You Gotta Fight for Your Right to Party." I don't want to be left with an empty baby book and faded memories.

The truth is, you think you will always remember those adorable, precious things your child does and every detail of each momentous event. You won't. That's why I always have my camera ready and I make a note of it. Sometimes it's something quick jotted down to jog my memory or a more detailed account with exact quotes.

Here're a few things I made note of that I didn't realize I'd already forgotten:

- On 6/26/02 Logan, 2 ½, sings Jack and Jill with Daddy and when Daddy asks him why Jack fell down the hill Logan says, "Gravity."
- On 12/21/02 Whitney, 1 ½, climbs out of her crib for the first time—naked.
- The first time Whitney, 3 ½, hears her echo she asked, "Do you hear my voice somewhere else?"
- Logan, 5, on the way up to Tahoe complains, "I have a yawn stuck in my ears."
- In April of 2007 Whitney learns to tie her shoes and Logan learns to blow a bubble gum bubble.
- 8/14/05 Logan, 5, catches his first lizard at the river.
- 2/29/08 Whitney, 6, calls a boy for the first time.

So, I may not have my children's first years neatly wrapped up in a completed baby book, but that doesn't mean I've missed a thing. The growth chart of penciled dashes, dates and initials on my laundry room wall proves otherwise. So does the faded, red, awkwardly shaped heart cut by three year old fingers taped to my bedroom mirror. And the tiny cement encased handprint stepping stones on my doorstep still tell a story that continues to unfold.

Did Someone Say Adult Conversation?

Momservation: Anyone who says they love the infant and toddler stage is not currently in the infant and toddler stage.

☺   ☺   ☺

It has been a wonderful experience staying at home with my children and being a part of their day to day development and growth. But it can be very isolating. And Momma needs to talk to someone who can do more than follow you around with their arms outstretched crying "Up!" and screeching "Elmo!" at the TV. Taking my toddlers out with the intention of stimulating their environment has, surprisingly, done the same for me.

Suddenly, there was a secondary benefit to taking my kids to the park and other places moms visit that I hadn't anticipated. Adult conversation! In taking my children somewhere that will possibly enrich their minds and allow them to learn and play I have stumbled upon great places to meet other women that I have a lot in common with. I've found that having something in common is a great ice breaker and lends itself to friendship.

Besides having children in common, I'm meeting other stay-at-home or working part-time moms (with the availability to push a swing for what sometimes seems like a quarter of our lifetimes), and we have found ourselves drawn to a place that will create a diversion long enough to formulate the next plan of attack.

You can't help but to be drawn to any adult presence at these activities. Adult conversation during the day becomes as precious as gold. It usually starts with friendly acknowledgment and routine questions about the children playing with each other:

How old is yours? Do they go to school yet? Needed to get out of the house too, huh?

Sometimes there's bonding over embarrassing behavior:

Sorry my kid bit your kid; Yeah, I'm sorry my kid threw tanbark in your kid's face.

It can lead to discussions about what you've tried for discipline or other issues your dealing with and finding comradery in struggling with the same issues. That's how I met my friend, Nancy, at our neighborhood park.

Other times there can be a connection with another mother because of the work we did before we were able to stay home with our children. It almost becomes like swapping war stories when we've reminisced, "Yeah, back when I was teaching fifth grade, you think having two is rough, I had a classroom of 34!" And, "I used to think getting up for work at 6 a.m. was hard, but now my littlest one won't sleep past 5:30!" That's how I met my friend, Kristin, who was also a teacher.

There's even been times when my child plays so well with another child, like they've been best friends forever, that I feel I should learn from my child and get to know the mother of the playmate with similar uninhibited friendliness. That's how I met my friend, Kim, at gymnastics. We were both sticking to polite, quick conversations while our kids tumbled and called out to each other. I took a cue from my son and made it a point to learn the mother's name, at least. Not only did I learn her name, but found out our husbands were in the same line of work and our friendship took off from there.

Children are so wonderfully adept in the aspect of making new friends. They haven't realized in their innocent world that rejection can lurk around any corner. They don't size people up first to make sure they fit certain self-perceived qualifications. They don't worry about fumbling for the right thing to say or if a conversation is going smoothly. They can just walk up to another child and see a friend.

I'll never forget the time I thought I was witnessing my

two year-old daughter's first form of rejection in seeking a friendship. I was sitting back watching her in the sandbox with one eye and watching my son across the playground with the other. Two older children came and sat down at the other end of the sand. My daughter, Whitney, in all her unreserved friendliness asked the newcomers, "Do you want to play with me?"

My heart wrenched when I heard the boy reply, "No. We don't want to play with you."

It took everything in me not to jump in and try to shield Whitney from further ugliness from this boy and give him a few ugly words of my own. I was prepared to open my arms to a crying daughter, providing a safe haven away from rejection.

Instead, to my amazement and absolute pride, with hardly a moment's hesitation Whitney announced, "Well, I'm going to play with you." She then got up and walked over to sit right next to the two children who I thought had just crushed my daughter's heart.

The surprised boy and girl looked at her as she continued digging in the sand next to them. The girl then started shoveling too. The boy scooched away a bit, but Whitney didn't give up. She just scooched closer and kept filling her bucket. Giving in, the boy started filling the bucket too.

Looking back on that day I realized Whitney had provided a good metaphor. Life is like playing in a sandbox. If you want to get the most out of it, you just gotta dig in. And you never know where you're going to meet your next best friend, so don't be afraid to walk up to that other parent and say, "Is it a one shot or two shot espresso day for you?"

Potty Training Master Supreme

Momservation: It's not the size of your diaper bag that matters, but what's in it.

☺   ☺   ☺

Here is my story as the resident Potty Training Master Supreme in my circle of influence (okay, friends and family). A title earned because my son was fully potty trained—even through the night—at twenty-two months (my daughter about the same age too).

Friends were jealous. Family was impressed. Everyone wanted to know my secret.

The question was did I go for the Mother of the Year fabrication or did I cop to my dirty little secret?

Ah, heck. Who cares how I did it? The kid was practically washing his own underwear at two!

"Tell us! Tell us!" they would beg, frustrated with their own futile efforts.

It was time to share my secret. "Bribery," I confidently admitted for all to hear.

"But I've tried that," my friends would concede. And I would hear all about the M&M jar in the bathroom; the bag of suckers waiting for successful peepee in the potty; promises of unlimited Elmo watching for number two in the loo.

"No," I instructed in my best Zen Master voice. "You must get to the root of what drives your child. What makes them tick? What do they truly covet over all else? What will they do anything for not just once, but on a regular basis? And when you have discovered what drives their little one track minds…"

The moms crowded closer, leaning in, hanging on my every word. I had earned their respect as Master Potty Trainer

Supreme.

"You have to follow through with it no matter how many times you have to drive to Toys R Us and spend over an hour getting down each bike for your son try out in the bike section."

"Is that what you did?" someone asked incredulously.

Squaring my shoulders, looking each of them in the eye I admitted, "Yes. Yes, I did."

"Every day?"

"Every day."

"For how long?"

And like a general who has earned their stripes I let out a long sigh. "Two weeks. Two long weeks of checking for dry and clean underwear. Clearing the calendar of all planned events to head back to the trenches of Toys R Us. Bringing enough formula, drinks and snacks to keep him and his infant baby sister content. Dragging myself off to the toy store again and again, when I just wanted to relax and read my People magazine."

"But didn't he throw a fit when it was time to leave?" The crowd was still amazed.

"Ah, but it wasn't the toys that made him tick. It was the bikes. It didn't matter that he had one at home. His favorite thing to do was trying out the pretty new bikes with training wheels at the store. The best selection just happened to be at Toys R Us."

As looks of skepticism crept up and before I lost the faith of my followers I proclaimed, "There is no shame in bribery! Forget what your mothers have taught you! For heaven's sake we buy salad in a bag now!"

There was a murmuring rising through the group. I had to go for the clincher to secure my crown as Potty Training Master Supreme.

I pointed at Michelle. "You! Ashlinn loves babies right? Michelle nodded. "Promise her you'll take her over your sister-in-law's to hold the new baby every day if she keeps her Dora the

Explorer panties dry. Bring Kathy Starbucks so she'll let you."

I pointed next at Jen. "Meghan loves books. Tell her you'll take her to the book store every time she wakes up from naptime with a dry diaper. You'll have to miss Oprah, but you can record it."

I looked at Kim. "Hannah can never get enough Pirate's Booty. Let her have it with breakfast, lunch and dinner if she'll keep those Hello Kitty underwear dry. She has the rest of her life for healthy meals."

Faces lit up with hope. Cheers of appreciation were shouted out. I thought they were going to carry me around the park on their shoulders.

Surprisingly, I felt very little guilt for bringing my friends down to my level of parenting through bribery.

As I waved good-bye and led my son away hand-in-hand I whispered to him, "We can go to Baskin-Robbins if you promise not to tell Mommy's friends that Mommy wasn't potty trained until she was four."

Diaper Bag Chronicles

Momservation: It's not the size of your diaper bag that matters, it's what's in it.

☺   ☺   ☺

I'll always remember the day my daughter, Whitney, was born on April 4, 2001. Because two years to the day after she was born I got rid of the diaper bag for good and celebrated by buying a new purse.

Go ahead and laugh, but you always remember the day you got to trade your pack-mule hump for a trendy purse again.

It's been many years since I've had to tote around a survival pack of diapers, wipes, Desitin, changing pad, extra onsies, clothes, and Bob the Builder underwear, sippie-cups, Goldfish, bottles, formula dispenser, Cheerios dispenser, back-up carseat clip, sunscreen, Mylicon drops, burp cloths, teething rings and favorite toys.

I still get a tear in my eye remembering the joy of being set free from the weathered pack of infant/toddler gear (actually an REI backpack chosen for its gender neutral coloring—for Daddy toting—and quick-serve sippie-cup holders built in to the front).

It was Monday, March 31, 2003 and Whitney had kept her underwear dry for over a week (as noted in her baby book—unfortunately her last entry). I didn't want to jinx it by saying it aloud, so I sent a note to my husband across the dinner table (this is what we did before texts). It read:

IF WHITNEY MAKES IT TO THURSDAY KEEPING HER PANTS DRY, I THINK WE CAN DITCH THE DIAPER BAG.

Hubby looked up at me, arched an uncertain eyebrow, then scribbled something back. It said:

ARE YOU SURE WE'RE READY FOR THIS?

I nodded. One more check that my 2 and 3 ½ year-olds were still busy getting spaghetti everywhere except in their mouths, then I wrote back:

YOU'RE WATCHING THE KIDS FRIDAY. I'M GOING PURSE SHOPPING.

See, tears again! It really was a life-changing experience.

I still have that purse—a beautiful, chocolate leather, Jack Georges, shoulder bag with handle option—and it will always be ranked up there in nostalgia with first kiss, first love, and first car.

Even though the purse still has Goldfish crumbs crushed in the bottom and has the scent of fermented apple juice. Despite the Dora the Explorer and Bob the Builder emergency underwear, wipes, favorite toys, sippie cups, sunscreen, extra car seat clip and bribery candy stretching it out a bit, it still looks great!

Preschool Panic

Momservation: It's easier to look back with nostalgia when you haven't just changed a diaper and regularly get a full night of sleep.

☺   ☺   ☺

I still remember the day my motherhood innocence was ripped from me like a "Binky" from a baby. There I was at the park following my first born child around the playground, making sure he was safely navigating his still wobbly little self. That's when my friend, Sacha, dropped the bomb. "I'm going to go visit some preschools today!" she announced with unrestrained enthusiasm.

Spitting out my Starbucks I think might have been my reply. I believe her son might have started walking the day before. "Don't you think it's a little early to be worrying about preschool?" I said trying to regain my composure.

"Oh no," replied Sacha, "I've had Pudding Pie on two waiting lists since he was born!"

I was getting ready to break the news to Sacha that her Type-A personality might have reached new heights, when my other girlfriend wandered up carrying her little crawler. "I just picked up a flyer for Little Tykes Preschool the other day. I'm thinking of putting Suzie Q on the waiting list."

Suddenly, the ladies at the park were in full talking over each other steam about what preschools in the area they heard were good and how long the waiting lists were. I felt my head spinning as I looked at my little guy who just added the word "juice" (actually jooz) to his short vocabulary. I was sure one day my obviously brilliant child would end up at Harvard or Stanford, but I didn't realize I needed to get the ball rolling yet.

"Do you think I'm too late getting Logan on a waiting

list?" I found myself panicking.

Wanting the best for our children has come down to putting our children on preschool waiting lists at birth. On the big imaginary check-off list of all we want to provide for our children to give them the best shot at not ending up on Dr. Phil, a good education is near the top. Before it meant saving for a good college. Soon it trickled down to making sure the kids went to a good prep school. Then, why wait? You can't count out those formative primary years, maybe a private school is best! And here we are today, pitching tents in school parking lots the night before kindergarten sign-ups.

For those of you whom I just ripped the proverbial Binky from because your baby or toddler is not on a preschool waiting list, don't dive for the keys just yet. Although, it is true, in our community preschool pre-registration has climbed to new hysterical heights, likely a spot for your child in a good preschool can be found without putting them on a waiting list in utero.

The good news is there are usually quite a few preschools in most communities, both parochial and secular run, as well as Head Start programs. More good news is daycare providers can be another form of preschool. The bad news is, no matter the school or daycare provider, there is likely a waiting list. But wait, there's more good news! It's JUST preschool.

The frustrating news is that the reason many of these waiting lists are so long is everyone is hedging their bets and putting their child on every school's list. One friend, for example, had her child on waiting lists at seven different preschool programs. Besides worrying her child wouldn't end up in a local preschool, she couldn't decide which program was the best fit for both her and her preschooler.

"I'm not sure if I want a program with parent participation. Do I want just preschool or continued education through eighth grade? Do you think a small, intimate, one-on-one setting is better or a larger one with more resources? I really like the established preschools, but I don't want to have to pay an arm and a leg for private preschool! Should I do a 3-day or 5-day program?" She couldn't decide so she did the waiting list lottery, hoping the decision would be made for her.

There are many mothers out their like my friend, and though it can be anxiety producing to realize your kid is 75th on the waiting list, it is amazing how, come fall when it's time for school to begin, holes start appearing like Swiss cheese as parents pick a school and finally remove their child's name from all these lists.

A good rule of thumb for choosing and enrolling your child in a preschool is to do a little homework. But it can wait until about a year before you'd like to have your child start school. Word of mouth is always a good start.

Next, go visit the schools that seem to fit you and your child's needs. If it seems like a good fit, then put their name on the waiting list. Two schools are usually more than adequate. It provides a first choice and a second choice. If your child doesn't get into your first choice, another gentle reminder, it's ONLY preschool.

It's not a race to start your child's education. I know a few moms who decided against preschool altogether in favor of providing their own enriching environment and savoring their child's youth. A healthy start doesn't necessarily mean preschool; a loving, attentive environment where children have an opportunity to grow and learn with confidence and validation is just as rewarding. With occasional trips to the zoo, fairs, parks and museums you're already adding more to your child's growth than a formal preschool does.

I ended up taking a cue from my son who doesn't like change. I kept him in Ms. Cindy's daycare program he was already comfortable with that was providing kindergarten readiness, structure and social stimulation. He thrived in the small, intimate environment.

My daughter, on the other hand, had already grown bored with Ms. Cindy's one day Mommy break daycare program by the time she was ready for formal preschool. My little spitfire was ready for the great, wide world so I moved her to a pre-kindergarten program that she absolutely loved and thrived.

And by the way, of the dozen or so preschool-age children in my mommy group, all that chose to attend preschool got into one regardless of when they got on a waiting list. Almost every preschool in the area is represented in our group along with kids that are right on pace without it.

Now if I could just get Sacha to back off the SAT preparation classes…

Not *Just* a Mother

Momservation: Motherhood may be the most challenging thing I've ever done, but it sure is the best ride in the park.

☺   ☺   ☺

In early 2004 my dad called to tell me I absolutely must record Oprah that day. I don't usually watch TV during the day, so Dad knew I wouldn't be watching and even if I was, my children wouldn't allow me the peace to watch the show.

My dad excitedly told me Maria Shriver was going to be on The Oprah Winfrey Show and he thought I'd find her inspiring and insightful. Dad, being my biggest champion in life, always told me I could achieve anything I strived for. He felt that fellow Type-A, Maria, and I were sisters in a parallel universe.

As I cradled the phone to my ear with my shoulder, poured another endless cup of apple juice for my son, hissed out of the corner of my mouth to my daughter about breaking the rule of talking to mommy while she's on the phone, and realizing the breakfast dishes were still in the sink, I thought "Yeah, I'll get right on that." Knowing though that my dad, later, would want to know how I liked the show, I hurriedly threw a tape in the VCR and promptly forgot about it for a week.

I'll admit right now, I did not vote for Arnold Schwarzenegger for California Governor. And all the fuss about Governor and First Lady of California sightings in Sacramento had grown as stale to me as the Goldfish crackers in my car seats. Always trying to separate myself from the trend, I was resisting all things Arnold and Maria. I was in no hurry to watch this tape.

Finally, one nap time I remembered about the Oprah tape and grudgingly gave up reading the daily paper to watch this show that was supposed to be so inspiring.

This is where the music crescendos and the glow of enlightenment shines down on my illuminated body. I got it! I got what all the adulation was about.

Maria was my soul sister! She was driven and competitive like me! She wanted to have it all like me—career, family, successful marriage, cute shoes. She was a mother also struggling to balance her own goals and aspirations with those of her family. Okay, she was funnier than me and quite a bit wealthier, but she could laugh with her pal Oprah about the insecurities of her life like I do with my girlfriends!

Where she had me at "hello," though, was when she said she wanted women with families to stop saying, "I used to be a (fill in the former career), but now I'm JUST a mother."

It was as if Maria had been standing over my shoulder eavesdropping at a wedding I had just been to when I said those very words with *teacher* filling in the I Used To blank. I stood up and threw off my veil of underestimation and shouted at the TV, "That's right! I A.M. a mother, and I'm a darn good one!" Then I added, "I can still be a teacher, AND I'm even a writer now!"

I was up with people and on the Maria bandwagon. It was like I was at a revival and I was throwing out the "You go girl!" and "Amen Sister!"

Shortly after that, when I saw *Sacramento Magazine* with Maria on the cover I quickly bought it anxious for more words of wisdom and inspiration. I even remembered this book Dad had bought me years ago by Maria. It was called *Ten Things I Wish I'd Known—Before I Went Out into the Real World* and it had been gathering dust in my nightstand drawer along with the other books I'd been meaning to read. Who has time with a three and four year old? I pulled it out and devoured it.

Again, I found a nugget of wisdom that struck me profoundly. In one of the final chapters Maria suggests writing down things that have given you joy in your life and reviewing it every so often to remind yourself to find happiness and laughter when things are weighing you down. I used to be a religious journal writer, but once I got caught up in my career and then my children it fell to the wayside. I always found journal writing and reviewing my thoughts cathartic and her words reminded me to get back on my path. So all this might sound like a big love letter to Maria Shriver, but really it is a love letter to myself and other mothers out there who sometimes feel as though they're losing sight of themselves and their ambitions while being a mother and wife. Maria is calling us to arms! As Oprah suggested to our First Lady of California, this is Maria's agenda and her message has been heard loud and clear by me and I'm an enlightened disciple spreading the word:

We aren't JUST mothers. We have the best job in the world with the best benefits—our children. Some days it ain't pretty, but I wouldn't trade my job with Bill Gates.

California First Lady, Maria Shriver and me

Trip vs. Vacation

Momservation: The amount of leisure in a vacation is in direct proportion to the age of your children.

☺   ☺   ☺

I'll never forget my husband's and my first summer vacation together as a married couple. His family rented a beautiful two-story cabin overlooking Lake Tahoe with a magnificent deck view jutting out over a rocky cliff. At night we sipped cocktails on the deck while watching the sun go down, later heading off to the casinos until luck or energy ran out first. We'd sleep in after our late night, get up in time for brunch, play a few rounds of Scrabble and let the day decide our course. Leisurely vacation at its finest.

Enter children.

I'll never forget our first "vacation" to the same Tahoe cabin once we were the proud parents of a 20 month-old boy and three-month old girl. It began with buying a roof rack for our SUV. Then a baby gate for the top of the stairs. Followed by a Review of Hazards meeting with my husband where he flagged the beloved deck as a caution zone because he had noticed some rickety railings and potential for some nasty splinters. Plus, the rocks out front looked dangerous, lots of sharp-cornered furniture, hot BBQ, and falling dangers from the loft railing and stairs. It pretty much narrowed down to leaving the poor kid in his port-a-crib for safety.

After the car was packed with strollers (umbrella and double), port-a-cribs, bouncy seat, booster seats, Baby Bjorn, backpack diaper bag, favorite toys, favorite food, cans of formula, a half a dozen bottles and enough diapers and wipes to fill two suitcases, we decided we would buy, once we got there, the rest of the stuff that wouldn't fit in the car.

"Well, do you think we're ready for our vacation?" I asked as we drove off, the back end of the car riding low.

"This is not a *vacation,*" my husband replied tersely. "This, is a *trip.*"

And boy was it some trip. The beautiful two-story cabin with the magnificent deck view morphed into a potential death trap at every turn with a toddler zipping around making sure we did not rest for one leisurely minute. Our days were dictated by the same schedule and need for routine for our children that we followed at home. The only difference was there were some pretty pine trees out the windows and a spectacular view if you were able to steal a minute to look at it without a toddler trying to lunge through the railing to the chipmunks below.

I remember waving everybody off to the casinos as we stayed behind with the kids. And the night we took my mother-in-law up on her offer to watch the kids the baby was up screaming throughout the night, dooming any other shot at getting out again.

There, of course, had been no sleeping in because the kids were up at the crack of oh-my-god-what-time-is-it? thirty. So we spent hours trying to keep them happy and quiet until the rest of the house woke up smiling and refreshed.

At the end of it, tired, disappointed and just wanting to get back to home turf advantage, I decided *trip* might have even been too nice of a word to describe the experience.

That "vacation" experience and similar comparisons by our friends with children (i.e. toddler throwing up all over Mommy on plane with no changes of clothes, rental car place unable to supply promised car seats, having to return early due to sick children) has led to a healthy debate:

At what point do these family trips once again take on the leisurely air of a vacation? And more importantly, why do we keep subjecting ourselves to them until we reach the turning point?

A mathematical theory has been kicked around. The amount of leisure in a vacation is in direct proportion to the age of your children. The younger the children the deeper you are in the realm of trip. The older the kids are, the more likely you will be able to find time to actually sit down and think that this could actually be a pleasant vacation. The amount of planning, organizing and executing is constant.

So if these are the Trip Years, don't forget to pack an extra set of big girl panties for yourself.

The Young and the Thankful

Momservation: It's understandable why kids have a hard time with the concept of gratitude when there are yams and green bean casserole on their plates.

☺   ☺   ☺

My kids and their preschool-age friends are asking more questions where they are really using their little brains to make sense of the world and their place in it. It gets increasingly trickier to explain things in a way that will make sense to them, further their knowledge, but not overwhelm them.

This was evidenced recently when we discussed the upcoming November holiday. When the inevitable "What's Thanksgiving?" came up with my five year-old son I decided to forgo the tricky pilgrim/Indian/first Thanksgiving route and go for the What We're Thankful For route. I tried this:

"Thanksgiving is where we celebrate with our friends and family what we are thankful for."

"What's thankful?"

"Thankful means we are happy for what we have." Okay, stepped into a teachable moment here. "What are you happy for Logan? What are you THANKFUL for?"

"I'm thankful for Christmas."

Not a bad thing to be thankful for. "Anything else?"

"I'm thankful for Momma and Daddy and Kyber and Whitney and myself and my fish and my toys."

He seemed to have caught on to this thankful stuff. I was amused that he put the dog before his sister in the thankful category.

Later, I explained to three year-old Whitney what thankful meant and asked her what she was thankful for.

"I'm thankful for going to see Santa Claus because I can get a new baby if another one gets broken. But I already have a lot," she conceded.

I was starting to see a Christmas pattern here. "Anything else?"

"I'm thankful for my toys, my princess dresses, my Barbies and my Nemo bag." She thought for a minute and seemed to come up with a new word that I think must be a combination of thankful and appreciate. "I'm preeshful of Momma and Dada and Logan and Nana..." then she proceeded to list everyone in our family including extended cousins. She finished it off with, "And I'm preeshful for watching TV."

Since this seemed to be a cute dialogue I decided to not only ask my kids what they were thankful for, but their preschool friends too.

Meghan, 4, was thankful for her toys and new house. She doesn't have a new house, but her friend Hannah does and so she thought she should be thankful for it.

Tommy, 4, was thankful for Mommy. Just Mommy. With a little more prodding he said, "I like going to parks and Willie's." As in Willie's Hamburgers.

Katie, 2, without hesitation said she was thankful for, "Waffles, pancakes and Taco Loco."

I was seeing another trend here. In fact, the rest of the kids all had food somewhere on their list.

Jack, 4, was also thankful for food, but added milk as well. He also was thankful for snails, "Except when they eat my plants."

Mathew, 3, was holding a bag of cookies when he was asked what he was thankful for and he replied, "These and goldfish." As in crackers. When asked if there was anything else he was thankful or happy for he added, "I'm happy right now."

How can you not be thankful when life is that simple?

10 Ways to Teach Kids Gratitude Beyond Thanksgiving

1. **Say thanks.** Teach kids early the kindness of saying "thank you" and the habit of telling people you appreciate them. Acknowledging a person's effort makes both of you feel good.
2. **Don't waste.** Educate kids to be thankful for modern conveniences like clean running water, abundant food sources, and flip-of-a-switch electricity by practicing conservation. Remind them to not let faucets run, turn off lights that are not being used, and not waste food by only taking one bite.
3. **Go green.** Instill green habits while they're young and to be respectful of the place we call home. Protect our planet and natural resources with things like watching paper consumption, refilling non-plastic water bottles, or choosing to walk/ride bikes instead of driving
4. **Donation box.** Have kids decorate a box to keep in the garage. Encourage them to deposit toys they don't play with, clothes they grow out of, or things they don't need into the box to donate. Let the kids choose which organization to bring it to when it's full.
5. **Thank you notes.** Don't allow kids to use a gift until they write or help write a thank you note. It's a great way to avoid it being put off or never gotten to and instilling the value of saying thanks.
6. **Chores.** Kids learn to appreciate the work Mom and Dad do by helping out. Doing chores around the home like keeping their room clean not only teaches responsibility, but also respect and appreciation for a roof over their heads.
7. **Go play.** A healthy body is not something to be wasted sitting on the couch watching TV, in front of a computer,

or playing video games. Appreciate not having any physical limitations by getting out and playing.

8. **Save Pennies.** Have your child save their money for something they want. The act of saving, delayed gratification, and buying something with their own money will teach them to value the item more.

9. **Say "No."** Giving kids everything they want instills a sense of entitlement. Learning to live without things they desire teaches them they can survive with what they already have.

10. **Give Love.** Like the Beatles said, "Love is all you need." By regularly showing affection, telling kids you love them, and taking any opportunity to give them a hug or kiss kids learn the most basic form of gratitude is to feel loved by someone.

God Rest Ye Weary Toddler Mom
(God Rest Ye Merry, Gentlemen)
A Mommy Modified Christmas Carol

Momservation: If the threat of Santa not coming and a tattle-telling Elf on the Shelf is the cornerstone of your discipline strategy—good luck with January.

☺   ☺   ☺

A few years back during the Christmas holidays I was lamenting to my dad how I was going to survive Christmas with two young children, or more specifically, how my holiday decorations would survive. The Christmas tree had been tied to the wall with fishing line so my toddlers couldn't pull it over, my favorite breakable decorations were up high and kid-safe ornaments had been put down low on the tree. But, I could still not save Christmas from being broken, slobbered on or redecorated all over my house.

I told my dad, "You know I could re-write the '12 Days of Christmas' about all the holiday decorations the kids have damaged, dismantled or destroyed. On the spot, I started reworking it. "On the first day of Christmas my toddler broke for me…the carrot nose off of Frosty."

We both had a good laugh, but then my creative gene kicked in and I added, "You know, I'm going to do it. I'm going to create a new song." And that's how it started. I ended up going through my childhood book of Christmas carols (which I had hidden from toddler hands) and one by one modified them from a mother's point of view.

Below is a crowd favorite from my collection *Mommy Modified Christmas Carols*. I hope you'll sing along…

God Rest Ye Weary Toddler Mom

1. God rest ye wear-y todd-ler mom, It is the end of day, For lit-tle ball of en-er-gy is finally put away: To rest their tiny for, tomorrow's end-less play:
   O Pints of Ben and Jer-ry's, Ben and Jer-ry's, O pints of Ben and Jerry's

2. From God, our Heav-en-ly Fa-ther, A bless-ed ba-by came, And un-to first-time par-ents brought routines of the same: How many times mo-re must we play that game?
   O Pints of Ben and Jer-ry's, Ben and Jer-ry's, O pints of Ben and Jerry's

3. The mom-my of a whirl-wind mov-ing all the time, What next in their lit-tle mouth with Moth-er find? Just one a-dult con-ver-sation before I lose my mind:
   O Pints of Ben and Jer-ry's, Ben and Jer-ry's, O pints of Ben and Jerry's

PLAYDATE
My People Will Call Your People

Momservation: If I take your kid for a few hours so you'll take my kid for a few hours, you can call the mommy-gets-a-break-get-together whatever the heck you want.

☺   ☺   ☺

Let me give you a definition of *playdate* when I was a kid: Being forced to turn off the TV and go outside to play with whomever I could find on my street or else I was going to be put to work.

I actually lived on a pretty good street, this big U of young families with lots of kids to stumble across. My very best friend lived three houses up. My back-up friend for when my best friend wasn't home lived one more house down, across the street. If I didn't find someone to play with, I was still not allowed to step foot in the house unless I was bleeding or had brought someone to help me clean my room.

Granted, I was lucky enough to live on a block where there were over a dozen kids between my older brother, me and my little sister's ages that I would probably encounter if I just stepped outside. Or if nobody was outside, I could just start riding my bike up and down the street until someone would see me and come outside to play.

There was no organization. There was no date book needed with little color-coded highlights, tallies and flow charts of whose turn it was to come over to play. There was no iPhone, Blackberry, Palm Pilot or even Rolodex needed to keep track of potential playmate families and available dates. Life seemed simpler back then. Good Lord, it was only the 70's!

Now, not only do I have my own calendar that threatens to envelop me on daily basis, but I also have to keep track of my own children's separate social calendar. The closest thing I have to social on my calendar is Wednesday playgroup at the park where I catch up with other moms—which, technically, is a social date for the kids that I've mooched in on.

Playdate. I remember the first time I heard that word. It sounded so Yuppie and pretentious. This was back when I was an upwardly mobile, unmarried, Hey Ya Wanna Go To Reno This Weekend? kinda gal. You know, the 90's. Playdates sounded so rigid and scripted and I remember thinking, *"No kid of mine will ever suffer through those."*

Hang on a sec, let me look at my children's calendar over here: Monday—playdate at best friend's house; Tuesday— playdate at our house for Logan; Wednesday—playdate at our house for Whitney; Thursday—playdate for both kids here so they will stop sobbing that it's not fair that the other has someone over to play and they don't; Friday—both kids gone at playdates, Jackpot! Okay, so it's the new millennium. Gotta get with the times.

Before I get blacklisted from everyone's playdate list for griping about organized play sessions, let me say this: I could not function without them. In true organizational mommy fashion here is my list of reasons why, in descending order of importance, and with cute little bullets:

☺ Unlike when I was younger, I don't feel comfortable letting my six and four year-olds wander the streets looking for someone to play with.

☺ Playmates are hard to come by in and around our block. And best friends live in different neighborhoods.

☺ My kids fight less, occupy themselves better and have so much fun playing with their friends that I become irrelevant and can actually get something done.

☺   Reciprocation! Ahh, sweet silence and productivity when the little darlings are off playing at someone else's house.

☺   Great social skills for the kids. Interacting with different personalities, rules and expectations while practicing good behavior is an excellent proving ground. (I know this should be higher up, but self-preservation kicked in.)

☺   Helping fellow mothers live a sane existence. We're all in the same boat, so everyone grab a paddle and row. (This should be higher up too, but safety first!)

So, yes, some days when I am nearly drowning in a sea of commitments and things to do for my kids and myself, scheduling a playdate is the foot that steps on my head and dunks me underwater. But other days it is the life ring that someone has tossed me to make my day just a little bit easier.

The modern definition of playdate does involve some advance planning, organization and memory (I am still in fear that I will one day leave someone's child at school who I was supposed to bring home for a playdate). We live in different times and the modern landscaping of parenting has evolved in so many different ways. I've signed on to become a hands-on parent for the joy and enrichment it brings both my kids and myself. I accept the challenges that come with it, but I also bask in its rewards.

Like tomorrow—both kids off at playdates and Mommy's off to get a pedicure!

Little Fashion Don'ts

Momservations: The only certainties in life are death, taxes and that your children will at some point embarrass you.

☺   ☺   ☺

Have you ever wished you could have a little asterisk over your child's head with a disclaimer on the back of their shirt? It would say something like:

* I chose this ridiculous outfit, hairstyle and/or accessories to wear today and in trying to not undermine my self-esteem my parents are letting me out in public like this. It should not be a reflection of their parenting abilities or lack thereof to let me out of the house in this manner.

Just the other day at the park my friends and I were each lamenting our children's choice of self-expression at the sake of our respectable mommy images. One of my friends was cringing over her daughter's insistence on parting her hair Alfalfa-style with barrettes holding back her plastered down bangs, something she did herself and thought looked absolutely stunning.

My other friend had thrown her hands up in surrender as her daughter came sashaying up in a lovely sundress that she had now been wearing for a week straight, unwashed and all.

And, of course, there was my son wearing his way cool Harley Davidson tank top that fit him perfectly—two summers ago.

To be honest, since we knew we were going to be among friends, we let our little fashion don'ts out of the house without a fight. Although, one girlfriend confided that she hasn't had to worry about her daughter going out of the house in her favorite horrible outfit (the one that made her look like a boy) since it mysteriously disappeared one day.

This group of friends, choosing to remain nameless, the black bars across our eyes, are victims of our children's fashion faux pas. We have all agreed to be plastered across the Fashion Don't pages in exchange for our children feeling wonderfully independent, beautiful or handsome and full of self-confidence in how they have chosen to express themselves.

However, laying a few ground rules is fair game. With one family I know the rule is: When it's your friends, you wear what you'd like. When it's my friends, you wear what I like.

In my own house, Mommy overrules any outfits, hairdos or accessories for any social occasion where the whole family is getting dressed up. This includes my husband. I think he might have the most vetoes collected out of everybody.

Sometimes though, you just have to cringe and bear it. Like the time my mom picked up my sister from kindergarten after my brother had given up arguing with his baby sister and let her go as is to school. Out pranced my sister from the classroom, obviously feeling fabulous in a ridiculously frilly dress cinched at the waist with a belt that made her look like a human sausage. My mom's pantyhose puddled down to her ankles. Mom was mortified as the teacher eyed her with disdain, but in the end all she could do was laugh at this adorable little girl who thought she had dressed herself as a princess.

There has been more than a few times in my own household where I was desperately wishing the Garanimals from my youth would make a comeback. I'm sure my kids would buy into the fun of matching a giraffe top to a giraffe bottom or lion shirt to lion pants just like the old days. I wouldn't have to pull reverse psychology on them or make up fake rules, trying to trick them into a matching, presentable outfit.

"Are you sure you want to wear those rainbow striped tights with sandals and a sundress? I don't think your preschool's dress code allows tights with more than one color in them."

Or, "Oooh, cowboy boots with shorts and a tank top. Nice outfit. I bet everybody at the park is going to wear that today too. I have a feeling no one's wearing jeans with their boots though."

Of course, it would be easier and less embarrassing to dictate every outfit our children wear, making them our little ambassadors of the perfect family image. But squashing their budding self-expression for the sake of outward appearances, a very adult neurosis, would be a shame and a missed opportunity in building self-esteem. Letting kids dress and groom themselves is an opportunity for them to navigate their own personal identity.

Seeing our children take their first tentative steps in establishing a self-identity should make us proud and be seen as the reward of a job well done in raising confident, independent and self-assured individuals.

And who am I to shoot down someone who wants to wear black Converse high tops with flames with her sundress to the park? I spent the eighties in neon pink and green from head to toe with matching visors.

I looked fabulous I might add.

Works in Progress

Momservation: Parents need to look at their kids with hope in their potential, not judgment of their failures, and trust that they are works in progress.

☺   ☺   ☺

A horrible realization dawned on me the other day. My children…aren't perfect. The just as brutal follow up conclusion was, if my children are not perfect, than I am not doing a Mother of the Year Award job raising my children. I was already preparing my speech.

Now, of course, I didn't think my children were flawless, but I thought my high expectations of manners, polite interaction and let's face it, likeability, were being reasonably met. It occurred to me that my children were turning out to be the equivalent of book smart, but not street smart.

In theory, they were prepared to be absolute darlings with such teachings as:

- Don't (yell, grab, hit)
- Use your words
- Cover your mouth when you cough
- Say please and thank you
- Friends share

But my kids had been trying out these teachings mostly on each other under strict review from Mommy and Daddy. When they hit the playdate circuit, despite all the repetition, rehearsal, and occasional pop quizzes, everything they learned apparently was instantly forgotten.

Case in point: Sharing suddenly came with clauses and fine print.

"But I don't want them to play with that, it's new," from my four year-old son.

And, "They can't play with that because it's special."

So I asked, out of sheer morbid curiosity, to see where this was going, "Okay. What's not special then?"

I was met with extended silence. Then, "Why can't they play with Whitney's toys?"

Meanwhile, the friends had gone off to Whitney's room since Logan's had been stamped with museum status. Three year-old Whitney, not quite grasping the concept that when you invite friends over to play you actually play with them, is screaming one decibel shy of breaking the sound barrier, "Now look what you did! Get out of my room! Get out of my room!"

It didn't get any better. Coping and decision making skills, I soon recognized, were also low and close to nonexistent under pressure to actually use them. When Logan re-designated his swords as "not so special" and regrouped his friends, then Whitney had an academy award nominating breakdown of "Nobody will play with me!"

Once I got her to stop looking in the mirror to see how she looked while she was crying, I tried to reintroduce the lesson *If You Want a Friend, Then You Need to BE a Friend.*

Next, Logan thought it would be cool to show his friends how fun it is to throw blocks around. He didn't start to see the ill advisedness of his decision until blocks started bouncing off his head with nobody listening to his cries of cease fire because they were too busy laughing at each slapstick moment and agreeing, "This IS fun!"

I was finally saved from continuous evidence of my failure as a teacher of manners, morals and values when I served lunch and put in a video to distract them. I reviewed my parental progress report for the day and knew it was time to shred the Mother of the Year speech:

Display and Use of Good Manners - F
Sharing - F
Making Good Choices - F
Art of Distraction - A+

I was actually glad to have witnessed these failures in execution in the privacy of my own home and away from the pitying glances of my peers. Although, I cringed at the thought of our little guests' interpretations and how it would be reported back home. I could just see the mothers' confused faces trying to make sense of it all.

"You weren't allowed to touch anything in the whole house and Whitney was in Timeout the whole visit?"

If this horrible playdate had taken place at one of the houses of my children's friends, I know I wouldn't have gotten a true reporting of how awful they could be.

I'm sure, trying to spare my feelings, I would have gotten a mild mannered report like, "Well, there was a little trouble sharing, but they were fine."

Nobody wants to be the one to say, "Your children were bratty, bossy, overly emotional and obviously living in cave-like conditions for the last three years of their lives."

Plus, a true test of your children's manners and likeability aren't really tested in an unfamiliar environment. Their shyness and reservation in a new situation is easily confused with politeness and compatibility.

Later, when I had banished my kids to naptime despite really wanting to lock them in their rooms until they emerged well-mannered, polished adults, it occurred to me:

They aren't adults. A long way from it at three and five years old. When I pushed my adult expectations aside for a moment I was able to see that what I thought was unacceptable behavior for preschoolers was actually normal behavior. I didn't have to like it, but just accept that they are works in progress.

Even though I wanted my kids to be a similar representation of the adult I had become and mirror my own values, I had to remind myself that it took me a good fifteen years to get there myself. It took a lot of mistakes, missteps, embarrassing situations and even punishment to find my way. It also took the guidance of two parents who loved me enough to not only weather those hard times with me, but also put in the time and the patience to instruct me, model for me, correct me and redirect me with firm, but loving hands.

I imagine my mom and dad's parenting report card at times had a few deficiencies on it thanks to me, but they gave me the room and the time I needed to grow up and learn from my mistakes while still letting me be a kid. And I think I turned out all right.

Now I just need to step back and remove my adult expectations from my own kids and put achievable kid goals in front of them. I need to put the proper timeline on it. I need to accept that there are going to be bumps and setbacks along the way. I can't expect my kids to learn all lessons before they're capable. I need to look at them with hope in their potential not judgment of their failures and trust that they are works in progress.

And so am I. One day when my kids have achieved my hopes and dreams for them of becoming well-rounded, contributing, personable adults, I hope to have become a more open-minded, patient and forgiving person. And maybe then I can work on my speech for Lifetime Achievement Award.

Calling For Backup

Momservation: Today I have met my match in two munchkins who stole my heart wearing Bob the Builder underwear and singing Five Little Monkeys all day.

☺   ☺   ☺

I sent out the call the other day. The need to call for reinforcements can sneak up on me, and other times it is not a matter of if, but when. It's just nice to know that in times of crisis, he's got my back.

"Honey..." I begin. The key is to stay calm, not panic. "I'm going to need you to come home a little early today."

That phrase right there is like the Bat Signal going out. The response is routine, no hesitation, no judgment. "How early?"

"How about 3:30?"

"Can you make it until four?"

"I don't know, things are looking pretty bad. I don't know how much longer I can keep it together,"

"All right. Stay calm."

"I am calm! Do I not sound calm to you?" I begin to shriek.

He's like the composed 911 dispatcher, cool and collectively giving out instructions in a reassuring, soothing manner. "Okay, where are you?"

"I'm in the bedroom."

"Is the door shut?"

"Yes."

"Okay. Good. Is everyone safe?"

"So far, but if you don't get home soon, I can't make any promises."

"All right, stay with me now. Where are the kids?"

"I finally got them outside. It was bad, Honey. God it's been bad..." My voice starts to break.

His voice raises just a hair, but he remains cool. "Keep it together, Sugar. I know you can do it. I'll be home soon and then you can go."

"I don't know if I can make it," I begin to sob. "You don't understand. It's just so awful... He... She..."

The breakdown starts to get to him. It always does. "Oh no, Sugar. Don't go there. You don't need to tell me about it. It'll just make it worse. Stay in your room. Keep them outside. I'll be home in fifteen minutes. Can you make it?"

"Yeah," I squeak. "I'll try."

"Great. Good girl. I'll see you in a few."

"Thanks, Honey. I appreciate it."

"No problem." And I know he means it.

That right there is the call for backup. The distress call that goes out when it's Kids-10, Mommy-0. When I've reached into my secret stash of patience and come up empty. The days when I'm doing more yelling then breathing. When the needs of my children have spilled over my levees of love and support. The times when unconditional love threatens to draw up a contract.

The solution for me is to get away and recharge my batteries. To hear my own thoughts again that have been drowned out by a constant barrage of sentences beginning with "Mommy..." To have moments of silence and remember what if feels like to not be interrupted. To not have anyone need me for a few hours. To escape the routine of caring for someone else's needs besides my own.

It may mean losing myself in a movie with a big tub of popcorn and Junior Mints or leisurely browsing the isles of Barnes and Nobles. It could be hopelessly trying to squeeze my butt into some trendy jeans at Forever 21 or getting lost in a Sudoku game in the food court at the mall. It doesn't matter where I go or what I do, just that I get away and find my sanity. And it's amazing how many times I find it with some really impractical, but way too cute shoes at Nordstrom.

My husband understands this. We have a mutual respect for each other and our jobs within the family. I know I can't frame a bathroom, install windows, or put up crown molding and baseboard in a day and make it look easy. He knows he can't go dawn to dusk catering to multiple and unending needs of two young children from wiping butts to wiping tears and everything in between without crying "Uncle."

As mothers and fathers we all have those days when parenting overwhelms us. When Super Mom is reduced to a puddle of tears and Super Dad has to admit, "I don't know how you do this every day." It's not a sign of bad parenting or out of control kids. It's a reality of raising a family. Some days the joys make your heart ache with happiness and other days you have to call for backup.

That's where my husband comes in. As a stay-at-home mom some days he is my savior at the other end of the hotline. He is nonjudgmental of the days when I do send the distress signal and appreciative of all the days I run our family with superhuman efficiency and organization. He is a true partner who even after his own long, hard day will say, "Don't worry about it, Sugar. I got it from here."

Together, raising our family, we make a great team like Batman and Robin, Superman and Wonder Woman, or Mr. Incredible and Elastigirl. Although, we do argue sometimes over who is the superhero and who is the sidekick.

But we all know the answer to that one, ladies.

Camp Have-a-Lot-of-Fun

Momservation: When a stubborn storm front of routine hits chances of summer fun, brace yourself for a chance of meltdown and 100% public humiliation.

☺   ☺   ☺

My son does not like change. He was a routine type of guy from the instant he was born demanding his feedings and changing every three hours on the dot. Later, when I realized a store had discontinued his favorite socks I dashed around like a mad woman in a three county radius pleading, "You don't understand! I have to have Dickies, no seam, crew socks, size small or my mornings will be hell!"

My son's meltdowns when something was not just right, not how he had grown accustomed to operating or not comfortably predictable were like Tornado Alley. You could see all the conditions were ripe for the storm, you could prepare yourself for the worst, but you just couldn't get out of the way. I was glad they usually happened in the privacy of my own home where I could ride out the storm and clean up the mess without it hitting the Mommy Group news circuit.

Little did I know there was going to be an F5-rating storm in my future.

It was called Camp Have-a-Lot-of-Fun and it was a morning day camp for preschoolers with weekly theme titles like "Splish, Splashing Fun" and "Dinosaur Days." It promised a great time with friends, singing, games, crafts, and adventure. Shoot, I wanted to go!

Now, I admit, I did not tell my son that I had signed him up for this camp, trying to head off the inevitable refusal. I did sign him up though with his security blanket—his four year-old sister who would try anything and like it—just to assure him I wasn't throwing him to the wolves by sending him on this new experience alone.

It was also selfish because I was really looking forward to my first taste in five years of having three glorious hours, five days in a row, to do what *I* wanted to do. I was ready to slap the sunscreen on them, give them a hug goodbye, and head for the nearest coffee shop with my People magazine.

The first day of camp, I presented my best sales shtick to my son while he was distracted by breakfast. "It's called Camp Have-a-Lot-of-Fun! All your friends from playgroup will be there! You get to dig for dinosaurs today down by a creek!"

"Will Whitney be there?" was his apprehensive question.

"Yes, your sister will be there too."

He shrugged and continued eating. I cautiously studied his face. No signs of disturbance brewing. I backed up slowly, waiting for any missed signs of trouble. The air felt safe, and I practically skipped back into the kitchen to make their lunches for camp.

The drive over was more pumping up of camp and hesitant, but curious questions from my son. My daughter wanted to know if I could leave her there all day instead.

As we pulled up to the camp drop-off, there were parents and children everywhere looking like a frenzied ant hill. We found a parking place, walking to the big, grassy area where everyone was meeting. With all the commotion, I missed the winds of change blowing.

Suddenly, there was a gut-wrenching wail next to me. Every head in the park whipped in our direction toward this distressed sound to see whose kid must have been run over by a car. I, too, turned and looked down in horror at my son.

And there, in a rarely captured on film display, was the mother of all public meltdown, the screech swirling out of his mouth, rising violently in the air, "Why did you sign me up for Camp Have-a-Lot-of-Fun?"

As he crumbled to the ground, caught in his own emotional storm he sobbed, "Why are you making me Have-a-Lot-of-Fun?"

Amidst the chuckles of irony, and contagious spin-off tornados from frightened campers, I decided right then and there I was done with the destruction of ruined moods and off-on-the-wrong foot days. I was pulling up stakes and moving out of Tornado Alley.

I hissed at my son in a way he had never heard, effectively stopping the beast in its tracks. "You will get up. We will go meet your camp leader. You will have **fun** and I'll be back at noon to get you."

Startled by my changed tactic of calling him out instead of gently coaxing toward a new direction, Logan got up and compliantly followed through with my instructions. I then decompressed at a local coffee shop and after some therapeutic shopping, returned at noon for my kids.

My son came running up to me. "Did you sign me up for next week of Camp Have-a-Lot-of-Fun? It's Pirate Week!"

Disaster averted. It's safe to come out now. At least until conditions develop for the next Big One...

Babysitter Blues

Momservation: Find yourself a kid obsessed with American Girl Dolls and put them on retainer now—they grow up into the best babysitters.

☺   ☺   ☺

You gotta get 'em young. And studious. And preferably totally uninterested in sports. You want the one who would rather write a term paper than score those Justin Timberlake concert tickets. Because if you find the one who discovers boys, high school dances, Friday night basketball games, and worst of all…love, they'll be the ones going out on Valentine's Day while you're stuck spending a romantic dinner over nuggets and fries with the kids.

Ah, yes the babysitter blues. Let's sing it together, shall we?

Feelin' kinda frisky
Like to start it off right
Think I'll see
If I can get a sitter tonight
The neighbor kid's busy
The college girl too
Can't call Mom again
What's a kid strapped couple to do?
Got the babysitter blues, oh yeah

But wait, let's say you do get a sitter! Planned way ahead because it's a big night: party, concert/show tickets, annual fundraiser, or the other guaranteed date night—your anniversary. Got the newly minted teenage neighbor eager for a first gig, dirt cheap. Maybe the college student who figures she can study as soon as the kids are in bed. Or your faithful go-to gal—she's rarely turned you down, but it'll cost ya in the big bills.

Then you get the call. So sorry, can't make it. Sick, contagious, unexpected relative visiting, gotta finish that term paper due tomorrow. All code for "That cute boy finally called and asked me out" or "Everyone who's anyone is going out and you can't pay me enough to miss it."

Got on my low cut top
Thankfully still in style
Haven't worn these pumps and push up
In quite a long while
Just got the call
The sitter's a no go
Frantically dialin'
But everyone says "No"
Got the babysitter blues, that's right

Every good, healthy marriage needs its regular date nights. But a word of caution: watch out for babysitter referrals from friend. What's wrong with a good referral you ask? Sure, it works out fine most of the time, but then it'll happen—I guarantee it. It's the Race to Get the Good One. It's a party everyone you know is going to and your best couple friends wouldn't miss. And the very people who referred you to your best sitter, are now your worst enemy. Do you RSVP first? There's no time! Pick up the phone and call that sitter before your BFF (babysitter lingo for Best Friend Forever) does!

Got the invitation
Better make that call
A moment too late
And Cinderella's missin' the ball
But the mailman hit me
Last house of the day
"You drop the Smith kids
I'll give you twice what she pays"
They've got the babysitter blues, uh huh

There is that one ace up the sleeve though. The relative babysitter. If you have one at your disposal, you are the envy of parents everywhere. Want to go away for the weekend? No problem. Last second plans? No worries. Cost you more to stay out past midnight than eating at Ruth Chris? Not if you have Nana. If you don't have parents, childless siblings or a favorite aunt who live nearby, I suggest adopting your elderly neighbor.

Neighbor's got a boyfriend
Co-ed's got a fake I.D.
Too slow on the referral
Won't pay $15 an hour for three
Throw out a call to Momma
She knows how to do me right
Not only will she take 'em
But they can stay the night
Ain't singin' the babysitter blues no more!

So in review, you can't have too many babysitters on reserve. Hoard them and collect them like a priceless Picasso collection. As soon as you hear of that teenager that moved in down the block, snap him up. Guard your best sitter with your life and instead of referring her, just give her more of your business. Pick one to overpay so you will always have a guaranteed back-up sitter. If you don't have family close by, tell them the real estate market is improving, their grandkids aren't getting any younger and you heard your in-laws are thinking of moving here.

That last one should do the trick.

Choices, Stimulation, Creativity, Oh My!

Momservations: You get two choices: "No" and "Did you not hear me the first time I said, 'No'?"

☺   ☺   ☺

I blame the parenting magazines really. They led me astray during my weakest, most vulnerable time. Those magazines I turned to first in idealism, then in desperation searching for wisdom and guidance on how to raise the perfect first child they knew I was going to have.

I consumed the pages of those magazines like a woman falling off her diet with a bag of Oreos. I was sure I was going to be an enlightened, hip mother raising brilliant well-behaved children. I was going to transcend my mother's common sayings like, "And how do you expect me to pay for it? With my good looks?" or "Hey! Who wants to play the Silent Game?"

I was going to use teachable phrases of, "Honey, that is expensive. Let's figure out how many weeks you need to save to be able to afford that," or "Can you please tone down your voices and find something constructive to play?"

These magazines were going to tell me how to be the perfect parent—who wouldn't trust a periodical with the faces of impossibly beautiful and angelic babies on its cover each month? I followed each article to the letter with smug certainty that my overachiever personality was going to yield enviable children.

Oh, how the high and mighty shall fall.

My biggest downfall heading advice from some cherub-faced magazine was to give your children choices. "Giving your child a choice will give them a measure of control over their lives and keep them from acting out in defiance of consistently strict guidelines they feel compelled to test the boundaries of," said a parenting magazine.

Choices! Let them have choices! What clothes would you like to wear today, Pumpkin? Shorts in the winter? Sure! Motherly intuition tells me to protect my child from the cold, but the magazine instructed: let them experience the consequences of their decisions as long as it won't harm them.

In theory, yes. Reality: I am convinced children don't grow cold receptors until they are at least ten. I now fight regularly with a six year-old boy who wants to wear shorts and tank tops in any weather, thus causing me to lug around sweatshirts hoping he'll come to his senses and cover up.

And don't even get me started on food choices! Who knew that offering either peas or corn was the training ground to become a short order cook?

Another unending trail I was led down by parenting magazines was to provide lots of mental stimulation for your baby. "By sitting down and guiding your infant or toddler through hours of repetitive play, you will stimulate their intelligence, problem solving skills and awareness of their environment."

In theory, yes. Reality: my first-born child who benefited from hours of mind-numbing repetitive play and constant stimulation provided by his guilt-racked working mother is aware that his environment is not being stimulated unless it involves someone interacting or watching him. Translation: the kid doesn't know how to entertain himself!

The magazines also taught me that you are no one if you are not creative with your child. "When you add creativity to any endeavor, making art projects together, turning a walk into a nature hike, letting your child help make dinner, you provide an invaluable learning tool and diversity to your child's mental growth."

And once again, it's a good theory in principle. The reality check I am cashing every day goes a little something like this:

- An art dresser overflowing with colorful paper, ribbons, buttons, beads, glitter glue, jagged scissors of every design, feathers, foam paper, popsicle sticks, fabric and anything else on sale at Michael's and two children telling me, "I'm bored."
- Asking my kids if they want to go down to the river but they'd rather go to the Kid's Club at the gym.
- Giving cooking instructions through clenched teeth as I clean up the broken eggs from the floor only to have my kids give up midway to go catch Drake and Josh on TV.

I tried. I really tried to be the perfect parent. I blame my failure squarely on the shoulders of every parenting magazine being carried around in diaper bags across America by first-time parents.

Perfect parent, of course, is an oxymoron. Raising kids is the biggest learning curve there is and it lasts a lifetime. The Cliffs Notes to parenting magazines is this: When you care enough to try to provide the best possible opportunities and experiences involved in raising a family your parenting is perfect, whether you succeed or not.

So, after the first child when you're seasoned and wise through experience, you learn to reach for People Weekly on the magazine rack instead, hoping for time to read it in the bathroom as you're screaming at your precious children, "When the door is shut, that means I want privacy!"

Wise words to live by, Mom. You should start a parenting magazine.

CHAPTER 2

School Daze

Momservations®

Top 10 Rules for Adults from Kindergarteners

1. **Be an eternal optimist.** Since so many experiences are new, children can't wait to see what each has to offer with intrigue and excitement.
2. **Every experience is an opportunity to learn.** Kids know there is always something new to learn.
3. **Tell it like it is.** Kids don't gossip behind each other's backs but just come right out and say, "I didn't like that."
4. **Don't forget to have fun.** Children approach life with the intent to have fun.
5. **Don't be afraid of things getting messy.** Kids don't see a mess, they see an experience.
6. **If you do make a mess, you need to clean it up.** They might be kids, but rules are rules.
7. **Be quick with an apology.** Children seem to instinctually know that if they hurt someone saying "sorry" goes a long way to make things better.
8. **The best accessory for meeting new people is a smile.** Kid 101.
9. **To make a friend be a friend.** When children encounter the face of a peer they always see a potential playmate. No judgment, just "Hi! What's your name?"
10. **Holding a grudge isn't worth having one less person to play with.** A child is eager to forgive and forget so the playing can continue.

The Saga of AM/PM Kindergarten

Momservation: If you're waiting around for parenting to get easier, you're going to be waiting a long time.

☺   ☺   ☺

The letter came in the mail a month ago. We'd been waiting eagerly for it. Actually, that's not true… *I'd* been eagerly waiting for it. Nobody else really cared. Especially not my 5½ year-old son.

When it finally arrived in the mailbox my husband announced its arrival with, "I think that letter you've been waiting for is here."

I dove at the mail and held the letter out, noting the return address from Logan's new school. I hovered over it like it was a letter from Harvard, closing my eyes and praying that the words said, "Welcome and congratulations for beating out 68 other applicants to AM kindergarten."

I desperately wanted my son in AM kindergarten. Apparently, so did every other mom at kindergarten registration. When they instructed anyone who had a "hardship" case to turn the paper over and write out the details on the back of their enrollment form, the wave of air pushed through the multi-purpose room was like the leading edge of a cold front as everyone quickly flipped papers over trying to get their sob story down first. Including myself.

Actually, that's not true. I used to teach fifth grade and I decided when I had kids I wasn't going to be one of the pushy, overbearing parents that dominated my nightmares about showing up to teach class naked. So, at registration I simply marked the AM box and jotted a little note next to it that said, "Whatever is the best fit for Logan."

I was actually rather proud of myself for resisting the urge to flip the paper over, begging for my mornings free as I had grown accustomed to with both my kids going to AM preschool three days a week.

By kindergarten assessment, three months later though, I had found out my daughter would be in a five mornings a week pre-kindergarten program. When I thought of Logan also being in a morning program, I practically fainted with pleasure at the thought of having five mornings a week to get things done. I envisioned myself no longer having to write past midnight when everyone who wanted me to play with them had gone to bed (that includes my husband). I pictured myself getting a consistent exercise routine going. I dared to imagine actually reading the day's paper before the day was over.

So at kindergarten assessment when they told the group of parents assembled that SOMEBODY'S kid had to be in PM kindergarten, everybody in the room including myself thought, "Not mine." The teachers again mentioned writing down any hardship cases for AM on the back of the student information sheet, and being the prolific writer I am, I put down my moving sob story.

So here we were, the moment of truth in my hands. A small audience of my husband and mom circled around me as I excitedly opened the letter from Logan's school. Logan declined the invitation to come over, waving me off for Nova on television. Actually, that's not true, it was Sponge Bob.

I read the first line aloud:

"It was impossible to honor all the many requests we had for AM kindergarten, and hope you will agree that the proper placement of your child is the most important consideration."

I kept reading trying to decipher if this was a rejection or a confirmation. When there was more administrative mumbo jumbo

I quit reading aloud a silently scanned the following paragraphs looking for the AM/PM designation.

"Okay, yeah, whatever. Is he in AM or PM?" I almost shrieked. I scanned to the bottom of the page where there was a sticker added with Logan's name and his teacher's name. "Great, Mrs. So and So, but is she AM or PM?" That time I did shriek.

Don't get me wrong, I was deeply concerned as to the quality and qualifications of his designated teacher that would be molding my child's first perceptions of his schooling career. Obviously, she must be the Gifted and Talented Program teacher. But I was desperate in my rising panic for her to be an AM teacher.

Now everyone was over my shoulder trying to help me find the words designating my son's kindergarten time slot.

And then I saw it in the last paragraph. The teachers' names and what classes they taught.

"He's PM," I said quietly trying not to sound disappointed, hot tears stinging my eyes.

I looked up at my family and they had the pitying glances reserved for someone whose fish just died. You know, trying to validate their sadness, but it's just a fish.

Finally I said, "Well, I did say I wanted what was best for him…so this must mean he's in an accelerated learning program."

I knew it meant nothing of the sort, but it was the only thing I could tell myself so I didn't burst into tears. I had just gone from having three days a week to get my freelance writing and other little slices of adult freedoms in…to none.

I rushed to pick up the phone like an addict desperate to find their next score.

"I need to know what Meghan got. I wonder if Ryan's mom is home. I know if Hannah's in that class it's got to be accelerated. I wonder if I can find someone at the school on Saturday and make sure this is right."

The voice of reason made me put down the phone before I could dial. That would be my husband.

"It doesn't matter. Logan is going to have a great kindergarten experience whether he's in AM or PM. He's going to love his teacher no matter who they are. And if none of his friends are in his class, he'll meet 19 other new ones. It's just kindergarten. Let's save the battles for when it really does matter. And we can work something out so you can get your writing done during the day. Things happen for a reason and it isn't until afterward that you realize it all works out for the best."

Actually, that's not true, he didn't really say all that. But those are things we came up with later after I was done having my pity party. Once I got over the sting of my disappointment and put my own selfishness aside I was able to see reason.

I'm still not sure how it will all work out, but I am looking forward to walking my son to and from school, which I wouldn't have been able to do if he was in the AM class. I will also have one last priceless year of one-on-one time with my children, something I know I'll look back on and cherish when my kids would rather be with their friends than to be seen with me.

Plus, I did find it funny that in my girlfriend's school district all the parents wanted PM and she got AM.

Actually, that's not true. She did get PM and I was jealous her kid got in and she got the free time she wanted.

Independence Day

Momservation: Being a parent means teaching your children to be independent when all you really want to do is never let them go.

☺   ☺   ☺

I'm gonna cry. My biggest baby started kindergarten last month. I was so worried about him not being ready and now it turns out, I'm the one who's not ready.

Wasn't it just yesterday that this little guy with chubby little cheekies and leggies used to look up at me with arms outstretched asking, "Hold you?" when he wanted to be picked up? Now all of sudden he's picking out a Harley Davidson backpack for the first day of school with his spiked hair and Converse high tops.

It was just last year when I drove him by his future school to get him used to the idea of the transition from preschool to kindergarten. His apprehension nearly broke my heart when he asked, "Mommy, does kindergarten have windows?"

Perplexed by his question I replied, "Well, yes. Why?"

"So I'll be able to wave bye-bye to you when you leave me," he said bottom lip quivering with tears in his eyes.

Hang on, I need another tissue.

So there we were at the first day of kindergarten, I had prepared myself to do the tough love of prying his little fingers from my leg and firmly encouraging him to interact with the other kids and not be shy with the teachers.

As soon as we walked through the classroom and onto the playground he wrestled his hand from my grasp and ran for the monkey bars without a glance back.

"Logan, I'm going to go now, okay?" I called after him, worried he'd panic when his excitement wore off. "Logan?" I had to call again.

He waved me off without turning around. I'm still not sure if the hot tears stinging my eyes were tears of pride or rejection.

Wasn't it just yesterday when I was the overwhelmed first-time mother in Target, racing to get my shopping done while the baby was still sleeping? When those seasoned mothers would smile at me knowingly and say, "Treasure this time, they grow up before you know it," I wanted to flip them off and tell them I'd see them at the 1 a.m. and 3 a.m. feeding treasuring with me. Now it seems like an evil prediction.

Nearly six years have gone by in my first born's life and it may not seem like a lot of time in the spectrum of a lifetime, but as a mother I see it as one third of the way to him leaving me for something or someone else when he turns 18.

I love that he needs me right now. I love how the last thing he wants to do before he goes to sleep at night is give his mommy a hug and a kissie. I love that when everything seems to be going wrong in his little world, he thinks I can fix it and he wants me to. I love that he thinks nothing of telling me, "I love you so much, Mommy," and "I don't ever want to leave you Mommy."

So I guess it's not the threshold of starting kindergarten that I'm having a hard time stepping through. It's the transition into independence I'm aching over.

I know that as he starts school, he's going to learn so many wonderful things and skills and life lessons. He's going to grow in so many ways in his first formalized year of school, physically, mentally, socially, and emotionally. I would be sad if he didn't. But it is so hard to know that as he grows into the amazing person I know he will be, that he will be growing away from me. He's going to quickly realize that there is a world out there besides

Mommy and desire to be a part of it. Yet my world will always be him and I'll be fighting to keep him in it.

I can't even look at teenage boys right now because they represent the road my son is so quickly traveling. It makes my heart ache to think this little guy with the squeaky, sweet voice, his favorite blankie still constantly by his side, and an unabashed love for kitties will, before I know it, cast all these things aside as he grows up and into himself. The voice of reason (that would be my husband) tells me I will enjoy every stage of my son's growth and there will always be something wonderful about him to cherish, but I know at age 13 he's not going to stop everything and run over to me when I ask, "Can Mommy have a kissie?"

So just like when I got the letter for kindergarten saying my son was going to be in PM class instead AM class, I'm pulling myself up by my bootstraps and trying to shake off the selfishness and self-pity.

I will not hold my children back because I want them to stay my babies forever. I will embrace that my value is not tied to whether or not my children need me. I will not burden my children with my difficulty in seeing them grow independent, but will only show them my joy of seeing them soar to their highest potential.

But I'm going to need to buy some stock in Kleenex.

Fairy Fiasco

Momservation: Preparing for the moment when my kids realize the true meaning behind Santa Claus, the Easter Bunny, the Tooth Fairy and Kid Rock's lyrics to "All Summer Long."

☺   ☺   ☺

First let me say, THANK GOD it wasn't his first tooth.

But I do believe it was the second or possibly the third lost tooth in our house when the Tooth Fairy missed her date with destiny and forgot to show up. And not because the little guy didn't fall asleep fast enough, or because the Tooth Fairy fell asleep during the news (though that was part of it).

No, just like all the times the Tooth Fairy took a load of wash to the laundry room, received a phone call, got side-tracked and forgot to return to the task at hand to maybe catch a little Oprah, the Tooth Fairy once again got side-tracked and plain forgot there was one very excited little boy with a tooth waiting in a special little tooth box for the BIG EXCHANGE.

Burned forever on my brain like a searing brand "L" for Loser, I will never forget the sad, (okay, heartbroken—oof, that still hurts), expression on my son's face as he nudged me awake that morning. With total disillusionment he quietly said, "Momma, the Tooth Fairy didn't come last night. How come she didn't come?"

My heart sank into my stomach and I silently started cursing the Tooth Fairy that she was FIRED. I was going to have to cover her blunder for her.

First, I assessed the situation. "Did you check everywhere, honey? Under both pillows?"

"Yes."

Okay, can't slip back in and hide it under the other pillow.

Second, time for excuses. "Oh, honey. Maybe a lot of kids lost teeth yesterday and she had too big of a workload. I bet she'll come tomorrow for sure. Do you think?"

My first born, five year-old son nodded a disappointed agreement.

Okay, he bought it. But there were unshed tears sparkling in his eyes. God, I could just pummel that Tooth Fairy!

Third, buy some time. "You want to go watch a little TV before I make breakfast?"

He nodded his head again, then slowly left the room. I waited for the sound of the TV to come on. As soon as I heard it I jumped out of bed and went to Plan B.

I actually just learned of Plan B, Tooth Fairy Division, a few weeks earlier at playgroup when a mom shared her story of the Tooth Fairy falling down on the job.

What a ding dong, I thought. What kind of Tooth Fairy would forget to do the BIG EXCHANGE? I looked in the mirror. Big ding dong staring back at me.

So, the plan was to put the dollar inside the pillow case, explaining that the Tooth Fairy got a little lost.

Fourth—Shoot I don't have a buck! Not even four quarters!

Tip-toeing into my son's room, I actually stole a dollar from his piggy bank to put inside the pillow case. I grabbed a marker and wrote I.O.U. on my hand to remind me to pay him back.

Fifth, initiate Operation Restore Faith. I slipped the money inside his pillow case but then realized—what about the tooth that was still there?

I got the marker again and a piece of paper and wrote, "Dear Logan, I thought you might want to keep your tooth like the first time, so I left it for you." I even wrote it in big, loopy cursive—very fairy like.

I raced back to bed, and got in like I had never left. I called my son to come back. I tried to look sleepy and act like I just had a thought as I was laying there (Meryl Streep eat your heart out).

"Hey, honey, did you check INSIDE your pillow case? I've heard that sometimes the Tooth Fairy can get a little lost."

"I didn't!" my son said hopeful. He dashed back to his room. I was beginning to feeling redeemed.

"She came! She came!" I heard him shout. "And she left a note!" He came back in for me to read it. Before I could though, he asked, "But, what about the tooth?"

"Well, let's read the note," I said giving myself bonus points for the addendum to Plan B.

So, he was happy and the day was saved, but I still had lingering guilt that I had to resort to Plan B. There was still one last thing to do.

I called my husband at work. "Why didn't you remind me?!" I accused as soon as he picked up the phone. "You can't put this kind of responsibility on a woman you've nicknamed Side-track Sally! You didn't even leave me a dollar!"

"You didn't ask for a dollar," he sputtered.

"See what I mean?!"

"Honey, what are we talking about?"

I relayed the whole horrible incident and he assured me I hadn't scarred our son for life, and applauded me on the save. I told him there was an opening for the Tooth Fairy and encouraged him to take the position.

He declined the offer telling me to give the Tooth Fairy a second chance. "You'll laugh at this someday," he added.

And, of course, he was right. I have laughed with other moms about it and the lengths we will go to preserve the traditional joys of childhood.

But Santa Claus better skip the news and have two alarms set.

Thank God

Momservation: The Golden Rule: Don't do it if you wouldn't do it with Momma standing right there.

☺   ☺   ☺

Okay, I'm going to lay it all on the table right now. I'll admit, we are not a regular church going family. In fact, why don't we just remove the word "regular." My husband and I were both raised Catholic—in that we have the guilt, not necessarily the church time under our belts.

It's not that we're not a spiritual family. I have my direct line to God dialed up every night thanking Him for my happy, healthy, safe-from-harm family. Also, that I will try to be more patient tomorrow and give another shot at going a day without raising my voice. Well, okay, running to shut the windows so the neighbors don't hear me yelling at my kids.

Actually, my husband and I have had discussions about how to introduce faith and spirituality into our home. It is an important value for us and we feel strongly that with or without church our children will have a solid, yet fluid belief basis. We decided we would just roll with the punches and introduce such intangible concepts as God, Heaven and Spirit in small, age appropriate doses as it presented itself.

It started off pretty easy. At Thanksgiving we would talk about being thankful for our gifts in life, including our gifts from God. My four year-old daughter, our more spiritual child, initially challenged us initially with some very thoughtful questions like, "How did God know you were going to be my Mommy?"

At the time, we were able to field her questions and lob back simplified answers that satisfied her curious mind. For example, I told her, "God picked me out special just for you." Piece of cake.

At Christmas, we talked about baby Jesus and who he was. I'd buy or check out some books that touched on the true meaning of Christmas that fit closely with our faith and would use storybook examples as a bridge to any gaps in my teaching. A dash of Santa, a touch of Jesus…God, I mean—gosh—these kids were turning out great!

When the kids got older and the questions started getting tougher about who exactly this Jesus fellow was and where exactly was Heaven and how come we can't see God, but he can see us…I turned to a Christian book store and bought books with titles like *Who Made God?* and *Someday Heaven*. I'd like to say it helped, but to be honest, I think they got so bored that they pretended to understand so I would stop reading these books to them.

I was still feeling pretty good, though, with my competency in raising faithful children despite our lack of parochial attendance.

And then the fish died. Yes, there's nothing like your child's first experience with death to slap a pop quiz of spiritual aptitude on you.

First, I thanked God it was just a fish. Then I turned to my 5 ½ year-old son whose body was shaking with heaving sobs, my heart aching for him, and decided it was time to step up the religious education, hoping deeper meaning would provide him some level of comfort. Here's just a little snippet of how well it went:

Mom: Honey, I know you're sad your fish is gone, but he's in a better place.

(It wasn't even his fish, it was his sister's. She was in bed blissfully unaware in her four year-old state of mind that she should be sad that her fish just got flushed. She had closure with, "Bye, bye Fishy!")

Son: Where did the fish go?

Mom: He's in Heaven, Honey. (Fish in heaven? Not sure. Sounds good.)

Son: How can he be in Heaven if Daddy said we flushed him to the ocean?

Mom: Um, well, fish go to a special Heaven. Ocean Heaven. (Curse Daddy. Where is he anyway? Let him field some these questions!)

Son: Why did he die?

(Okay, bought Ocean Heaven! Moving on!)

Mom: Oh, Honey. Everything dies. Things don't live forever. (Sensing teachable moment with aging family dog, I go for it.) Even our doggie isn't going to live too much longer. But just because we lose them, doesn't mean we stop loving them.

Son: Kyber's going to die?!

(Uncontrollable sobbing. What was I thinking?)

Mom: The dog's fine! The dog's fine! I'm just trying to say… Hey, want to get a Slurpee tomorrow?!

Needless to say, there is a reason why I was a public school teacher and not a Catholic school teacher.

In all seriousness, in wanting the best for my children I know they are going to need a strong moral compass, a solid belief system and the safety net of unquestionable faith to get them successfully through life. It's a confusing, wonderful and horrible world out there and I will do whatever is necessary to prepare my children emotionally, physically, educationally and spiritually for what lies ahead.

I take any opportunity to thank God for my children. Without any hesitation I can say having children has made me a better person. I pray regularly that I will do right by these gifts from Heaven. That I will be able to do everything in my power to provide for them a solid introduction into everything necessary to be a good human being with a full, productive, happy life on earth…and beyond. In order to do that I know I must teach them, no matter how tricky and hard it can be sometimes, to have faith and thank God for our blessings.

I know we still have our work cut out for us though. The other day while driving my daughter home from her parochial preschool, she told me in an exasperated tone, "I don't know why we sing a song thanking God for our snack. We should be singing a song thanking the grocery store. THAT'S where food comes from."

A Mother Is Never Surprised to Find...

Momservation: You better make it good, because it's nearly impossible to surprise a mother.

☺   ☺   ☺

Welcome to the initial installment of A Mother is Never Surprised to Find... Where the second you become a mom, things cease to amaze you because kids like to keep life interesting. The list of things your child will do, say, or pull to little or no reaction from Mom is endless, but I'm going to have to put a cap on it here, cause I've got a Costco run to make.

A Mother is Never Surprised to Find...

- a turtle in the bathtub when you don't own a turtle
- objects in a poopy diaper that weren't served in a previous meal
- a lost sippy cup with curdled milk buried in the sandbox
- a dead frog in the freezer
- two months' worth of milk money on the bottom of a backpack
- her son trying to leave the house in a duct tape shirt
- her daughter trying to leave the house with badly applied make-up
- a live snail collection in a shoe box in the closet
- her bra being used as a water balloon sling shot
- an empty milk jug put back in the refrigerator
- a cube of butter being eaten like a popsicle
- her dining room chair propping up a bike jump
- her daughter shaving her stuffed animals with her razor

- a Lego in a clogged drain
- tadpoles in the toilet
- poop and vomit can shoot across a room
- an already colored coloring book wrapped up as a gift
- the cat dressed in doll clothes
- the dog in a pair of boxers
- a ceiling fan being used to shoot things across the room
- dried boogers on a headboard
- her couch cushions outside on the trampoline
- Daddy's tie being used as a fly swatter
- the leaf blower tied to a skateboard
- her toddler brushing her hair with the toilet bowl brush

Feel free to add to the list. But I'm telling you now, I won't be surprised.

Vacation vs. Trip

Momservation: Definition of hope: "One day we'll look back at this and laugh."

☺   ☺   ☺

Don't hate me because I'm writing this from the beach. Okay, go ahead.

But before you move on, let me paint my picture for you, because I want to give hope to mothers everywhere who are still taking "trips" rather than "vacations" when they try to travel with their children.

That used to be me.

I will never forget that first major "vacation" Hubby and I took with our two kids under two. We were going only an hour and a half up the hill to Lake Tahoe. But not only was our Ford Explorer filled to capacity with diapers, toys, strollers, baby food, baby supplies (there is not enough room here to list everything, so I'll stop now), we had to buy a cargo carrier for the roof to get it all in.

As we were pulling out of the driveway I asked Hubby, "So are you excited for our first vacation as a family?"

"This is not a vacation," he growled at me, "this is a trip."

And for years to come we would have many more trips.

But as I sit here on a deck overlooking an Aptos beach on a glorious 90-degree day, a cold beer at my elbow and BBQ sausages on the grill, I'm looking over at my six and seven year-old children. Watching them contentedly throw a ball around after digging in the sand for sand crabs and playing in the surf for hours, I've realized—I have finally arrived.

It is truly a vacation. There is relaxation. I can sit for long stretches without having to entertain, distract or hover over my children. The balance has finally swung in my favor where it is actually more fun than work now to try and take a holiday with the kids.

And the only reason I put fingers to keyboard at this very moment is to give myself an electronic pinch that this moment is reality and not fantasy. That there will be a record somewhere that this is actually happening, because I thought it never would. I also want to give my comrades in the trenches of motherhood a ray of hope, that those dark days of trips will one day dawn into a glorious, magnificent vacation.

Actually, really, as I'm hoisting another beer, I'm indulging in the fantasy that I am a New York Times best-selling author and this is how I write my novels.

10 Free Indoor Activities for Maximum Fun

Momservation: You're guaranteed to have a good time when you entertain yourself.

☺   ☺   ☺

The western United States is doing its impression of a frying pan right now. In Sacramento, where we live, going outside is like jumping from the frying pan into the fire. We aren't even venturing into our pool because it's doing its impression of a hot tub.

Years ago when my friend, Janine, moved to Arizona I questioned how she would survive the brutal desert summers. She explained it this way: "Like you do in the winter. We just stay inside."

Key difference though: You can count on restless kids being in school for good portions of the day in the winter. The longest days of the year seem especially long when you've got hot, cranky kids cooped up inside.

But I've got two words for you to help solve this dilemma: Diversionary Tactics.

And I've got another word for you that will seal the deal for locking yourself inside with restless, whining kids: Free!

Here's a list of **10 Free Indoor Activities for Maximum Fun** (to beat maximum heat) that can be modified for any age level:

10 Free Indoor Activities for Maximum Fun

1. **Make ice cream in a bag.** If you have milk, sugar, vanilla, kosher salt, ice and zip lock bags you're already good to go without a trip to the store!

2. **Board game stations.** Have Rumikub set up on the dining table, Sequence on the living room coffee table, Pay Day in one bedroom, Sorry! in another bedroom, and finish with Gestures in the master bedroom (or whatever games and rooms you have). You can do speed rounds, wager rounds (we bet state fair ride tickets), winningest player, or just for fun!

3. **Get crafty with Pinterest.** Whatever your resources are or whatever your fancy is, there's something for everyone: packing tape postcards, homemade lava lamps, create and eat veggie trays that look like Sesame Street characters, paint your nails to look like Converse High Tops, carving a watermelon like a pumpkin...what will you make to feel so clever and creative?

4. **Interactive movies.** Pick a favorite or popular movie and assign crazy hijinks to perform whenever a certain word is mentioned or scene appears. Ex: Monsters Inc. Anytime you hear "Sully" you thump the table with your hands. Anytime you hear "Mike Wazowski" you do scary feet. Anytime a child screams everyone runs around the house screaming. Anytime you hear "Boo" you hug the person next to you.

5. **Cards only.** Play for points, pennies, bragging rights, or loser does the other siblings' chores, but only card games allowed: Rummy, Crazy 8's, Spoons, Speed, Double Solitaire, Blackjack, War, Spit, Uno, Hearts...go one on one or play as a group, but I guarantee your kids will get hooked and keep playing them all summer.

6. **Make forts.** Pillows, blankets, mattresses, anything's fair game as long as it's put back. Then bring in a board game,

cards, iPods, iPads, or drinks and snacks and enjoy Mom letting you tear up the house without getting mad!

7. **Hall ball.** If you have a bocce ball or croquet set and a hallway you're good to go for a modified indoor game! (i.e. softer throws and hits) Wickets can be pushed into bars of soap to stand up for croquet and a closed door or end of hall stands in for a wall for bocce ball. If you don't have these outdoor sets, you can improvise with tennis balls, whiffle balls, or baseballs and use wire hangers for wickets and baseball bats for mallets.

8. **Penny pitch.** Everyone gets a pile of pennies (or quarters for high rollers). You stand 7-10 feet from a wall. You pitch your penny trying to get it closest to the wall. Whoever's penny is the closest gets all the pennies.

9. **One-Four-Twenty-Four.** It's not gambling with dice it's teaching math and finance! Buy-in is 10 cents. Everyone takes a turn rolling six dice. You get up to six rolls and you have to pull out at least one die every roll. During these rolls you need to get a one and a four to "qualify." With the rest of the dice you 're trying to get the highest cumulative points to win the pot. It doesn't matter which roll you pull out a 1 and a 4, but you have to have it all by the last roll—the qualifier with highest total points wins the pot.

10. **Indoor scavenger hunt.** Break into teams to find different lists of items that can be found around a house. Set a timer and pick a prize for the person or teams who can find the strangest or funniest things found in a home.

An August Reminder

Momservation: You can't always do it right the first time. But if you appreciate that there was a first time, you did something right.

♥   ♥   ♥

August is a tough month for me. It's not because the kids are going back to school and back to the grind of coordinating schedules, homework and extra-curricular activities, although that is daunting. What is it anyway with kids going back to school so early in August? What happened to the unofficial end to summer and start of school after Labor Day? Okay, don't get me started here.

Seriously, August is tough because it is my own personal yearly reminder to cherish my children, take joy in each of their smiles, laughs and giggles. It reminds me to be grateful for the opportunity to see them make mistakes and watch them grow from them, to drink in their innocence and be refreshed by it. It whispers to me to feel blessed to be a parent and the reward of overcoming the fights, the challenges and frustrations to get to that sweet spot of bursting with pride over your precious charges.

But why do I need August to remind me of this? I need my August memory because it is easy to love your children when they are being good and sweet and wonderful. It is when they test your patience, when they are less than angelic, when they fight, when they whine, when they need you even when you feel you have nothing left to give, when parenting seems like too tough of a job description for what you thought you signed up for.

What gets me through those times when I'm having difficulty summoning my mommy compassion and unconditional love is August 1983. It is what makes me a better person, a better parent, and someone who I think has earned the right to pass on a few words of wisdom.

August 10, 1983 is a day I use to remind myself that having children to yell at, argue with me, turn my hair gray, test my patience, make my life more difficult, and run me ragged is better than having no children at all.

That day has meant different things to me over the years and guided my life monumentally through its various stages, but it took on an entirely more profound meaning when I became a parent.

On that day over twenty years ago now, I lost a sister, which is devastating in its own right, but my mother and father lost a child—something my heart recoils at, my mind races away from, and my spirit whimpers in fear of when I even try dip my toe in what that experience must feel like as a parent.

My little sister was born August 21, 1976 and died ten days before her seventh birthday in an accident in our home. Now days they have safety plugs on hair dryers and a permanent tag that warns of all the things we did not do that day a blow dryer fell into my sister's bath. In an instant, lives are forever set on a new course, for better or for worse.

I've tried to choose for better, but with my son quickly approaching his seventh birthday, old fears resurface and the unimaginable question whispers in my ear like buzzing mosquito, "What if this is all I got?" It is a question I feel both bitter about being forced to contemplate yet blessed to have long ago gained such a clear perspective.

So when my friends give me the greatest compliment a parent can ever hear, "You seem like such a good mom. You are so patient and good with them," it is not without conscious effort and appreciation for the ups and downs of parenting that I constantly strive for and am aware and checking myself with.

Tomorrow is not promised. Your children are, despite some days to the contrary, a miraculous gift—little reminders of heaven here on earth, physical representations of unconditional love. You, as a mother, may have given birth to them and, as a father, was a partner in conceiving them, but somewhere, in a way we here on earth have a hard time wrapping our brains around, these precious souls chose us to guide them, love them, and cherish them.

So get to it. You don't need an August to remind you of it. I hope my story can be your August. On those days when you're looking for your children's receipts to send them back, stop and ask yourself, "What if this was all I got?" Then go kiss them, hug them, and take another look at that mischievous sparkle in their eyes.

Funny how fighting can become music to your ears.

Me and Sommar, age 6

Kindergarten Contrasts

Momservation: Boys and girls are different but Snack Recess is loved by all.

☺   ☺   ☺

This time last year I had my oldest child finally realizing that he wasn't being thrown to the wolves by being forced to start kindergarten. He had not been at all happy about leaving the safety and comfort of preschool and was not buying my pitch that kindergarten would be a fun and enjoyable.

I was so relieved after his first day of kindergarten when I asked him how his day went and in typical boy and future teenager fashion explained in detail, "Fine."

I knew then that I should've gone into dentistry because getting any kind of detail about his days in school was going to be like pulling teeth. As we walked home, I continued to gently prod him for any signs of emotional damage or hints of joy about embarking on his new frontier. But alas, the only thing he seemed to get slightly excited about was what was served for snack.

This is not to say he didn't enjoy kindergarten. He actually really liked it. But after being married to his father for ten years, for whom my son is a carbon copy, I have come to learn how to interpret Aloof Male. It is not necessarily what is said, but what is observed.

For example, first, I noticed my son became eager to go to school and do homework. Second, he didn't cling to me or show any sign of resistance at drop-off. And third, I overheard him tell his sister, "Kindergarten's pretty fun, Whitney. We have a guinea pig."

This year is my youngest child's turn to begin her elementary adventures with kindergarten. So after the experience of nearly having to shoot my son with a tranquilizer gun to get him through the front door of kindergarten, I started probing early for signs of apprehension in my daughter.

I was certain she was going to be fine with it since she dove into pre-kindergarten like ants on a picnic. Bless her little heart, she is a carbon copy of me, and she is the definition of teacher's pet with her love of school and pleasing the teacher.

So imagine my surprise when I asked her in August if she was excited about starting preschool and she said no. When I asked her if she was nervous she said yes. And without getting out my dentistry kit, she revealed why.

The divergent roads of life traveled by boys and girls flickered before me as my five year old daughter, in typical female and future teenager fashion, took a deep breath and with flamboyant animation complete with hand gestures and eye rolls explained, "I'm nervous I won't make any friends. I didn't have any friends when I first started in Mrs. D's class and it took me a long time to make friends in Mrs. D's class, but then everybody ended up being my friends. And what if people are mean to me or don't like me? If Alex isn't in my class or David or Ben, then I won't have any friends. But if they are all in my class then we can all be friends and then it will be okay because then I will have friends."

After listening with veiled amusement to my far from friendship challenged daughter, I counseled, "Honey, I don't think you will have any problem making friends. You just look for a friendly face on the first day of school, sit next to them and say, 'Hi, I'm Whitney. What's your name?'" She seemed satisfied with this solution to her angst and I was happy not to have to reload the tranquilizer gun.

The point is both my children were afraid to start kindergarten for fear of leaving what was familiar and comfortable. But my son was nervous out of emotional immaturity and my daughter for social fears. There are plenty of research and studies out there also substantiating these differences in male and female experiences with education.

It is just another example I've noticed of boys and girls being wired differently. Both children had valid reasons from flip sides of the coin to be apprehensive about kindergarten and I wanted to make sure as a parent I validated their fears, but then gently pushed them on their way and out of the nest. It's interesting that no matter how hard we work to create similar and equal experiences and opportunities, it just has to be recognized that it will always be interpreted uniquely to their inherent perspectives.

But enough with the psycho-babble—my babies are leaving the nest! I am officially a stay-at-home mom, with no kids at home! I'm going to cry…no wait, I'm going to go grab the paper and eat a bowl of raw brownie mix in blissful peace and quiet.

And my daughter, for those of you who need closure, bounced out of her first day of school with a gaggle of giggling girlfriends in tow.

Houston, We Have a Problem

Momservation: I think my kids are going to become astronauts because there is nothing left on this earth for them to fight about.

☺   ☺   ☺

You know as much fun as kids can be, sometimes they can really suck the fun out of things.

Bring them down to the river to look for ladybugs and they start arguing over who gets to hold the jar. Soon it becomes a one-upmanship to see who has caught the most ladybugs.

"I've got 15!"

"Oh yeah, well I got 17!"

"No you didn't because three flew away when you tried to put them in the jar, so I'm ahead!"

"You're a cheater! Mom!"

Take the kids to get ice cream and soon it's a showdown over who gets to order first, whose got three licks more ice cream, whose flavor tastes better.

"Mint chip is the best!"

"Mint chip's boring. Chocolate fudge brownie is way better."

"You're a do-do."

"You're a ding-dong."

"Mom!"

I'm pretty much ready to cancel Family Movie Nights because it traditionally starts with an argument over which movie to rent:

"I want to see *Monsters vs. Aliens*."

"We've already seen that. I want to see *Sandlot*."

"Well we've already seen that 50 bazillion-jillion times. No way!"

"Mom!"

Followed by a wrestling match in the kitchen over who captains the popcorn machine:

"It's my turn to dump the popcorn!"

"No it's my turn!"

"Mom!"

Finishing with me shutting off the movie early because someone won't stop touching someone or quit hogging the covers:

"Mom, tell Logan to stop touching his pinky toe to me!"

"Mom, tell Whitney to get her hair off my side of the bed!"

It's times like these, when the kids suck the fun out of what should've been a nice family moment, that I end up shouting, "You know I don't have to be doing this! I could be doing something a lot more fun by myself—like cleaning bathrooms or folding laundry!"

To which the kids know they've really crossed the line now and immediately fall into order.

Hammy Heartbreak

Momservation: Pain is the price of love.

♥   ♥   ♥

Rough week this week. Our beloved Hammy, the diabetic hamster, went on to the big exercise wheel in the sky.

And I had one devastated little boy on my hands which in turn devastated me. Holding Hammy's fading little furry body in his hands Logan sobbed, "This is the worst day of my life!"

I don't know whose heart ached more—his for Hammy or mine for my son.

The day Logan's cousin gave him a hamster for his eighth birthday only nine months ago (without checking with Mommy or Daddy first, mind you), it was love at first sight. How could we say no to a child who has so desperately wanted a fuzzy, little kitten from the moment he said, "Meow-Meow kitty" at a year old—who now recognized this fuzzy little dwarf hamster as its surrogate?

Oh, and how he loved Hammy. Every morning he would collect her from her cage, rubbing his cheek along her calico fur proclaiming, "I just can't resist her! She's so cute and soft!"

He even created her own special jingle. So many times I'd hear him sing, "Hammy is the cutest, cutest, littlest, littlest, sweetest, sweetest, prettiest, prettiest Hammy!"

Logan diligently cleaned her cage, he was her fierce protector from overzealous young visitors, and every night he and I made sure she had fresh food and water before he'd call out to her cage on his dresser, "Night, night Hammy. I love you."

So when I noticed Tuesday morning that Hammy seemed more sluggish than usual, a creeping dread ran through me. The same dread I had some weeks ago when I realized we had an unwell hamster—diabetes, common in dwarf hamsters. I thought we had held off the inevitable with a change in diet and care. But that morning I knew…this was the day my son's heart would be broken.

Later, when I realized the end was near, I called Logan and his sister in to break the news and say good-bye. It was excruciating to witness his devastation and it took everything in me to hold it together to provide him a measure of strength and comfort in his time of raw despair. One of my toughest motherhood experiences to date.

Later, after many tears and a giant Slurpee to ease the heartache, we laid Hammy to rest in my flower wagon in front of Logan's bedroom window—where he could always see flowers blooming in her memory. Then we put his favorite picture of him holding Hammy in a frame where her cage used to be on her dresser.

The hurt is still fresh, the loss still raw, and the sadness lingers like a wet blanket of fog. And that's just Mommy aching for her son's first lost love and the tears he still cries.

Will there be another hamster? My heart can't take it. It looks like a cat may finally be in our future, because despite me being allergic, at least I know it should live a good dozen years before I have to deal with it going to the big cat nip patch in the sky.

Summers Past and Present

Momservation: Run up a hot street in bare feet, throw a water balloon, or scrounge for change as the ice cream man gets closer and you'll feel like a kid again.

☺　　☺　　☺

I actually feel bad for my children.

It's not their fault their generation of parents just aren't comfortable letting kids venture too far from home in search of the cure for summertime boredom.

My kids have listened with envy to all the thrilling stories of summers past from my own generation and their grandparents—where kids could run free without checking in until dusk, swimming was done in waterholes with no adult supervision, risky adventures were hatched out of boredom and little supervision, and we all survived to tell about it.

At night when oral histories are the favorite request over bedtime books, my children listen in rapt amazement at things we used to experience as kids.

There's Gammy's tale of growing up in swamps of Pascagoula, escaping the heat and mosquitoes, a passel of brothers, sisters and cousins ranging in age from six to twelve at the edge of a water moccasin infested swamp. All summer long they rode that rope swing perfecting their aim over the submerged roots of the Cyprus tree to the sweet spot in the center of the waterhole. It wasn't until a neighborhood kid hung on too long and dropped right into a water moccasin nest there that they realized they'd been flirting with such danger.

And to think I feel like I'm putting my children's lives at risk if I don't sunscreen them every time they head for the pool.

There's also Grandpa's story of he and his cousin taking their brakeless go-cart up the hill five blocks from Cannery Row in Monterey and hoping for the best on the way down. They would position one lookout on Lighthouse Avenue, the busiest intersection, but as for the other four blocks, well, evasive steering and crashing luckily never had to be tested.

Makes worrying about my son riding his bike to his friend's house down the street seem a little tame.

I spent many childhood summers down at the local creek in Concord. With no air-conditioning or pools to escape the heat my brother and I would troll barefoot through the littered water looking for bottles to recycle, scooping up tadpoles and draping ourselves in moss to look like The Creature from the Black Lagoon. We would refresh ourselves in shoulder deep water only found under the bridge, by now a good mile from home and out of range of the "come when I call you" rule. But we always made sure we were home by dark, the last line in the sand of being busted.

My kids have waded the waters of our local creek in search of tadpoles and adventures. They always come when I call them because I'm right behind them. And everyone's wearing Tivas.

My husband also has tales of stretching the limits of the stay within earshot rule growing up in Burlingame. He and his buddies would ride their bikes down to the local canyon spending the day building forts in the thick brush and trees. Sometimes they'd see how many snap turtles they could find that people had dumped in a lake near there and sometimes they'd hop the fence of the local golf course to collect balls out of the water hazard to hit around later. He'd always be back by dinner and whenever his mom asked him what he'd done that day he'd say, "Not much."

I always know what my kids have done that day because I've usually planned it for them.

It is a sad testament of the world we live in today that unless I have orchestrated some safe and sane summer adventure, my kids would be restricted to their own front and backyards. A little overprotective? Probably. Could I let them test the boundaries of safety and precaution without consequence? Maybe. Do I have grounds for my concern and paranoia? Definitely.

How about every time I ride my bike or jog through my neighborhood I have seen cars treat stop signs as optional? How about the sex offender registered under Megan's Law one street over? Or that my kids couldn't hear me call for them over the roar of speeding traffic on a major street near us or the constant buzz of leaf-blowers?

I recognize there are two extremes here. Somewhere in between the days of negligent supervision and overprotective parenting is the answer. But until I feel comfortable with the common denominator of my children's maturity and responsibility and suitable summer diversions, I feel best planning their summers and being a part of their fun.

Of course, I still let them get bored so they'll learn how to create their own fun and adventures. But the craziest I've let them get so far is going out of the house at dusk without mosquito repellant.

Pace Yourself

Momservation: Why do people never ask men how they are able to balance work and family?

☺   ☺   ☺

On your mark, get set, go! School is in session and you're officially out of the blocks.

School clothes, school shoes, and school supplies have been bought. Kleenex for the classroom has been donated. You've filled out emergency cards, field trip forms, and made donations to PTA and for science. You've already been signing off on homework and reading logs and after some early jostling over making lunches and getting to school on time, the race to get back into the school routine seems to be going well.

But just when you think you've settled into a comfortable pace, it begins: the push to volunteer at your children's school. We need a Room Parent! We need a Field Trip Parent! We need an Art Docent! We need volunteers in the classroom! We need you on PTA! We need an Auction Chair! We need a Fall Festival Committee! We need help with Beautification, Staff Appreciation, Procurement, Art Night, Movie Night, Dance Chaperones....the list of help needed so your child has the perfect school experience in endless.

Suddenly, you're feeling the tempo speeding up and you get caught up in the pack sprinting toward the finish—which depending on how many kids you have can be at least 12 years ahead! But you're not comfortable pushing the pace. You're already exhausted with all your other work and family responsibilities.

Besides, you really have no interest in being room parent. You really don't have the time to get involved in PTA. You don't really have the ambition to be Procurement Chair. You'd like to do a field trip here and there and maybe volunteer in the classroom when you can, but then the pressure mounts to keep up with providing the best possible school experience for your children.

In panic the pack works into a frenzied pace. Nobody is stepping up! They kids won't have art! We don't have enough drivers! The kids won't have class parties! The Auction is our biggest fundraiser and the kids need new laptops to stay current! The classrooms are over-crowded, who will read with all the kids? We don't have enough volunteers to run the games at the Fall Carnival! The campus is a mess, the teachers don't feel appreciated, the dances are under-supervised, and nobody shows up to the PTA meetings!

Before you know it you are sprinting to bring gluten, sugar and nut-free cookies to the classroom party. You are racing to cover your shift at the Fall Carnival. You are at the school on a Saturday spreading mulch. You are running feverishly to get restaurant gift cards and donated golf clubs for the Auction. You have packed your SUV with children for every field trip. You have listened to hundreds of kids read and become an expert on making staff feel appreciated. And you are solidly in the front pack that is 10% of the parents doing 100% of the volunteer work.

By the time your kids are in high school you are exhausted by the pace. You drop out in sight of the finish line.

But the reality is, as important as the formative years are, the prep years are critical. Where your kids end up in life and how they spend the last years leading up to adulthood really is cemented in their last four years of schooling—when grades really matter, support with course work and good study skills matter, college entrance exams matter, and academic, sports, performing arts, motivated ambition and school pride and spirit matters.

So before you grasp that volunteer baton in kindergarten, full of energy and excitement to give your children the best possible school experience and support remember this:

It is a marathon. Not a sprint.

Pace yourself. Start slow with what you're comfortable with and work up to a big finish which is really this:

You have supported a happy, healthy, best-prepared young adult for their future. And you all can feel good that you gave your very best right to the end.

Of this race. Next call: 18-23 year-old guidance and support. Good luck.

Missing: Patience. Reward Offered

Momservation: If patience is a virtue, my general moral excellence has a big blemish on it.

☺   ☺   ☺

Many times I've caught myself being in a rush for my kids to grow up.

And I'm talking more philosophical than just not wanting to have to change diapers anymore. Although, no one can be faulted for wanting a kid to hurry up and learn how to wipe their own butt.

More like, I thought toddler years would be easier than the demands of infancy. I thought grade school years would be easier than chasing around a toddler. Now I'm finding the grade school years aren't any easier, they just present a different set of challenges.

Unfortunately, if there is any patience to be found in my body, my daughter snatches it and smothers it, foreshadowing the teenager she will become if I don't hurry up and learn how to do this patience thing.

Sometimes I'm anxious for my kids to mature so they'll understand things with a wisdom that buffers them from frustrations of inexperience.

Or I see the seed of their potential and I become anxious to see them blossom into who they will one day become.

I find myself impatiently excited for them to experience all those wonderful firsts in life.

My husband believes the reason our son rolled over, crawled, walked, talked, and did everything early was because I put him through baby boot camp. True, I was impatient to witness these firsts, but it was because I wanted to experience these milestones before the day care provider did.

But when I see that my eight year-old son can almost fit into my shoes and we're shopping in the young men's section; or my seven year-old daughter writing songs about heartbreak and first kisses; and their step stool for the sink shows the dust and cobwebs of decommission, I feel like I'm being penalized for my impatience.

A lesson in careful what you wish for.

It makes me say desperate prayers of penance that I'm in no rush for my kids to be the next Michael Phelps and first woman president.

But thank you Lord, for whizzing me through those days of sitting in the Target bathroom waiting for the tinkle in the toilet and poopie in the potty.

Appreciating the Little Things

Momservation: You know you're a mom when the top of your gratitude list includes bathroom doors that lock for stealing moments to yourself.

☺ ☺ ☺

It's the month of thanks, but for busy parents it can be hard to feel grateful when all you want for Christmas is a chance to sleep in and not have to drive anyone anywhere.

In these hectic times of raising kids—where there's a constant hunt for that missing part of a uniform, rushing to the store for the forgotten materials for a school project, and emergency arrangements for carpool because you just can't get there in time—sometimes it's just enough to appreciate the little things. Like:

- A seven-hour school day releasing you from around-the-clock attention, supervision, and care given to a hyperactive preschooler.
- And the crock-pot—for being able to check dinner off your list by 7 a.m.
- Or the microwave. Hot meals in minutes—it's invention should be lauded right up there with the discovery of fire.
- Baby wipes. The affordable all-purpose cleaner, make-up remover, stain-lifter. They're not just for baby bottoms anymore.
- Costco. If you can't buy it at Costco, it doesn't exist.
- Plus Target—it's almost like that best friend that's always there for you.
- Last minute babysitters. Special place in Heaven for those who give up a relaxing night on the couch with Netflix.

- Pizza. Or chicken that comes in the form of a strip, nugget, or finger. Go ahead and throw mac and cheese in there too. For those days when you just don't have the fight in you.
- Yoga pants. Because it looks like you're giving more effort than just throwing on sweats.
- Pre-graded cheese, premade salads, prepackaged everything. I don't know how my mother raised a family without them.
- Starbucks. Because damnit, I'm worth it too.

See? That wasn't so hard to find some glimmers of gratitude to shine through the never-ending demands and exhaustion of parenthood. It even makes it easier to appreciate the people in your life.

Like the friends…who will tell you when you have something in your teeth, that maybe it's time to ditch the yoga pant uniform, or who bring your kid home when you forgot soccer practice was over pretending that was the plan all along.

Your husband…who pretends that left-overs is just what he was hoping to have for dinner, tag-teams nagging at the kids so you don't always look like the bad guy, and who still thinks it's funny when you point to the laundry basket when you tell him his socks are in the "dresser."

Grandma and Grandpa…who show up for soccer games that are really a group scrum around the ball with time-outs for referees tying shoes, who will take the kids to ice cream so you can shower and go to the bathroom in peace, who almost always are that last minute babysitter.

Your kids...Because life is so much more colorful with them in it. They may make life messy, but if you didn't get messy in this life—you didn't really live it.

Momservations®
Santa's Watching You

- If it can't be found on Amazon, it doesn't exist.
- Scoring the season's hottest toy for your kid is the equivalent joy of a child waking up on Christmas to find out they were on the Good List.
- As far as Santa's concerned, you've got to believe to receive.
- Naughty is way more fun than nice, but don't tell the kids.
- Clothes for Christmas are right up there with lima beans for dinner.
- Letting your kids help with wrap Christmas presents is an exercise in patience but not letting them help would be like kicking a puppy.
- If you have toddlers, either put your favorite ornament away for another year or go ahead and throw it on the ground right now and get it over with.
- The perfect Christmas card photo will be snapped the day after Christmas.
- A Christmas cookie taste so much better than cookies from the rest of the year.
- There should probably be a limit on pictures you can take for Baby's First Christmas.
- The end of a candy cane fits perfectly up a nostril. This is an important discovery if you're a toddler.
- There is no better re-gift than when your kid wraps up something from their room in a heartfelt gift to Mom.
- If we're not all kids on Christmas then we're missing the big picture.

Resolutions Meant to Be Broken

Momservation: It's never too late to water-down your expectations for yourself.

☺   ☺   ☺

I don't know about you, but I don't need New Year's and broken resolutions to make me feel any worse about myself. I do a pretty good job of it on a daily basis as evidenced by a never ending To Do List that mocks my continually interrupted productivity. Some days I put things on the list that I've already done just so I'll have something to cross off.

So this year, instead of making a list of resolutions I hope to stick to, I'm making a list of routines that I hope to be broken. Instead of setting myself up for failure I figure I'd have a better chance at being wildly successful padding the books in my favor. Take a look:

A Mother's Resolutions Meant to Be Broken

- Continue to race out the door at the last second for school trying not to pass on the habitually late gene to the children.
- On a regular basis grab a rotisserie chicken from the grocery store minutes from dinnertime with instant mashed potatoes, bagged salad, and bakery bread to pass off as a home cooked meal.
- Never remember where I left my keys, sunglasses, or iPhone.

- Curse daily about having to walk, feed, play with, and pick-up after the dog that everyone in the family promised to help take responsibility for.
- Nag the kids constantly to brush their hair, teeth, take a shower, and get to bed on time.
- Every time I do laundry threaten to not wash socks that aren't turned right-side-out or that the kids will start doing their own laundry if they can't learn to just put their clean, folded, clothes away,
- Randomly burst into tears near that time of the month and cry about how no one appreciates all that I do.
- Spend hours being creative in the kitchen to come up with a healthy new meal for my family that everyone will hate.
- Yell at everyone but myself for not unloading the dishwasher again.
- Continue to insist that Subway sandwiches accompanied by Powerade or a McDonald's meal with Apple Dippers substituted for fries is a decent dinner on the go.
- Vacuum more often so that the dog doesn't go crazy trying to attack the unfamiliar object.
- Add to my stash of belated birthday cards.
- Make sure to write all activities on the calendar and highlight in color codes then always forget to look at it.
- Run out of laundry detergent, bleach, and stain remover on a regular basis to avoid laundry.
- At least once a month drop kids off at wrong practice times and places.
- Buy birthday gifts at the last minute arriving late for parties because I picked the slow check-out line.

- Fill-up the DVR with shows I refuse to let my husband delete thinking one day I'm going to watch them.
- Try to see just how few groceries I can have in the house before I REALLY need to go shopping.
- Continue forgetting to empty the memory card and charge the video camera for important games, recitals, and other momentous events.
- Regularly nag the kids about living in a pig sty of a room as I kiss them goodnight.
- Drive around daily in a filthy car inside and out driving my husband insane that it doesn't occur to me to take it to a car wash.
- Never throw anything away, ever. Ever. (My husband made me add that last "ever.")

Wish me luck! Here's to a new year of traveling on a road of broken promises. If not, no big deal. It seems to be working for me.

Where Do Hamburgers Come From, Mommy?

Momservation: Trying to protect your kids from the truth is like leaving the liquor cabinet unlocked—if you think they won't find out you must like watered down Vodka.

☺   ☺   ☺

I wish I was a vegetarian.

Today, on the Hamburger Farm field trip with my son's second grade class, I had to look a Black Angus yearling cow in his big, beautiful, long-lashed eyes and tell him, "I'm sorry I will be eating you in a few years. I just can't say no to your delicious flanks. That and Ben & Jerry's Chocolate Fudge Brownie ice cream."

Thankfully, I was the only one distressed by this circle of life moment.

I was the picture of over-protective mother making sure I chaperoned this great Hamburger Farm field trip adventure, worried my son would find out where hamburgers really do come from. I was ready to cover his eyes and plug his ears to preserve his naiveté. No more magical hamburger stork, the truth revealed that Mommy and Daddy do it all the time and like it—eat slaughtered beef.

The trip started innocently enough with a petting zoo, corn pit (think ball bit with corn), and giant slides and tires to play on. The farm provided a BBQ hamburger lunch that I hoped was not fresh. Then we took a train to an acre in the shape of a hamburger that produced all a burger's natural ingredients. The kids started by grinding some wheat, saw some budding green tomatoes, pulled up some onions, tasted some lettuce, and getting a good look at the more fortunate dairy cow and her loins of cheese.

When the guide proceeded to tell us the dairy cow's neighbor was a Black Angus cow used for beef, I held my breath, scanning the faces of 20 second graders. But no quizzical looks appeared, no hands shot up with clarification, no child seemed disturbed with this revelation (if in fact, it was). No, the moment of truth was saved when the cow distracted from his own fate by taking a well-timed peepee, to the delighted gross-out of a passel of 8 year-olds.

As the guide moved us on to simulated milking of a cow, the only kid who did absorb just exactly where hamburgers come from said to no one in particular, "Now all he needs is a piece of cheese on his nose."

So, in the end, my kid still believes in Santa Clause, the Tooth Fairy, the Easter Bunny and that he didn't just pet his lunch at a petting zoo.

I sure hope they don't have a Victoria's Secret field trip in middle school.

Why Not to Spring Clean

Momservation: If the Lord had meant for us to do spring cleaning, He wouldn't have given us closets.

☺   ☺   ☺

It's the first full day of spring and I'll tell you what I'm **not** going to do:

Spring cleaning.

Why should I when I can still reap the benefits of Out of Sight Out of Mind that a closet door affords me? I may be barely able to shut a few of them, but that's nothing that a DO NOT OPEN sticker can't handle.

I've had a decorative tile prominently displayed in my home that declares a personal philosophy that I long ago adopted:

Good mothers have sticky floors, dirty ovens, and happy kids.

I think I need to etch on there – *and closets stuffed full of disorganized crap.*

I've long banked on the fact that my kids are going to remember the days when we dropped everything to go fly a kite, check out if there're butterflies at the river yet, or rode our bikes to see the rainbow of tulips our neighbor plants every year. Not whether Mommy kept a wicked clean and organized closet. They are not going to care if my blinds and ceiling fans were dust free. It won't bother them that I have expired canned goods, stale crackers and cookies, and never used spices in my pantry.

When they one day have kids of their own and are reflecting back on what to bring to the table from their own childhood, I hope it's the belief that these moments are precious and clean closets can wait.

To an extent. I certainly don't want us to end up on an episode of Hoarders or Clean House with Niecy Nash.

But the first day or the first weekend of spring should be celebrated by going out and playing with your kids, not cleaning house. Try some from this list:

Things to do with Your Kids Instead of Spring Cleaning

1. Plant a strawberry garden to harvest in the summer.
2. Look for lady bugs and caterpillars in the tall, green grasses.
3. Skip rocks at the river, pond, or lake or feed the ducks.
4. Ride bikes to go get Slurpees at the local 7-Eleven or gas station convenience store.
5. Fly a kite.
6. Go on a neighborhood scavenger hunt for blooming flowers to press between book pages.
7. Go cheer on a local baseball or softball game that your kid isn't playing in. Make sure to stop by the snack shack.
8. Play Frisbee.
9. Go to a local park and play Hot Lava Monster with them on the playground equipment (or whatever else their imagination invents).
10. Try to watercolor the sunset.

Here's to a layer of dust on top of your hutch so thick you can make dustmen.

Momservations®
Happy Birthday to You

- There's pretty good odds the guest of honor will nap through their one year-old birthday party.
- No matter how you wrap it, new clothes just don't register the excitement of a new toy or even a cardboard box.
- Reserving an inflatable bounce house for a party is a modern day rain dance.
- Never turn your back on frosting tester.
- The amount of money spent on a birthday party seems inversely proportional to the likelihood of said birthday boy/girl coming down sick the day of the party.
- Buying extra party favors, strangely enough, still does not guarantee you won't come up short at the end of a party.
- It is virtually impossible to get through a birthday party without someone crying.
- It's a good weekend when you don't have another birthday party to go to.
- For each additional child you allow to be invited, add an additional half hour of fighting over the completion of thank you cards.
- Any amount totaling over $50 in Target gift cards for a child is a waste and should be contributed to the greater good of the family.
- A slumber party for girls requires a completely different survival plan than a slumber party for boys.
- It is possible to have too much of a good thing evidenced by the melt-down of the birthday girl or boy.
- A gift worth giving is a gift worth receiving is a gift without a gift receipt being re-gifted.

Playground 1, Daughter 0

Momservation: If you can make it through childhood without stitches, breaking, fracturing, or spraining something, you didn't have enough fun.

☺   ☺   ☺

I think right up there with the fear of coming out of the bathroom with your skirt stuck in your underwear, is a mother's fear that her instinct was wrong and a trip to the emergency room was in order rather than a Band-Aid, a kiss, and instructing "just shake it off."

It's interesting how lax you get as your children get older. When my kids were little I thought a paper cut needed stitches. Any fever I was sure was the first stage of the West Nile Virus. A rash—the reemerging of Small Pox. A bump on the head, I was waking that kid every 20 minutes and checking pupils.

I once saw an ad in a magazine where a child was wrapped in bubble wrap—a sight gag on parents trying anything to protect their children. I thought it was an advertisement and I wanted to know if bubble wrap suits came in extra small.

I'm not sure when it happened, maybe after the first set of stitches. Maybe after the dislocated elbow. Possibly after seeing my son crash his dirt bike or a giant goose-egg rise out of his forehead. But at some point I realized my kids were pretty tough. They took a lickin' and kept on tickin'. I could keep them bubble wrapped on the couch or I could let them be kids and deal with the injuries one Band-Aid and kiss at a time.

Enter Whitney at age 8 and thanks to her older brother, Logan, tough as nails. Those two play like puppies and in the ensuing rough-housing Whitney has lost two teeth, gotten two stitches, dislocated her elbow and had countless other injuries all in the name of a little fun.

I was sure that out of my two kids, if there ever was a broken bone, it was going to be Whitney and somehow involve her overzealous brother.

Well, I was right on one count. It was Whitney, but her brother had nothing to do with it. Although she said, "It was at his baseball game, so I can still blame him."

It ended up being a playground injury—she slipped off a bar and broke her fall, and her arm.

At first when Whitney came up to me, not even a tear in her eye, to tell me she hurt her arm and thought it was broken, I nearly brushed it aside ready to remedy with a kiss. Especially since I was engrossed in the excitement of Logan's championship game. No tears, no big deal.

But after I got her some ice, thinking it was more to sooth her fear than her injury (Band-Aids, kisses and ice cure almost any ailment), Whitney started sobbing in pain. Way out of character. Everyone I had take a look at her arm thought it looked okay. But my mommy instinct was ringing like Spiderman's spidey sense. We did our RICE: Rest, Ice, Compression and Elevation and I got a doctor's appointment.

When I took Whitney to the doctor first thing the next morning, I had no doubt her arm was broken. I even asked her what color cast she was going to get. When the doctor delivered the confirming news, I felt a surge of validation that I got it right. I actually felt like I should've earned some sort of mommy badge of excellence for knowing this wasn't just a drill and what to do in case of a real emergency.

On the way out of the doctor's I asked Whitney what she thought of being first to the finish line of broken bones.

On the mend and back in usual form, a sly grin spread across her face, "Now," she said, "My brother can't touch me."

(Not So) Proud Parenting Moment

Momservation: Parenthood is a journey made up of little moments that make you gaze upon your child, turn to your spouse and say, "Whose kid is this anyway?"

☺   ☺   ☺

I like to think I'm doing a nice job raising my children. That at this point in the game I've firmly implanted some good morals, values and expectations. And most of the time I can look at my kids and honestly feel pride and satisfaction that these kids are going to do alright.

Other times I just pray I haven't messed them up too bad.

So the other day, I see a teachable moment and pounce on it. I figure I can give my kids a hands-on lesson by showing them what taking responsibility means (instead of yelling it at them while laying waste to teaching them to watch their tempers).

I was doing laundry. I HATE laundry. If I had the money of Oprah I'd just buy new clothes and underwear every day. Or if I had the body of Jennifer Lopez I'd just walk around naked.

So, there I was, wasting my precious time on this earth by Shout-ing out stains, and my kids go moping by because I made them put away their clean and folded clothes themselves.

"Hey, I got a question for you," I say to them. "Do you think Mommy likes doing laundry?"

"No, you HATE laundry," they say in unison. I'm not sure if I'm pleased with their perception or mad at myself for not setting a good example with a better attitude.

"Please, don't use the word "hate" – it's not a nice word," I say. Then I make a mental note to self: *Quit using the word hate—it's not a nice word. Probably should quit saying God d*** it, too.*

Despite their unfortunate, yet accurate, choice of words they stepped right into my teachable moment.

"Mommy doesn't like laundry, but I do it anyway, right?" They both nod. "That's what taking responsibility means. It means doing things because you should, because they need to be done, or because it's the right thing to do. You may not always like it, or want to do it, or it might be hard and no fun, but you do it anyway."

This is where my Proud Parenting Moment (PPM) happened. And if there was a font for sarcasm you would know already my kids didn't suddenly light up with understanding and drop everything to help fold clothes.

No, instead this little conversation unfolded:

Whitney says, "I HATE laundry. I never want to do it."

Logan then declares, "Well, you better learn to like laundry Whitney, because one day you're going to be a mom."

Says Whitney, "That's why I'm not getting married until I'm like, 64."

To which Logan replies, "Then you're going to be a lonely old lady who talks to her cats."

Whitney just shrugged and walked away, satisfied with that option.

But just to make sure my son didn't continue down this early wrong course of thinking laundry was women's work, as soon as Hubby got home I shoved a basket of clean clothes at him.

"Make sure you fold this in sight of your son, please."

The High Wire Act of a 3rd Grade Book Report

Momservation: There are a lot of parents walking around out there with A+'s on book reports, dioramas and science fair projects.

☺   ☺   ☺

Had to help my son with his third grade book report project this last week. Here's what went well with it:

- **He was prepared.** The book was read well in advance. He had an idea of what he wanted to do to meet the criteria for an advertisement billboard. He wanted to buy the poster board and get started well before the due date.
- **He was receptive to guidance.** Since he had never done this type of project before and he's only eight, he realized Mommy might actually have some valuable advice and strategies worth listening to.
- **He managed his time well.** He worked on it a little each day of the week so it didn't become overwhelming. There was no rush to finish it and he had time to set it aside if he grew frustrated.
- **In the end it came out wonderful.** It was actually a third grade-level production, driven by his own creativity and eight year old capabilities without too much interference by Mommy.

Here's what didn't go so well with the book report project:

- **Creativity is not his specialty.** He is a human calculator, but when it comes to arts he is a minimalist. He has no interest in putting a little extra effort into an art project or upping the bar beyond kindergarten stick figures.
- **Creativity is my specialty.** I had to physically remove myself and drew blood biting my tongue so that this would

not become the best third grade book report I have ever done.

- **He wasn't always receptive to guidance.** The fact that Mommy used to be a teacher holds no water in this house. Apparently, I know nothing and his teacher knows everything. The kid can be as stubborn as his mother.
- **The "Giving Your Best" talk and semantics.** It is a tightrope walk between pushing your kids to do their best and not eroding their self-confidence when they think they are. I think I finally found the right words after we had a joint melt-down over the supposedly finished project. Here's what I told Logan when he thought he was done and I thought he could have done a little more:

"For each grade of school there are higher expectations of what you should be able to do. Just because it worked in second grade doesn't mean it's still good for third grade. You've learned more so you should be able to do more.

"Tomorrow, you will probably see three types of book report projects: Ones that look like a little more effort could have been put into it. Others that look like a third grader gave their best effort. And a few that will look like their parents really enjoy doing third grade book reports. I want yours in the second group. So, this project is good, but how can it be made better?"

Later, on my volunteer day in the classroom, I got to see all the book report projects. There were some that could've used a little more effort. There were many that looked like a third grader gave their best effort. And there were some where Mommy and Daddy are going to get an A+.

And with little interference and a bit of guidance from Mommy, my son's project was right where it was supposed to be with his best effort and he was proud of it.

For that I think we both deserve an A+.

Double Digit Panic

Momservation: You know you've gone overboard on a birthday party when it becomes more work than when you gave birth to the birthday boy or girl.

☺   ☺   ☺

It's October. That means it's officially fall. When it's fall in our house that means three things.

One, we're full swing into all-soccer-all-the-time. At any given moment with our family someone needs to be at practice, coaching practice, at a game, cheering a game, washing stinky soccer socks, pulling dirty uniforms out of the laundry and giving them the sniff test, searching for a lost _____ (fill in the blank with cleat, shin guard, ball, water bottle, etc.), and trying to get dinner on the table amidst all this soccer chaos while trying to make sure homework gets done too.

The second thing fall means is the beginning of the silly season when Mommy busts out her seasonal/holiday decorations and transforms the house into (depending on how you view it) a wonderland of seasonal celebration or a Macy's Thanksgiving Day Parade gone horribly wrong by exploding in our house. Either way, it's like the annual holiday parade in New York—fun, entertaining and festive at first, but after a while you're ready to change the channel and move on. Plus, you feel sorry for whoever has to clean up everything afterward.

But the third and biggest thing fall and October usher in for us is my son's birthday. Now, if you're just joining this regularly scheduled program, you may not understand what that means. However, the preceding paragraph may have given you a clue I have a tendency to overdo things.

This is not any normal birthday though! This is Logan's 10th birthday. This is my first born baby's transition into double digits. It is Mommy having a heart attack because her baby is growing up too quickly as evidenced by a decade going by in the blink of an eye. It is the gateway to preteen. It marks the downhill run toward 18 and my baby eventually leaving me (although, I did have him sign a waiver saying I will always be allowed to call him my baby).

I know to Logan this is a huge milestone in his young life. I clearly remember it myself—when you roll that age odometer into double digits you officially leave baby stuff behind and ascend to the proverbial big kid playground. To anyone under ten you are worthy of worship. To anyone over ten, they can't lump you with the little kids anymore and have to bring you along. In the mind of a ten year old, double digits means you're practically an adult and might as well be since you know everything already anyway.

As Mom and a member of the double digit club for, let's just say a number of years, having my son hit ten years old feels like someone has suddenly hit the fast forward button on parenthood. And I don't like it.

Where were these button pushers when I could've used them during the sleepless and insanely mundane repetitive newborn years? Or the toddler years when I had two kids under two and a good day was when I got to brush my teeth and/or take a shower. Or even the early school years when I had only seven minutes a day when I didn't have my opposite schedule pre-kindergartener and kindergartner with me.

For me, this is when it's really getting good. Before children, when I fantasized what having a family would be like, this is what I pictured. Semi-self-sufficient kids enjoying a life of school, sports, friends and family togetherness. A house full of youthful chaos, hectic mornings, crazy afternoons, kids running in and out, shuttling to events, cheering in the crowd, beaming with pride, basking in the glow of their success, being there to support them in their failures.

These are the years when I want to spend time with them and they want to spend time with me. It's the years of shaping who they'll become, but witnessing their own personalities guiding the way. The years of preparing them for independence when they still can't imagine wanting to be free. The years of guiding their decisions while they still want your input.

Plus, I just really like my kids. Is it so wrong that I'm a little panicked because I don't want this time under one roof to end? (For you parents of teenagers, that was a rhetorical question.)

So even though this double digit birthday is a big deal for Logan, and I'll do everything in my power to make it special for him, it doesn't mean I have to like it.

Do you think renting a Monster Truck is overdoing it?

God Bless America and Other Expletives

Momservation: You have not earned your stripes as a mother until you utter the ridiculous, over-used, eye-rolling phrases your mother used to say.

☺   ☺   ☺

The other day I tripped over my daughter's soccer cleat I had asked her to pick up more times than I should've. "God Bless America!" I yelled both in pain and anger.

Then I looked around to see how my mother ended up in the room. Was that me? How long had I been using one of her favorite tag lines? When did I give up on my own bag of parenting tricks to reach into my mother's?

"I'll be darned," I said aloud.

Another one! I clamped my hand over my mouth before another of my mom's Momisms (as we liked to call them) could pop out. If a "Believe you me!" came out of my mouth next I was going to run and look in the mirror a la "Freaky Friday."

I always thought all my mom's common threats and sayings were like background noise. It seemed she was always yelling one of them at us, but you didn't pay attention until her tone changed or it was preceded by a "God Bless America!"

My mom was not a cusser. So if you did ever hear foul language come out of her mouth, you were about to be in deep kimchi (hot water/trouble) and you better run for the hills (in big trouble).

I used to think my mom's Momisms were silly rather than effective and was sure as a parent I would come up with better communication and expectations for my kids. Because you know, we always think we're going to do better.

131

But you know what? At some point we all turn into our mothers, hopefully giving her the respect and admiration she finally deserves. That's because loving your kids and wanting help and guide them into being the best people they can be doesn't change. It's every parent's wish to see their child succeed and be happy. And to that end, you will inevitably find yourself saying the things that parents have and will always say to their kids to keep them on the right path.

Even if it is yelling at the top of our lungs, "Do you hear me?"

And trust me, you don't want to reply, "Geez, Mom. The whole neighborhood can hear you." Deep kimchi.

Favorite Momisms and Their Meanings

1. If I have to tell you one more time...(said right before you've pushed it too far)

2. You have until the count of three...(but everyone knows you'll get the extra 2 ½ and 2 ¾)

3. Did you hear what I just said? or Do you hear me? (yelled at the top of your lungs)

4. I don't want to hear it...(so don't waste your breath)

5. I don't care who started it...(justice is not going to be served)

6. I sound like a broken record player...(this still gets the point across despite today's children having no idea what that is)

7. What, are your arms broken? (Warning shot over the bow, you better start helping)

8. Do I look like a waitress to you? (Can also be replaced with maid, chauffer, cleaning lady...)

9. What did you just say? (The calmer this is said, the bigger trouble you're in)

10. You get over here right now! (The last thing you want to do but to defy it would be bigger trouble)

11. Do you think I'm going to pay for that with my good looks? (too expensive)

12. I'll give you something to cry about...(empty threat but a warning none the less)

13. If you're bored I'll give you something to do...(worse than #14 because you are about to be put to work)

14. What is going on in there? (hide or run when accompanied by footsteps)

15. When your father hears about this...(bought some time until punishment, but may not be a good thing)

16. If I ever see you do that again...(got away with a warning this time)

17. You should know better than that...(maybe, but had to test it anyway)

18. What were you thinking? (that you wouldn't get caught)

19. Go to your room and don't come out until I tell you...(understood you'll still ask 50 times when you can come out)

20. What don't you understand about "No?" (it was worth another shot)

The Proof Is in the Pudding - Literally

Momservation: Obviously, you love one of your kids more than the other if someone has been dished an extra french fry at dinner.

☺ ☺ ☺

Careful, you're being watched.

I'm not talking about your neighbor's surveillance camera, or the slightly off bagger at the grocery store, or even your mother-in-law who suspects you just turn the towels around instead of washing them when she comes to visit.

We're talking about your very own children.

Whether you realize it or not they are watching closely (and very likely keeping a tally in crayon on the inside of their closet) for any sign that you love one of them more than the other.

And apparently, according to siblings, the signs are everywhere that you love one of them just a tad bit more than the other. Exhibits A-Z as seen through your children's eyes:

A. You let him watch 30 more seconds of TV than her before you made him get in the shower.
B. You gave her a kiss good-night before him.
C. His helping of pudding is 3 millimeters taller than hers.
D. You bought green bananas because she likes them that way best.
E. You gave him the extra french fry at the bottom of the McDonald's bag when it was her fries that looked like it was missing one.
F. You never let him watch Sponge Bob when he was little but she can when she's little.
G. One time you gave him 5 more Goldfish crackers in her snack cup than her.

H. You ALWAYS let her go first when it's time to _____ (fill in the blank).

I. You NEVER let her do _____ but he ALWAYS gets to (fill in the blank).

J. He got the first bite of the cookie dough batter.

K. She got to have a friend over and he didn't (regardless of no one being available).

L. His rice crispy treat square is bigger by at least a dozen crispies.

M. You ALWAYS drag him along to her performances (even though he chose not to participate).

N. You are ALWAYS watching his games and practices (even though she chose not to do a sport).

O. There are more baby picture of her than him.

P. There are more home videos of him than her.

Q. His chocolate chip cookie has more chips than hers.

R. You've made her unload the dishwasher possibly one more time than him.

S. He's had to clear the table when it was her turn.

T. There are more toys in her toy box.

U. He's got more 11 more pieces of popcorn in his carrying tray than her.

V. She got to pick the movie last time to go see.

W. He got to pick the movie last time to go see.

X. You laid in her bed longer at bedtime than with him.

Y. You gave him the chocolate donut with more glaze.

Z. You gave birth to him first.

Obviously, they're on to us. So this Christmas when you buy the exact same number of presents in the exact same dollar amount value, make sure you don't give yourself away by putting the prettier bow on his.

Mommy's Pity Party

Momservation: Locking yourself in the bathroom with a bottle of wine and People magazine may not be the solution, but it's a good start at throwing ideas at the wall to see what sticks.

☺   ☺   ☺

I invited my husband to the pity party I was having. He refused to put on the party hat I offered.

Mr. Voice of Reason apparently had other plans. He also pointed out he's been invited to these downer fests before and it's not worth the party favor (retail therapy). Plus, it always seems to revolve around my co-guest of honor, Monthly Friend, who does not get along with his wing man, Mr. Happy.

I had a great theme for this month's pity party too: I Don't Wanna. It was a hard choice between that and It's Not Fair. As in, I Don't Wanna clean the house because I will never have the satisfaction of seeing it clean for more than ten seconds. Or It's Not Fair I have to do ten loads of laundry when my dirty clothes make up 1% of the bulk.

The other dilemma I had planning for this come and bring your depressed friends party is how this would come across to my kids. After all, when they tell me they Don't Wanna I tell them, "I'm not asking you, I'm telling you. There are no options here."

Also, when they pull out It's Not Fair, I tell them, "Life's not fair. Get over it."

See where I'm going with this? My pity party theme was quickly morphing into Do As I Say, Not as I Do.

Normally, I'm a big believer in picking yourself up by your bootstraps. I think having the ability to shake things off and move forward is an invaluable life skill. There is absolutely no way you can protect your child from every inevitable hurt or injustice they will encounter growing up. How they handle these tests of life absolutely shapes who they become. It's not that there is a No Whimps policy in my house, but a belief that life will keep throwing the punches so you might as well learn to box.

In our house, Daddy has given the nickname Dukes First to our daughter. That's because when her older brother takes her out in the course of overly rough play, she doesn't cry and go tattle. She comes back at him dukes first, crying later. Of course, I don't condone this (we do have a strict No Hitting, Scratching or Pinching rule), but the point is the girl is both sweet and tough. Whether physically or emotionally knocked down by her peers, she lets it roll off her armor of confidence and pride. There is no retaliation because she knows you don't have to knock someone else down to stand tall.

My son is also coming along nicely learning to roll with life's punches. In fact, parroting his daddy he likes to say, "That's how I roll." He is literally not afraid of falling whether taking a physical leap or social dive. He knows a crash is inevitable, but how are you going to land that awesome bike jump or pull off that overgrown mop of hair as a hairdo unless you try it? Whether crashing or coming off as the hero, he owns it. "That's how I roll," he'll tell you.

My husband and I both try to model overcoming life's set-backs. We let our kids see we are disappointed when things don't go our way. We let them witness our frustration. We don't hide our tears when life's gut checks are painful and devastating. It is important for them to see life is not fair or perfect or without road blocks.

It is also important for our children to see how we handle being knocked on our tushies by a one-two punch of life and living. I want them to witness and learn how to get back up and step up to the challenge of turning a negative into a positive. I want them to believe giving up is not an option and not to be fooled by the path of least resistance. I want them to know it is possible to climb out of that dungeon of despair and join the real life parade already in progress.

I want them to see Mommy put down that batch of brownie batter and the biggest spoon from the drawer and hear me say again in triumph, "Kids, if life was easy, it would be pretty darn boring."

In the end, the pity party I threw on my behalf was brief and not well attended. And I couldn't have been happier about it.

Parenting Disney Style

Momservation: If we all parented like Disney runs their theme parks, we wouldn't need to go to the happiest place on earth—we'd already be there.

☺   ☺   ☺

Just got back from a trip to Disney World, and can I please tell you, I'm ready for Disney to take over the world. Nobody, I mean nobody, does customer service and clean, friendly fun like Disney. *These* are the people we need in charge.

I truly believe if Disney ruled the world we'd all be singing Zippity Do Da out our you-know-whats. Who cares if we were just sent over a proverbial 50-foot waterfall and now have to walk around for hours in wet underwear? Life is good! Just grab a turkey leg and head over to the next attraction!

Instead of casting a wary eye on strangers, we would warmly greet them with, "Have a magical day!" Peace would envelop the world like a big, warm hug from Mickey and be commemorated with a souvenir photo. All our frowns would be turned upside down simply by someone handing us a churro.

And all our problems would be solved by someone in a crisp, sharp Disney uniform saying, "How can I make your Disney experience more pleasant?" or "Let me take care of that for you."

I've now been to both Disneyland and Disney World and am absolutely amazed at what a smooth and fantastically positive operation it is. I think there is something to be learned here.

In fact, The Walt Disney Company thinks so too and actually has a Disney Institute where businesses can send their employees to become experts in the field of flawless customer service.

I've taken it upon myself to take a page from the Disney playbook and apply it to parenting. Below follows a list of ten ways to become a better parent by applying Disney philosophies. Because really, isn't the bottom line to successful parenting crowd control and an enthusiastic, motivated work force? No…well, it should be.

Have a magical day!

Tips for Better Parenting Disney Style

1. **Customer service rules in the Magic Kingdom.** The attitude in which you handle your kids' problems, worries, fears, desires, questions, curiosity, etc. sets the tone for "customer" loyalty, trust and respect. According to Jim Cunningham of Disney University Professional Development Programs, "The front-line is the bottom line. It's the type of service received that usually determines the decisions customers make."

2. **Attention to detail.** Be tuned into your children's daily lives and needs then be prepared to provide a positive, supportive, family friendly atmosphere. Explains Cunningham, "Everyone has certain needs…and certain emotions involved that determine what they do."

3. **Exceed Expectations.** Your children look to you as an authority, a leader, a role model, and a moral compass as well as for security, reliability, and stability. Make them want to follow in your footsteps and make it easy for them to have a clear example for right and wrong. Make home a good place they want to be.

4. **Keep it clean, friendly, and fun.** Whether talking about the top three expectations for Disney theme parks or your child's outside interests, parents and Disney are on the same page. To help achieve this goal, encourage your kids to get involved in extracurricular activities that explore

their passion while building character, skills, and confidence.

5. **Don't forget about safety, courtesy, show and efficiency.** Focusing on the four priorities for "guest" entertainment with Disney detail toward happiness will help your kids transition into safe, likable, self-respecting, and responsible adults.

6. **Have a well-trained, enthusiastic and motivated work force.** Get those kids excited about doing something productive! Disney believes an important key to keeping employees motivated is having great leaders who create an environment where people want to do their best. So go set a good example, let kids learn by doing, and keep a positive attitude Mom and Dad.

7. **Be aggressively friendly.** Say it with a smile. Even if you're telling your kid they aren't going to see the outside of their room for a week, telling them with a perky smile like they just won the lottery can take the sting out of it.

8. **Build loyalty.** According to Disney, the easiest way to build customer loyalty is by keeping the promise. Whether that means sticking to your word or sticking to your guns, kids need to know they can trust you and your expectations finding comfort in consistency.

9. **Have Plan B waiting in the wings.** When a flower, shrub or tree dies in a Disney park, there is one exactly like it already being grown to replace it. Always be ready to swap out what isn't working.

10. **Thrill and delight.** Don't forget to have fun. The easiest way to make your kids happy is to play and interact with them. Why do you think the Disney parks are so much fun? A family that plays together stays together.

The Politics of Santa

Momservation: If you have to ask where the party line between naughty and nice is drawn, odds are it's already been stepped over.

☺　　☺　　☺

Prior to the presidential elections I was trying to explain to Whitney, at her request, the difference between Democrats and Republicans.

"Basically, you have two groups of people who believe in two different ways to do things," I tried to explain as simply as possible. "Not one way is right or wrong, but just different beliefs."

I paused to look at her, gauging her response, hoping my answer was sufficient and she would go back to coloring. The last thing I needed was a political debate with my second grader and another person I couldn't talk politics with.

To my surprise, she not only got it, but summed it up this way: "Oh. So it's like Santa Claus. Some people believe in him and some people don't."

Suddenly, we were talking about one of the most important issues on our family ballot. I make it a point not to ask about people's potentially contentious beliefs like party affiliations or if they loved or hated VH1's "Rock of Love," but I needed to know which side Whitney was on.

"What do you believe?" I asked, trying to stay calm. But really, I wanted to know who had gotten to her. Who had messed with my daughter's innocence and prematurely tried to get her registered as a non-believer?

Whitney gave me a look that was an eerie glimpse of the future teenager she would become. It was coupled with a huff of exasperation at my obvious density, so out of touch with reality. "I believe in Santa Claus! But Sacsha and David in my class don't."

Excellent. She was giving me names. Now I could track these kids down and give them a piece of my mind for lobbying outside of their precinct.

"They don't believe in Christmas. They believe in Hanukkah," Whitney clarified.

Big sigh of relief—the equivalent of Green Party members. Valid party, but I'm not really too concerned their going to steal the election. The magic of Christmas was poised for victory, saved for another term, and I was relieved I didn't have to go on the attack against a couple of second graders and start a smear campaign aimed at their parents.

But it got me worried. My daughter was already grilling me about my party affiliation—tough questions about Santa were probably soon to follow. Add to that my son is now nine and a prime target for unregistered voter canvassers. The fact is both my kids are beginning to ask intelligent and thoughtful questions about this world that's starting to come into sharper focus for them.

My mother's instinct wants to steer them away from difficult topics, protecting their innocence and simple view of the world for as long as possible—there'll be plenty of time for them to deal with the realities and the weight that comes with expanded knowledge.

Still, I could see the point of the other side. How do you not lose your credibility and continue to impress upon your children the value of truth after they find out you've been lying and deceiving them for the good of the party?

I needed more information before I could decide which stance to take. To tell or not to tell? To choose reality over innocence, truth over idealism. I needed to know, at what age do you arm them with facts? At what point do you inflict harm by withholding the truth? When does it become necessary to advance their world and introduce them to reality?

Surprisingly, we still haven't had a frank discussion about where babies and chicken nuggets really come from, let alone the truth about Santa. I realized if I was still going to have some control over how my children's world is shaped it just might be time to sit them down and tell them what a hot dog is really made of and why Joan Rivers looks the way she looks. I know my children are aware there's more to the stories, but they've been content to let the spotlight of truth shine elsewhere.

Am I really ready to change their perception of the world forever? Are they ready and equipped to deal with it yet?

I conducted polls to help me decide. I also collected information from veteran constituents who'd been there before me—mom friends with older kids. I looked back into history, my own, and remembered the devastation of finding out too early about Santa and the influence it had on my development.

And I've made my decision. I'm joining my friend Tracy's party, the Undeclared whose motto is, "You've got to believe to receive." There's no commitment to the far left or right, but a safe middle ground until the kids are ready to take a stance.

When it is time, I will tell them. But the time is not now. They should be worrying about issues like do they want to play soccer or wall ball at recess? Is this person someone I want to be friends with? Could Sponge Bob take Mickey Mouse in an arm wrestle? Not the implications of turning their back on something they believed in with joy and conviction to step forward into a scary world where Santa Claus is just a representation of childhood innocence and it's time to grow up.

I choose to believe in innocence.

And that Sponge Bob takes Mickey easy.

New Year New Road Ahead

Momservation: Time marches on but mothers will always see babies when they look at their children.

☺ ☺ ☺

Who went ahead and told my kids they could go ahead and grow up? One minute I'm blissfully picking out their clothes, chopping their food into bite size pieces and taking them to see "Finding Nemo."

Next thing you know I'm sitting in "Paul Blart: Mall Cop," the gig is up that the really bad s-words aren't "stupid" or "shut up," and my eight year-old baby girl is telling me, "Today in class, Billy told me I was 'hot'."

And another thing—how come I can't remember the last time one of my babies called me "Mommy"? Now I'm just, "I-know-Mom-I-got-it-Geez."

How did I miss the road marker indicating changes ahead? One minute we're zipping along in feetsie pajamas and the next thing I know we're exiting for deodorant! We were just happy cruising along leaving cookies for Santa, putting teeth under pillows and laughing together at "America's Funniest Videos." Suddenly, we're flying down Reality Highway talking religion, politics, and current events. I thought I had plenty of time before merging onto The Birds and The Bees Expressway.

I think the reason I feel so off-course without a developmental GPS is because my oldest is only ten. We're talking staunch believer in the magical wonders of our holiday friends. Secure in his need for sleeping with his blankie and dozens of stuffed cats on his bed during a sleepover. Still a big fan of hugs, kissies, and "I love yous" at bedtime or anytime. There are no blinkers on indicating a sharp turn in maturity ahead.

So imagine my surprise when I notice he doesn't like to be seen naked anymore, suddenly declares himself too old for the kids' menu and kiddie rides at Disney World, and instead of watching cartoons in the morning he opts for "SportsCenter."

I should've had a clue we were turning down a different road when he opted out of an animated movie for "Old Dogs," deciding the mature themed movie was his new favorite. But just when I think I recognize the road we're going down, Logan throws in a U-turn: "The guy got hit it the weenie three times! It was hilarious!"

You see my confusion? Are we making a right, left or going straight here?

If we were talking my daughter at age ten this would be a different map altogether. Miss Independent, although tenuously holding on to her Santa belief system, continues to quiz me for cracks in my story—even going so far as to ask if Santa would still show up if she set out a video camera. This is also the girl who, at age three, when being scolded for the mess on the floor by missing the potty told me, "Well, now it's your problem Mom." I know exactly where I'm headed with this girl and I've got the emergency kit ready and waiting.

Part of the reason I sometimes feel lost and unsure of what road I'm on with my kids is when I start comparing directions with other parents. For example, I have friends who are much further up the road than me—comfortable letting their ten year old children stay home unsupervised for an hour or more.

My son doesn't like to be left alone even for five minutes in the car, parked at the entrance of the grocery store where he can see me waving at him from the postal line. And to be honest, I'm not comfortable leaving him alone yet.

I know parents who have already told their fourth graders in great detail where babies come from because their kids were seeking answers either from them or their peers.

My kids still think the proper name for boy and girl parts are "weenies" and "woo-woos" and believe procreating animals on the nature channel are just playing or fighting.

And then there's the whole PG and R-rated movies thing. I'm still doing guarded five-point family friendly inspections while many of their peers are quoting "School of Rock."

I may be proceeding with caution, but it's for good reason. I recently traumatized my kids by reading them the book "Ishi" about the last Yahi Indian thinking they would enjoy the fascinating history lesson. I had to stop reading it when they began crying because someone in the book died.

"How did you think it was going to end?" I asked startled by their response, thinking they understood what "last of his tribe" implied. Later, Whitney explained the book was hard for them by bringing back painful memories of all the loved ones they've already lost in their lives.

Ugh. Why didn't I see the Use Caution on Road Ahead sign?

My kids are maturing, probably faster than I'd like them to, but I certainly don't want to impede their growth and development by standing as a roadblock. I would love to keep them on familiar and comfortable roads forever, but I then I'd be in danger of going into a blind curve where I've misjudged the changing wants and needs of my growing children.

I'd just like a few warning signs to the road ahead.

Like: Beware of Falling Waistbands and Plunging Necklines. Be Prepared to Stop Foul Language. Caution Curves Ahead. Danger—Bumps in Road. Warning—Jack Black Movies.

The New Baby

Momservation: They say the true pain of childbirth fades otherwise mothers wouldn't have more children. Obviously, we also forget the pain of infancy and toddler years or else we wouldn't ever get puppies either.

☺   ☺   ☺

Right now I am dashing off this blog while the baby is sleeping. I only have a limited amount of time to try and accomplish anything because once she wakes up the baby demands my full attention.

There's the feeding. Then making sure she's gone potty. Some playtime for stimulation. Close supervision so she doesn't hurt herself or break something. Realizing there're more things I need to do to baby-proof the house. Hopefully after a few hours of that she'll be ready for her nap and I'll be able to sneak in a shower.

New baby? No, new puppy. But really, it's the same.

Oh, how quickly we forget the tied down, all consuming, rigorous schedule of babies, toddlers and puppies once we have left those years safely in our rear view.

I have always said the newborn years weren't my best genre. I still occasionally suffer some Post Traumatic Stress when I smell Desitin.

The toddler years I did better, because they're much more interactive and receptive to bribery.

The pre-kindergarten years I was like a relay runner sprinting to the next leg, giving it all I had because I knew I was almost done and I could pass the baton to California educational system.

And the school years have been my favorite yet. I still celebrate every year's Back to School day doing absolutely nothing unless it involves chocolate.

So why on earth would someone get a puppy, who was so desperate to not go through all of that again that she had her Hubby get a vasectomy on Father's Day weekend because it was the first date available?

Because puppies are the Clif Note version of early childhood. All the joys of adding another family member but with a quicker learning curve and they don't talk back.

Before I know it Little Miss Darby won't need to get up in the middle of the night. She's well on her way to being potty trained. She already will eat whatever I put in front of her. I don't need a babysitter when I leave her, just some good crate training. And after I play with her for a little bit, she just sits at my feet and lets me work. At nine weeks old.

My non-fuzzy kids are eight and ten years old. I still haven't gotten them to do that.

Sit, Stay, Do Your Homework!

Momservation: If your kids aren't mad at you or hate you at some point, then you're not doing your job as a parent.

☺   ☺   ☺

After recently bringing a puppy into our lives, I've come to realize there's not a lot of difference between raising kids and dogs.

(Cat's don't count because they just want you to leave them the hell alone—which I guess would mean there's not a lot of difference between raising teenagers and cats, but I'm not quite there yet.)

When your kids are little it is so important to teach them what the rules are, what's expected of them and what won't fly. Then you have to reinforce the behavior you're looking for with repetition, consistency and praise.

And treats are key.

Sounds about the same as training a dog, right?

I like to think I've got good, obedient kids. I take great pride in knowing we made it through the early years without one of them being known as "The Biter" or being blacklisted from any parks. So applying the same obedience strategy, I'm working hard to make sure our puppy, Darby, doesn't ruin my streak. Here are my basic rules:

Top Ten Rules for Obedient Kids and Dogs

1. **Nobody likes a biter.** Zero tolerance policy on aggression. Nip it (HA!) in the bud with severe consequences that don't include more violence.

2. **Play nicely with others.** If you can't play nice, then it's time to go home or have some time alone. If you want to have a friend, be a friend.

3. **Do what you're told the first time.** You undermine your authority if you allow anything else.

4. **Manners count.** Being on your best behavior at all times will earn you affection and respect.

5. **Don't beg.** It's a nuisance and it should never be given in to.

6. **Good behavior = Reward.** Positive reinforcement is a powerful tool. Love, affection and praise are basic cravings. And who can resist a good treat?

7. **Share with friends.** Selfishness should be discouraged because it can lead to other antisocial behaviors.

8. **Everything has its place.** Have designated areas for eating, sleeping, going potty, keeping toys, playing, etc. Consistency with these boundaries creates security.

9. **Make good choices.** Make it clear what your expectations are and reward for resisting temptation. Soon they'll be able to do it on their own.

10. **Set a good example.** Keeping your temper and frustrations in check will teach appropriate response and behavior and keep anxiety levels down.

Sneezing Out Your Belly Button

Momservation: Teaching your child to stand up for themselves shouldn't include teaching them, "If my dog was as ugly as you, I'd shave its butt and make it walk backward."

☺   ☺   ☺

Beware of girls with braids in their hair. Or ponytails. Or headbands. Straight and curly hair too.

Actually, just look out for girls in general.

They're mean.

My nine year-old daughter, Whitney, has been the repeated victim of bullying on the blacktop recently. This is surprising to me because she is no wall-flower and she's a tough cookie. Just ask her older brother who has the cuts and bruises to show for pushing his sister too far.

But, according to the principal, this is an ongoing problem with girls. The boys are easy. Fight, get over it in two seconds, continue with the ball game. But the girls—they're sneaky and they go for the emotional jugular. They tell you you're dumb, say your clothes are ugly, and that you're the only one not invited to their birthday party.

As a parent, besides wanting to storm the school and take out these girls Rambo style, my first instinct is to give Whitney some of my best lines to shoot back at these bullies in barrettes.

Like, "You may think my shirt is ugly, but I can change my shirt. You can't change your face."

Or, "I refuse to have a battle of wits with someone who is obviously unarmed."

And also, "You may think I'm dumb, but I can go to school to get smart. You're out of luck. You can't fix stupid."

But of course, I hold my tongue and do the standard parent mantra about sticking up for yourself:

- Did you use your words to tell them you didn't like what they said/how they were treating you?
- Did you ask them to please stop?
- Did you just walk away and try ignoring them?
- Did you tell a teacher/yard supervisor if you felt like you needed an adult to step in?
- If you've tried to solve the problem yourself and it isn't working, would you like me to step in?

The first time, after Whitney couldn't solve the problem herself, I went to the teacher and principal. The girl and her parents were talked to and, surprisingly, instead of dealing with a parent who thinks their perfect child could never do anything like that, the parents had the girl apologize and promise to leave Whitney alone. And she did. No retaliation. Happy ending—but truly the exception and not the rule to bullies (and their parents).

This most recent episode Whitney took care of herself. It went like this:

A girl cuts in front of Whitney and other kids in the tetherball line.

Whitney: Hey, you just cut. You can't do that.

Bully: So. Whatya going to do about it?

Whitney: You know, you're not going to have any friends if you treat people this way.

Bully: I can see you're just as annoying as your brother.

Whitney: Hey! You can insult me all you want, but you can't talk about my brother that way!

Bully: I can see you're just as stupid as your family (when Whitney told me this account she spelled out S-T-U-P-I-D because she's not allowed to use that word).

This next part, Whitney prefaced it to me by saying, "I don't know if you're going to like this part mom, but I said it anyway."

Whitney: If you don't shut up, (which she's also not allowed to say) I'm going to punch you in the nose so hard, you're going to be sneezing out your belly button.

Okay, first I tried not to laugh. Then I tried not to high five her. Then I tried not to say, "Now THAT's how you take care of business!"

Instead I asked, "So what happened then?"

"She left and went somewhere else," Whitney grinned triumphantly.

"Was that an original line?" I finally laughed.

"Got it off TV," she said.

"Effective," I nodded. Then after a momentary pause I felt it my parental good example duty to ask, "You weren't really going to punch her, were you?"

"Nah," she said. "It's just a line I've been wanting use and I finally got to use it."

And one I couldn't have said better myself.

Rolling Human Sexuality Class

Momservation: A mother should always ask herself first: Do I really want to know the answer to this question?

☺   ☺   ☺

First, I'd like to thank Kid Rock, Justin Timberlake, and Katie Perry. Without them and their provocative lyrics I would've never been able to simply drive to the store for bananas without getting an opportunity to educate my children about human sexuality.

Who needs the tedium of formulating a shopping list when we could talk about trying different things, smoking funny things and making love to a favorite song?

Or about the importance of bringing sexy back and why a girl might kiss a girl and like it.

So thank you for not letting me shirk my duty and putting these important discussions off until the kids actually don't believe in Santa or the Tooth Fairy anymore.

I'd also like to thank Nickelodeon, the Disney Channel and definitely TLC—I mean, they are The Learning Channel, after all.

And, boy, are my kids learning.

Learning that boys and girls should be preoccupied with the opposite sex, getting someone to like you and/or kiss you should take priority over all else, and that having six kids at one time or 19 kids and counting is a great way to get on TV.

But most importantly, I'd like to thank my Ford Expedition. How else could I tackle the uncomfortable subjects of puberty, sex, and drugs without your seatbelts that restrain, doors that lock, steering wheel to grip, front and back seats for a buffer, rearview mirror for just the right visual contact, and for providing an opportunity to clarify all the crap modern society puts out there in the time it takes to go get gas and a car wash?

Wow, I hope I'm not forgetting to thank someone…

Entertaining side note:

The other day when I was alone in the car with my nine year-old daughter, I decided after another racy song on the radio I better check in. So I cautiously asked her, scared for the answer, "Whitney, is there anything you want to ask me? Or maybe questions you have about things you and your friends might be talking about or don't understand?"

Watching her in the rearview mirror as she carefully pondered the question, I gripped the steering wheel, reluctant but ready to provide her with whatever answers she may need for her expanding world.

Finally she spoke. "Yeah, Mom. I do. How many presidents have there been?"

That's my baby girl.

I'm With the Band

Momservation: Your kid joining Band just might be retaliation for all the times you've told them to be quiet.

☺   ☺   ☺

I try to tell myself that behind every Paul McCartney, Eddie Van Halen and Dave Grohl there was once a mother with bleeding ears.

And so the next leg of my parenting journey reveals itself: The supporting of artistic expression by letting my kid join the school band. Because, you know, we're not doing nearly enough extra-curricular activities here in the Wheeler house.

So my nine year-old daughter, Whitney—she of no fear and King Kong confidence, decides she's going to jump on her first year of eligibility and represent in the wind instrument category in the likes of Louis Armstrong.

That's right. Trumpet. Not cute little flute or piccolo. Not the mellow clarinet. She goes for the instrument version of herself—loud and proud. Needless to say, she is the only girl in the section.

The first night of practice was actually comical. Students were instructed to start with just the mouth piece detached from the instrument to get the hang of the technique and beginning note. The noise coming out of Whitney's bedroom became a game of Guess That Sound:

- A Moped in desperate need of a tune-up?
- A swarm of bees with a stuttering problem?
- Whoopee Cushion dying a slow death?
- Daddy after burrito night?

Soon, you could hear Whitney had had enough with this amateur mouthpiece stuff. She wanted to get straight to the big gun. That's when the strangled sounds of what can only be described as a cow trying to pass a gall stone screeched from her room.

Straying from the one-note script, it immediately became Improv Night and Whitney was creating the sweet sound of an elephant with a sinus infection.

Oh, but it was Pied Piper music for 10 year-old boys because it immediately drew her brother to her room.

"Hey, Whitney, can I blow? Can I blow now?" I heard Logan beg.

There was some closed-door negotiations before more sounds of a moose in heat violated my ears.

Now I don't know if Whitney will go on to be the next Wynton Marsalis, or if I'll even survive the Beginning Band years, but I do know one thing. She could definitely have a fantastic career as a hostage negotiator.

She's got her brother caddying her trumpet to and from school for the right to play around with it for five minutes a day. She's also got me ready to give her anything to find a new interest.

The Gift Stages of Christmas

Momservation: Peace, love, and friendship are great, but a gift that hits its mark is even better.

☺   ☺   ☺

Nothing says Christmas is around the corner like the Toys R Us Great Big Book of Christmas showing up in your Sunday paper.

In October.

Nevertheless, I reserved the ad thinking I would have the kids do their fun annual tradition of circling things for their wish lists.

But then I realized—wait! We didn't do it last year. In fact, it had been a few years since a Toys R Us gift card had been relevant in their lives. I picked the thick circular back up and flipped through its full-color, glossy pages filled with happy children and their Elmos, Barbies, Legos, baby dolls, Star Wars action figures, Candy Land and Sorry! games, swing sets, miniature bikes, scooters and musical instruments.

I saw nothing my nine and eleven year-old kids still desired and plenty they had outgrown.

Wow. Had it really been that long since I used going through the isles at Toys R Us to pick out a toy as bribery?

Thinking back to the previous Christmas and the gifts that brought squeals of delight to my kids it occurred to me—we had indeed left the Toys R Us years and had entered **The Electronics Age**.

It was all about Nintendo DS, xBox, iPod, iTouch, cameras, phones, camera phones, and gift cards to Best Buy,

Game Stop and iTunes to get all the gadgets, games, and music that went with them.

It really made me miss the first stage of Christmas with kids: **The Anything Age**. This was the stage from 0-3 years when you could give anything to your child or grandchild and they would love it. For babies, as long as they could stick it in their mouth it was fantastic. For one year-olds the box the gift came in was equally magic. For two year-olds if you could throw it across the room in a tantrum or hit a friend over the head with it, it was perfect. And for three year olds it didn't matter what it was, they weren't going to share it.

At around four years old kids move into the next stage of Christmas gift giving: **The Everything Age*** (* Except clothes). This is marked by kids getting more specific in what they would like to receive and everything in the Toys R Us Big Book of Christmas should about cover it. Give them a pen and the catalog and everything on every page will be circled. Each year you will have to pry them off of Santa's lap as they go through their wish list without taking a breath, "...and I want Ninja Legos, and I want a Nerf Dart Gun, and I want a Razor Scooter, and I want a drum set, and I want..."

Somewhere around the age of nine, kids get pickier. This is **The Out & In Age**. Barbies are out, American Girl Dolls are in. Star Wars action figures are out, Bakugan are in. Elefun is out, themed Monopoly games are in. Razor push scooters are out, electric Razor scooters are in. Clothes are marginally acceptable but cutesy decals are out, favorite brands are in.

The stages of gift giving come swifter after that with each period becoming increasingly brief (and more expensive) as children move toward preteen and into the teen years when tastes and trends change as quickly as a texting teen.

You hit the aforementioned Electronic Age first with your wallet because no gift is cheap during these years. Which makes you think it should last a significant amount of time, but within a month it will become obsolete. It will also seem like you can never escape this stage because by the very next Christmas you will find yourself buying the exact same gift—somehow newer and better.

Before you know it you will be in **The Gift Card Age**. This is when the worst gift you could have given them before has now become what it's all about: clothes. And you, Grandma and Aunt Sally are nowhere near cool enough to get that purchase right. Or any other gift for that matter. So save yourself from digging out your Christmas receipts—gift cards to anywhere are fine, but including one to Forever 21, American Eagle Outfitters, Abercrombie & Fitch, PacSun, or Nordstrom's will make you momentarily cool again.

The final gift stage of Christmas is **The Cash Out.** The only thing your kids want from you now is money. Your teenagers are craving freedom and even a gift card is seen as an act of suppression by dictating where they can shop. And really, their craving of cash isn't much different than any other time of the year. The only difference is on Christmas it comes with a bow.

Or wrapped in the Toys R Us Great Big Book of Christmas.

The Cool Mom Dethroned

Momservation: If I wanted my kids to like me all the time, I wouldn't be their parent.

☺   ☺   ☺

I always pictured myself as "The Cool Mom." I envisioned having the right snacks, the latest toys, the rules that were strict enough for safety but lax enough for fun. I wanted my kids' house to be the place where neighborhood kids wanted to hang out. So much so that when we purchased the home we live in now with its spacious backyard and pool I truly believed it was the crown jewel in my quest to be The Cool Mom.

But the frozen pizzas are always bigger and the video games newer on the other side.

Recently, it dawned on me I just might be the female counterpart to the disillusioned "cool dad" in the funny new sitcom "Modern Family." Here I am thinking I'm dialed in to providing what every kid wants, meanwhile my kids are hanging out over at Blake's because his mom serves root beer floats for snack.

Of course, I'm only now realizing it's all relative. One child's abandoned playhouse is another child's Barbie Malibu Beach House. I just really wanted to be on the beach house end.

Why is it so important to me to have my kids and their friends wanting to hang out at our home?

First of all, because I have the security of knowing exactly where they are and what they're up to. Second, I know my rules are going to be abided by because it's under my roof. But mainly it's because it feels good as parent to know you have created a home where your kids want to be and are comfortable bringing their friends over.

But let's face it—kids like going over to each other's houses because there's always something they can have or do at a friend's house that they can't at home. And as long as you're not violating a major moral code, what's the harm of letting kids escape the boundaries of home for a few hours? Kids need a chance to practice policing themselves when they are away from home, learning to stay true to the values and expectations instilled in them.

You think I don't know my son shoots Airsoft guns when he's over at Brodie's house? Or that my daughter has doughnuts for breakfast when she spends the night at Hayley's? It may not be the way we roll at our house, but I'm comfortable that these occasional transgressions aren't going to undermine my kids' basic values about violence and healthy choices.

What I didn't count on is it's impossible to be a cool parent if you care anything about your kids. If you are truly watching out for their best interests and want to maintain a level of respect and authority, you can't be cool. You've got to set rules, enforce rules, take away privileges, establish boundaries, dictate schedules, approve choices, discourage inappropriate behavior, and make unpopular decisions. People who do that just aren't cool.

I may be a little jealous that Heidi, Becky and Julie are The Cool Moms to my kids, but then the crown switches heads when their kids come over. I become The Cool Mom because of the free reign their kids have to my gumball machine, holiday candy dishes and junk food drawer (to which my own kids have become immune).

That's The Cool Mom loophole. You can't be cool to your own kids, but you can be cool to their friends. That's because you don't have that responsibility over someone else's child. It's like being a grandparent. You can sugar them up and let them watch all the Phineas and Ferb they want and then send them home because it's not your job to enforce someone else's rules. It's just your responsibility to make sure they stay safe and don't learn any new bad words at your house.

But if there's anything I learned from gorging myself as a kid on white bread and Hawaiian Punch at my best friend Robin's, it's that if you're so strict you don't allow your kids to make their own choices, then they're going to sneak behind your back to test their boundaries.

I'd rather pass The Cool Mom crown to Michelle and know my kids are just at her house having their 15th Otter Pop.

Although a good Don't Ask Don't Tell Policy might help me loosen the grip on that crown while my kids really get the hang of making better choices.

Oh No You Din-int Just Judge My Parenting

Momservation: If I'm not going to win Mother of the Year, I hope there's at least a good consolation prize.

☺   ☺   ☺

Those who live in glass houses shouldn't throw stones...or think of switching to siding.

Don't judge until you've walked two moons in someone's moccasins...or go for it because now you're far away and you have their shoes.

It's always the people you know the least who judge you the most...doesn't that make it more fun?

Judge not if you're not ready for judgment...but that's not how this game works.

Everyone you meet is fighting a battle you know nothing about...that's why ignorance is bliss.

It is not until you become a mother that your judgment slowly turns to compassion and understanding. ~ Erma Bombeck

Now, that's the inspirational quote I'm looking for when it comes to judgment! Because there are no perfect parents out there. (Except for, maybe, Cindy Crawford and Randy Gerber if we're just judging on how the outsides look.)

Let's face it: All of us are winging this parent thing and hoping for the best. We're faced with decisions big and small every day for our children. At the end of the day you just hope you didn't pick the curtain with the goat eating the clothes off the clothes line over Door Number 3 with the trip to Tahiti.

Parenting is a never-ending series of decisions:

Do I let them watch Nickelodeon over PBS?

Should I serve lima beans or green beans?

Do I start them in kindergarten now or wait another year?

Should I tell them "yes" even though I really want to say "no"?

Do I call the doctor or wait to see how they feel?

Do I insist on switching teachers or make this a lesson in adapting?

Do I make them go back in the house and brush their teeth or just give them a piece of gum?

See what I'm saying? Can I get an "Amen, sister!" up in here?

At the end of the day I pray to God: *Please, let me have done more good than harm to my children.* But you know what else could help? If we would all just lay off each other when it comes to judgments—especially when it comes to parenting.

Can we all just agree that we're doing our best with the best of intentions and out of a place of love for our kids? And what that is and what that looks like is going to look different for everyone. Because the last I checked, none of us looked like Cindy Crawford and Randy Gerber…

While we're vowing to cut each other some slack and lay off the sideways glances, tsk-tsk head shakes, and mean-spirited gossip, here are some playful reminders about not judging:

Oh No You Di-int Just Judge My Parenting

- Don't judge unless you've never served Coco Puffs for dinner.
- Don't judge unless you've never sent your kid to school with a cold and told them to pretend its allergies.
- Don't judge unless you've never pretended to look for the money the Tooth Fairy forgot to bring and did a slight of hand to "find" it.

- Don't judge unless you've never put your kid in too small clothes and told them it was the new style.
- Don't judge unless you've never thrown a Bounce in the dryer w/ some dirty clothes and passed it off as clean.
- Don't judge unless you've never accidently given your kid a bad haircut and then tried to blame it on them for wiggling.
- Don't judge unless you've never sent your kid to school w/ a mayonnaise and mustard sandwich because you were out of lunch meat and cheese.
- Don't judge unless you've never dropped your kid's sandwich on the floor, picked the dog hair and lint ball off and then gave it to them to eat.
- Don't judge unless you never started a crock pot meal with things from the freezer that you can't identify under the freezer burn.
- Don't judge unless you've never accidently dropped an F-bomb in front of your kid and then bribed them with a Slurpee not to tell.
- Don't judge unless you never used fuzzy socks to sweep the floor.
- Don't judge unless you never protested needless laundry by tossing a can of Axe to your kid and telling them "good luck."
- Don't judge unless you've never forgotten to pick your kid up from somewhere and when you finally arrived pretended you got held up in traffic.

Feel free to keep the No Judgey-Judgey list going!

Sunscreen and Other Torture Devices

Momservation: Sunscreen application is a kid's kryptonite.

☺   ☺   ☺

There's a saying—what doesn't kill you will make you stronger. This doesn't apply to children.

If you go by the moaning, whining, crying and obvious suffering of a child who has to stand still for two minutes of sunscreen application you would think they were being tortured to death.

So when they survive this lather session to go frolic as they please, being saved from the much worse fate of a three-alarm sunburn, you'd think they would face the subsequent adversity of sunscreen application with new resolve and courage.

No such luck.

My kids are ten and eleven and they still hide from a sunscreen bottle like I just pulled out a bushel of broccoli.

It's not just sunscreen though. If you step into my torture chamber you'll find all methods of bringing unbearable suffering to my children:

- Making them dress up and smile for a Christmas card photo
- Making them finish everything on their plate that is green
- Having to flush the toilet regularly
- Wiping or blowing a nose
- Putting away their washed, folded clothes and shut their drawers
- Having to set or clear the table
- Having to sweep or vacuum a floor

- Making them get out of a swimming pool
- Cleaning their room or their own mess they made
- Taking a shower
- Brushing hair or teeth
- Taking a children's chewable vitamin
- Having to drive somewhere without watching a movie
- Wearing a sweatshirt or jacket
- Not being in control of the TV remote
- Running errands

And the most horrible, awful thing besides sunscreen to my children?

Bedtime. Certain death every night.

Group Therapy

Momservation: The sooner everyone realizes—if mom is happy, everyone's happy—this place will run a lot smoother.

☺   ☺   ☺

Dip me in salt and call me Margarita, I love Girls Night Out.

There's nothing better for a weary mother's soul than a "hall pass" for some girl talk, a good adult beverage, and food that is absolutely delicious because you didn't have to cook it yourself or clean it up.

My mom friends and I usually get together at least once a month to celebrate birthdays, catch a good chick flick, and for an actual, organized Girls Night Out. We've even given it an official title so our husbands can't balk at another outing.

"But it's Culinary Queens, Honey! You know I have The Queens every first Tuesday of the month. The girls are counting on me to bring 'Gramma's Chocolate-Chocolate Cake.'" And wine. Lots of wine.

I know dads get weary too, but it's not our fault that guys just don't know how to properly and frequently assemble in the name of good chit chat, gossip and venting. We women, after years of traveling in packs as teenagers, clumping in cliques, and going in groups to the bathroom, have learned there is no better way to deal with stress and manage anxiety like assembling a support group.

What better way to come together in the name of preserving sanity than by getting a bunch of gals together one night a month (preferably with wine) for commiseration and validation? It doesn't matter how fabulous your family might be, a night out as anyone other than Mom is essential to parenting mental wellness. Women—mothers—have figured this out.

It doesn't matter if we end up talking about our kids most of the time anyway. In fact, conferring with other moms about everything from picky eaters, to growth spurts that keep you running to Target, to the best brand of diapers or cheapest price in town for Pirate's Booty helps make our jobs easier by sharing advice and providing insight.

It's not just about talking shop though. We catch up on each other's lives because we've been too busy running carpool or organizing the school's fundraiser to pick up the phone. We find out the best places to splurge on a pedicure, who's got the cheapest hairdresser to cover the grays, which exercises tone your inner thighs, when not to go bathing suit shopping, and we ooh and ahhh over new purses, shoes and accessories.

Sure we also might air a few husband grievances. But when we realize everyone else's husbands don't turn their socks right-side-in before laundry either, or leave toothpaste spit in the sink right after you cleaned the bathroom, or pout like a little kid when they have to wait until after American Idol for a little sugar, then it becomes funny instead of frustrating.

Whether your Girls Night Out is Culinary Queens, Bunko, Book Club, Dining Divas, Scrapbooking, going to dinner, a movie, a bar, dancing, or finding a home where the kids have been cleared out—never doubt you don't deserve that time to laugh and play. Any smart husband knows, for family unity and harmony, you don't want to stand in the way of this.

Trust me, it's cheaper than therapy.

Treasure in my Junk Drawer

Momservation: It is the little moments that make life big.

☺   ☺   ☺

You think you'll remember, but you won't.

Sure, you'll remember the big stuff and the stories that will be repeated until it becomes family lore. But you'll forget the small stuff. The everyday stuff. The regular moments that make you stop and chuckle before becoming another layer of why you love this person more than you could've ever imagined.

Write them down Mommy and Daddy. After you've had that chuckle or that moment that you felt overwhelming love etching another notch in your heart, grab a scrap of paper, pencil, and write it down.

Trust me. These scraps of paper found years later in your junk drawer with unsharpened pencils, locks with missing keys, and sticky notes that don't stick anymore will be like finding treasure with a metal detector

First, you will feel excitement and joy that you found these precious memories—that they could've been lost but they weren't. Then you will feel a tinge of sadness—how could you have forgotten a memory that was so precious to you? But then you will be thrilled because you realize you are richer for having them. Finally, you will be grateful. Grateful that person in the past knew that one day those moments would be treasures and took care to preserve them.

Like when Whitney was four years-old and declared we lived in "Sacafornia."

Or this one from Logan when he was still a curious toddler: "Mommy? Does rain ever miss a spot?"

And the early evidence that Whitney would grow up to be a creative thinker: "Is a 'litter of kitties' because they're all over like litter?"

And the no one would believe us if we didn't write it down vocabulary of our toddler Logan: "That cookie was tremendous."

Or these funny exchanges on long car rides:

Whitney: "British accents are so cool. If I had a British accent I would never stop talking."

Daddy to our already non-stop talker: "And we're all glad you don't."

Logan: "Ow! I hit my elbow so hard it's ringing! Man, it won't quit ringing! I better answer it. Hello? Elbow? Are you okay?"

Whitney: "Do you think anyone ever robs a pizza place for the pizzas?"

Logan to Whitney: "Three words for you—Knucklehead."

I thought I would remember these instances that make me laugh all over again and make my heart ache for those moments they said would fly by me like a jet breaking the sound barrier.

But I didn't. I didn't remember them until I found these treasures sprinkled in my junk drawer with old pennies, lost buttons, and loose safety pins. And some of them—I still have no recollection of at all.

But I am so grateful that over a dozen years ago I stopped and said, "I better write that down." Just in case they are right. That it will all fly by in a blur and one day my funny little babies will be grown and my house will be quiet.

Write it down, Mommy and Daddy. Write it down.

CHAPTER 3

Preteen Testing Ground

Momservations®
Mom's Top 10 Rules for Kids

1. **Respect yourself and others.** This pretty much covers all other rules. But just to be clear...

2. **Own it.** Quit throwing other people under the bus and take responsibility for your choices.

3. **Just 'cause you can, doesn't mean you should.** "Seemed like a good idea at the time" should be reserved for tombstones.

4. **Lying only throws fuel on the fire.** Mess with the fire and you're going to get burned.

5. **Change is inevitable.** So quit your complaining and learn to adapt.

6. **Don't be a hater.** Ugly attitudes don't look good on anyone. Let it go - don't waste energy on carrying a grudge.

7. **Remember the Mom Test.** If you wouldn't say it, do it, or suggest it with Mom standing next to you – think twice.

8. **Do no harm.** Keep all hands, feet, arms, legs and other violations of space and privacy to yourself.

9. **Do something.** Don't just sit there – be helpful, thoughtful, considerate, generous, a friend, anything! Everyone's got something to give.

10. Enjoy the journey. It's not the destination that counts, but how you get there. So you might as well hang on end enjoy the ride.Management Decisions

Management Decisions

Momservation: Parents are the eyes that see the future until their children's eyes come into focus.

☺　　☺　　☺

I was recently talking in the driveway with my neighbor about our fuzzy babies. He's got an older Golden Retriever and I've got a young Labrador. Both are on expensive medications for chronic joint problems. We found common ground in our complaints.

Joking out of frustration I said to Dan, "If the kids didn't love Darby so much I'd give her free to a good home."

"Well, that there is a Management Decision," said the grandfather. "We made a 'Management Decision' with a Lab we once had. When our daughter, Danna was little we decided to tell her the old dog went to a nice farm to retire."

I wasn't about to make that kind of Management Decisions with Darby—we'd already decided to put her under the knife for better quality of life. For better or for worse she's ours and she's family. But I laughed, loving the term "Management Decision" for tough choices adults have to make for their kids.

It got me thinking about all the Management Decisions Trey and I have made for our kids so far and the tougher ones that will inevitably follow as we near the teenage years.

There was the Management Decision to wait to start Logan, with an October birthday, in kindergarten. Logan was okay with it, happy to stay another year at his beloved preschool. But it had been a hard choice for us holding our academically ready son another year. I still remember one of Trey's impassioned considerations: "He wouldn't be able to drive until he's a junior if we start him now. That's not gonna work."

Logan is now a thriving fifth grader and our Management Decision has proved wise.

But that's the problem with Management Decisions. The right decision, unfortunately, is not always clear. They can be tough choices for parents to make in the best interest of their child. Many times parents just have to go with their instinct of what will be the best projected outcome. At the time your gut tells you it's the right choice, but you don't really know if it will be. Usually, you know it won't be a popular decision and you'll have to deal with the fallout. But you hope your kids will one day understand that all decisions were made out of love, with careful consideration, and concern for their well-being.

Like the Management Decision to put our aging and ailing dog to sleep. The kids weren't ready to let him go, unwilling and scared to deal with the heartache of death. Trey and I cared for an increasingly immobile and incontinent dog trying to prolong the inevitable grief. Finally, a Management Decision had to be made. Trey took Kyber to the vet and I took the kids to John's Incredible Pizza Place to soften the blow.

To be qualified to make Management Decisions parents have the benefit of perspective and experience on their side. Kids may not realize it, but they have the benefit of not being faced with making real world decisions before they're ready. Parents take the hit so kids don't have to take the fall. One day they will thank you, but not today.

Not all Management Decision are heavy. Some are fun. Like deciding on an end of the school year trip to Disneyland. Or deciding with enough protective gear and following rules of safety, a dirt bike for your birthday gets a green light. And this year, letting our youngest child go away to sleep-over camp.

Some Management Decisions prove to be, let's say, a learning experience. Allowing Logan to keep an unauthorized birthday present pet—the diabetic hamster got out twice and lived less than a year causing more heartache than it was worth. Giving in to Whitney wanting to try cheerleading at age six—too much too soon, quitting before a single game cheered was an expensive mistake.

There is a looming Management Decision we didn't see coming. Logan recently told us he wants to go to the local private school for high school. All along we've been planning for the neighborhood public school.

Pay for high school or pay for college? Let's get through middle school first and the Management Decision about a cell phone and texting...

The More They Change, the More it Stays the Same

Momservation: If you're waiting around for parenting to get easier, you're going to be waiting a long time.

☺   ☺   ☺

Passing through the Salt Lake City airport on our way back home from our Montana Thanksgiving vacation spent with grandparents, Hubby and I saw a flashback of ourselves a decade earlier.

It was a frazzled and weary looking couple trudging to their next gate, the man with a backpack on his back (no doubt filled with airplane distractions), a toddler in one arm and car seat in the other; the woman pushing a collapsible stroller with an infant in an infant carrier with all sorts of baby and toddler paraphernalia swinging from it.

As we passed them with sympathetic smiles Hubby asked, "How far apart are they?"

"Twenty months," the man said sounding like 20 months ago he should have stayed on the couch watching SportsCenter instead.

Hubby and I glanced at each other with a knowing smirk. We had them beat. We nearly always have them beat. Nodding with his head toward our 10 and just turned 12 year-olds walking up ahead carrying their own luggage he said with camaraderie to the couple, "Ours are 17 months apart."

The man nodded his head in recognition of our mutual membership in the had-our-kids-ridiculously-close-together-club before looking at our loosely supervised kids with disbelief that one day that would ever be his experience.

"It gets easier," Hubby assured him. But then to not paint an unrealistic picture and show the battle stripes earned he added, "But there was a lot of crying in the beginning."

That was my cue. "Most of it was by me," I said toward the woman who looked about to cry. Then I reassured her, "You're in the hard part, but it goes by so quickly."

While one couple was thinking *too quickly,* another was thinking *not quick enough.*

As we caught up to our kids who had stopped to wait for us at the gate without being told we wished the couple good luck and encouragement to hang in there. Giving them a glimpse of their future Hubby said, "They're like twins by this age. They entertain and play with each other really well."

Smiling at our son and daughter who were getting the cards out in anticipation of a family Rummy tournament while waiting for our flight, I added, "They're a lot of fun."

Watching the couple struggle forward with hopeful smiles, I knew there was so much more I would've liked to tell them.

That it doesn't necessarily get easier, just different. That each stage comes with its own set of challenges. That one day you're worrying about ear infections and diaper rash and before you know it you're worrying about first crushes and broken hearts. And that all too soon we'll be staying up late hoping they get home safely, that they'll find someone who will love them as much as we do, and that they'll want us in their lives when they have lives of their own.

Dang it—see now I'm crying again over my kids! Some things never change.

California Mission Accomplished

Momservation: The threat of multiple California mission reports and science fair projects is the best birth control.

☺   ☺   ☺

Today is a day to rejoice.

It is right up there with the night my infant son started sleeping through the night the day before I had to go back to work again.

And the day we weaned my year-old daughter off the stinky soy formula and my toddler son off his sippie cup.

It is as joyful as the day I exchanged my diaper bag for a ridiculously expensive trendy, stylish purse because both my children were potty trained (although I still carried Bob the Builder and Dora the Explorer back-up underwear in it).

It is up there with my kids finally getting all their teeth, learning to barf in a toilet, and to say, "Mommy, my ear really hurts."

Today feels almost as good as the day my checkbook gave a sigh of relief because both my kids were in public school and we no longer had to pay for day care and preschool.

Actually, this still might be better.

Today, this glorious day, my youngest child is turning in her California mission report effectively putting behind us this horrible chapter of elementary education.

Now that this is finally over, I swear I will never set foot in another California mission again. At least not for educational purposes.

Two years in a row I sat with each of my children at the kitchen table, guiding them through their first major report. Helping reconstruct the facts of, essentially, Native American slavery, as a notable time in our state's history was just as torturous as an adult as it was when I was a fourth grader. Minus the musty smell of outdated library books.

I had flashbacks of being stuck at my grandma's kitchen table while everyone else was out playing, trying to finish my mission report due at the end of spring break. I had to write it in cursive and in ink which meant lots of mess ups and lots of rewrites. I cursed Junipero Serra's name and my misfortune of being born and raised in California.

But today—today all that is behind us. The nagging to get it done. Daddy harping that he didn't want this thing done at the last minute. The whining of how hard it is and not knowing where to start or what to say or how to say it. The kids begging me to type it for them. Me yelling at them that I already did fourth grade and I long ago finished MY mission report. And BTW, I didn't have a computer with spell check and cut and paste and snazzy fonts or the internet!

And the extra credit model replica of the mission? If Mom, the writer, got stuck with nurturing the written portion of this fourth grade albatross of the California education curriculum, then Dad, the contractor, got to be the foreman for the physical portion of the torturous journey. If we were going down, we were all going down together.

But just like the sore nipples of breast feeding, the long nights of no sleep, the days when the kids wouldn't nap—this, too, has passed: the fourth grade California mission report.

Hasta la vista, baby.

Mother's Day Wish List

Momservation: Forget Mother's Day—you're never more appreciated as a mom than when everyone runs out of clean underwear.

☺   ☺   ☺

My family is always looking to do something special for me on Mother's Day. Easy. I don't want to be a mother for Mother's Day. Just leave me be and let me drift along for a day with no mothering responsibilities. They just laugh and think I'm kidding.

But really, getting a break from being Mom is sometimes just the gift busy moms need.

When my son was an infant it was as simple as letting me have eight hours of uninterrupted sleep. When I had two kids under two years, whisking them away to let me wake up to a quiet house with the Sunday paper at my feet and time to enjoy it was just what I needed. As they got older, but their needs no less demanding, letting me slip off to the movies to see something not animated was a perfect treat. Now that my babies are preteens, I just want a cease fire for the day.

This year, though, I've decided to help my family out instead of keeping them guessing as to what would be the perfect Mother's Day gift. Like a wish list written to Santa, I think I've been a good girl so I've come up with some things I think I deserve.

When I asked my kids if there was anything they thought should be on my wish list for me to have a Happy Mother's Day, they pretty much thought I covered it.

Then my daughter asked alarmed, "Wait! Do we have to do EVERYTHING on that list?"

"Even one would be worth a hundred forced kisses from you," I said.

Then my son turned to his sister and dad and spoke the words he didn't even realize was my greatest wish: "We better stop giving her ideas."

Mother's Day Wish List

- Turn your stinky socks right side out before putting them in the laundry
- Make sure anything that misses the toilet gets wiped up. Especially the first 24 hours after the bathroom's been cleaned
- Not have sudden bouts of amnesia about whose turn it is to set or clear the table
- Don't wait until 8:30 p.m. on a Sunday to remember you have homework
- Realize that "just a little bit" of homework is never just a little bit
- Actually look for something before telling me you can't find it
- Don't ask me if your friends can sleep over or come over when they or their parents are standing next to me
- Stop thinking that momentary lapses in activity or conversations need to be filled with the distraction of a phone app
- Try new foods without threat or bribery or pretending you don't like it to validate the fight you put up
- Trust me when I tell you it's not something you want to learn the hard way

- Someone else come up with something for dinner
- Realize that folded clothes on your bed didn't appear magically and don't get put away that way either no matter how long you leave them
- The dog doesn't care who feeds her dinner or walks her so quit pretending it has to be me
- Believe that good hygiene can happen without someone nagging you
- Agree on a show to watch instead of monopolizing all the TVs in the house
- Decide fighting over the remote doesn't need to be a daily battle
- Accept that I'm never going to pay you or stop yelling at you to pick up your rooms and your things so save us all the trouble and just do it
- We don't live on a mushroom farm so stop leaving wet towels and bathing suits on the floor
- It would be nice to walk through the garage without having to navigate a maze of bikes, scooters, balls and dumped toys like Indiana Jones
- Don't tempt me to sell you on eBay by thinking you know everything with an eye roll and huffed, "I know Mom"
- Hug me every now and again and tell me thanks

A Mother Is Never Surprised to Find...Part II

Momservation: It's all fun and games until you hear the Mom Voice and freeze in your tracks.

☺   ☺   ☺

Welcome back to another installment of *A Mother is Never Surprised to Find...!*
Of course, this is an endless game we can play because kids will never cease pushing the boundaries of acceptable outcomes. That front cerebral cortex that makes rational decisions won't be fully developed until after college when they finally stop and think:
"Hey, maybe seeing if I can light my farts on fire isn't such a great idea." (In some men, this just never develops.)
Only the best of us are cut out for this Mom stuff.

A Mother is Never Surprised to Find...

- kids circled around a toilet to see if hamsters can swim
- someone standing on the roof with a sheet ready to try parachuting
- something frozen in the freezer that should not be anywhere near food
- calls for help coming from inside a sofa sleeper
- she is out of tape because it's all been used on her kids' faces
- a suspiciously missing favorite action figure buried in the garden
- shoes in the middle of the room that a child supposedly looked "all over" for

- kids getting ready to drop the cat off the roof to see if it's true they always land on their feet
- her make-up being used as finger paint
- evidence on the wall that a peanut butter sandwich had recently resided there
- contraband stashed inside pillow cases
- her bra being used as a water balloon launcher
- a kid wearing a hat made out of duct tape and leaves

Next Stop: Middle School

Momservation: Raising kids is just the first great ride in the amusement park.

☺   ☺   ☺

First they start to crawl. Then they begin to walk. Soon they climb out of their crib and then they start to talk. There's first smile, first tooth, first word, first step.

Then all of sudden you're going to middle school orientation.

For those of you still making first recordings in your baby books, I swear to God it goes that quick.

When I started writing this column, my son wasn't even in school yet. We were bouncing from park to park with our mommy group, hoping to make it through the day with a nap and nobody peeing the bed that night.

One day you're putting your kid's name on a preschool waiting list, the next day you're buying him a lock for his locker and deodorant for his gym bag. How can my baby already be going to middle school when it seems like just yesterday I was spreading Desitin on his cutie patootie booty?

I am scared to death for Logan to go to middle school. Why? Because I remember all too clearly what middle school was like. It's hormones in high tops. It's a social feeding frenzy. It's all about who's got boobs, and who's the hot dudes. I can't recall anything academic I learned in middle school, but I can still tell you who kissed behind the backstop, who got their period wearing white jeans, who asked who to slow-danced to REO Speedwagon's "Can't Fight This Feeling," and who got suspended for graffiti-ing their true feeling about Mrs. Tarshish, the evil Spanish teacher.

I'm not ready for my sixth grader to be exposed to all that while he's still putting teeth under his pillow and singing the "Do You Love Waffles?" song as he eats his breakfast. Especially trying to navigate the social mine field of middle school now with modern day booby traps of cell phones, texting, Facebook, and instant messaging.

Nearly twelve short years ago I was eagerly awaiting the birth of my first born child. Wondering if it was going to be a boy or a girl. If they would have Daddy's blue eyes or my brown ones. I imagined what it would be like to hear someone call me "Mommy" and to feel my heart flood with joy at the sound. I wondered what this little person's personality would be like and if they too would love pickles, the smell of a forest, and the bold orange of poppies. Or would they be their own person and choose mint chip ice cream over orange sherbet, early morning quiet over late night peacefulness, polite handshakes instead of warm hugs?

Like dumping out the cereal to find the prize inside, I was so eager for this child to be born and to hurry and grow up so I could see what kind of amazing person they would end up being.

Now I'm stomping the breaks. This is all going too quick. We whizzed past saying "Mama" for the first time, learning to ride a bike, first T-ball hit, first day of school. We already sped by new adventures of jumping waves at the beach, catching a snow-flake on your tongue, and the exhilarating fear of Space Mountain at Disneyland.

It's too soon for first school dance, first school crush, first broken heart. He's still too young and innocent to find out what the lyrics really mean to Lady Gaga's "Poker Face" and that the "s-word" isn't "stupid" or "shut-up."

And the worst part? Logan can't wait to go. He can't wait to have a locker, change classes throughout the day, have P.E. every day, and hang with his buddies in the halls of middle school. It seemed like just yesterday he was a happy little kindergartener telling me "I never want to leave Mariemont (Elementary)." Now he's actually excited for school to start at the end of this month! See—middle school changes people!

First they crawl. Then they walk. Suddenly they begin to talk. Then they're texting, IMing and Facebooking before you know it. Kids growing up is a bunch of bull-(real s-word).

The Parents' Guide to So Not Cool

Momservation: Potential embarrassment is a powerful bargaining tool.

☺   ☺   ☺

My son just started middle school this week. I have volunteered in my kids' classrooms since kindergarten. So I was planning to keep on truckin' and see where my services could be used at the middle school level.

Before I could ask for a sign-up sheet the school counselor informed an entire multi-purpose room of helicopter parents: working in the classroom—**so not cool**.

Before we could go buy a new lunch box for this year we were told by a veteran middle schooler: lunch boxes? **So not cool**.

Apparently, everyone's having hot and smashed food in brown bags in sixth, seventh and eighth grade. Obviously, so much cooler.

When my friends went to drop their daughter off on the first day of middle school there was a waving, cheering contingent of student leaders welcoming new students.

Getting ready to wave and honk back their daughter hissed, "Don't even do it! That's **so not cool!**"

Welcome to the middle school years parents. Be prepared to walk through a minefield of **so not cool**. Suddenly the rules have changed and what once was normal and okay has instantly become **so not cool**.

I present to you an initial list, certain to grow, with things that have become **so not cool** for preteens. If you choose to use it to save embarrassment or have a little fun, good or evil is your choice...

The Parents' Guide to So Not Cool

- Being seen in the classroom, bringing a forgotten lunch or assignment, being on campus or out of your car – **so not cool**.
- Bringing anything other than a plain, brown paper bag for your lunch – **so not cool**.
- Showing any sort of affection or that you actually like them– **so not cool**.
- Acknowledging or waving to your children's friends – **so not cool**.
- Offering any sort of help or suggestion in front of friends – **so not cool**.
- Complimenting friends' outfits and asking where they got them – **so not cool**.
- Jumping in on a conversation with their friends or sharing in a piece of gossip – **so not cool**.
- Basically doing anything other than breathing in front of their friends – **so not cool**.
- Trying to touch their hair, adjust their clothes, or point out a potential problem with their appearance – **so not cool**.
- Waking them up in the morning with the traditional gentle touch, hug, or kiss – **so not cool**.
- Asking about the opposite sex or if they think anyone is cute – **so not cool**.
- Accidentally catching them naked, dancing or singing in front of a mirror, applying deodorant or body spray, or checking their face out for zits/hair – **so not cool**.
- Leaving any sort of note in lunch, locker, or binder – **so not cool**.
- Being seen in an uncool car at drop-off and pick-up – **so not cool**.
- Trying to be funny, make jokes, or make conversation in carpool – so not cool.

Where's My Child Been?

Momservation: Middle names were invented so mothers could effectively yell at their children.

☺   ☺   ☺

Hello! And welcome to this edition of: **Where's My Child Been?** The frustrating game of clutter and ignored requests played by nagging parents all over the world!

A quick nod to our players in Holland with a shout-out to Greta who has tripped over wooden shoes left in the doorway for the 1000th time! We know where her child's been!

Don't forget our loyal players in France with a high five to Juliet for the brie and baguette left on the counter AGAIN! We know where your child's been!

And a special "Hello" to our Summer Olympics host Rio de Janeiro! Our newest player, Salvador, continues to have sand from the porch to the bathroom no matter how many times he says, "Por favor! No mas playa en mi casa!" We know where your child's been!

Where's My Child Been? is not a new game—it's been around for centuries! Mrs. Bonaparte yelled, "I know where Napoleon's been!" before telling him for the 1000th time to pick up his toy soldiers from the middle of the foyer. Mrs. Wright played hundreds of games of **Where's My Child Been?** before she got Orville and Wilbur to keep their kites and bicycles out of the den. And Mr. Cousteau stepped on his fair share of wet swim trunks and sea shells playing Where Has Jacque Been?

So are you ready to play? Rules are easy:

1. Discover items discarded around the house despite repeated nagging of your children to pick up after themselves.

2. If it's a good day hold up discarded item and yell: "I know where (fill in child's name)'s been!"

3. On a bad day yell: "For the love of Jesus, Mary, and Joseph (fill in child's entire name)! For the 1,000th time pick up these (insert item)! I'm not your personal assistant!" (Continued rant optional.)

4. If the child is not home: cuss under your breath, mutter about nobody ever listening to you while picking up discarded items. Deposit arm full of personal possessions into middle of child's bed (to be thrown on floor later for another chewing out at bedtime and a rant about forgetting to brush teeth for the 1000th time without being reminded).

That's it! Good luck and remember to smile! It only gets more frustrating the older they get! For hours of fun there's also **Where's My Child Been? Outdoor Edition** and **What's That Smell? Car Edition**.

Words of Wisdom

Momservation: Out of the mouths of babes is a short trip from out of the mouth of a parent.

☺   ☺   ☺

"Life's not fair—get over it."

My kids hear this a lot. So much, in fact, that if they start to whine, "That's not fair," they catch themselves before I can shoot back my usual retort.

We've got a lot of sayings in our house meant to course correct behavior as well as inspire our kids to be their best possible selves. Some are funny. Some are frank. Some are shouted. Some are not printable. Some we've adopted from our own parents.

But they are all meant to be sound bites to motivate, educate, validate, and provide perspective, direction and reality.

Growing up I frequently heard, "If you tried your best that's all that matters." I got this whenever I brought home a disappointing grade, lost a race, or missed out being the first, the best, or the winner.

At the time, I thought this mantra was another sign that my parents just didn't understand. Who cares if I tried my best? My best wasn't good enough! But it was also a clever double entendre—because if you didn't try your best, it was implied that you had no one to blame but yourself.

Now, with the perspective that only life experience and becoming a parent can bring, I understand the gold weight wisdom of their guiding phrases. These nuggets of truth and insight we impart while raising our children, either passed on or original, may fall on deaf ears when our kids are young (or obstinate teenagers) and further put us in the annoying category.

But the hope is it will sink into their consciousness to become the built in GPS system they will turn to when navigating the road of life.

I literally have some of these important life messages pasted on the walls of our home. In the bathroom: "Be the change you wish to see in the world." Gandhi.

In the kitchen: "Do not follow where the path may lead. Go instead where there is no path and leave a trail." Ralph Waldo Emerson.

I just got a new one from the movie *The King's Speech* that I think I'll put in the entry way: "My castle. My rules."

My husband has one he picked up from the new reality television series *Last American Cowboy*: "I'm raising you to be tough, not mean."

I asked some of my friends what popular sayings they use in their house (whether yelled in frustration or said with encouragement) that they hope their kids will take in on a conscious level, if not a subliminal one, if said often enough. Below is a sampling of local family words of wisdom:

"Work first, play later." The Mahoney family. Also, "If nobody's dead, it's not that big a deal."

"Know your worth." The Borg family. Also, "Suck it up."

"Your life experience is based on 10% of what happens to you and 90% how you react to it." The Dowd family, who simply reduces it down to "90-10" to get their point across. Plus, the number one family rule, "No freaking out."

"I love you. I'm proud of you. You can do anything in the world you want to do. Why? Because I believe in you." AJ Salvetti every night to his two young daughters. Also, "You get what you get and you don't throw a fit."

"The harder you work, the luckier you get." The Koerwitz family. Also, favorite family tongue-in-cheek words of encouragement, "If you don't win, you're not eating tonight."

"If you're always trying your hardest, it will always work out." The Lippi family. Also, "Why would anyone play soccer when they can play baseball?"

"Life's not fair—fair is where you buy balloons." The King family. Also, passed on through two generations of Marines, "The Seven P's: Prior Proper Planning Prevents Piss Poor Performance."

"Finish what you start." The Phipps family. But according to the youngest Phipps, Katie, it's, "Would you like some cheese to go with that whine?"

"Control yourself. You're in charge of your emotions." The Lewis family. There's also, "Show some gratitude," good at any volume.

"Risk/Reward." A simple phrase for weighing your options from the Hemond family.

From Ginny Dowd's friend, Tina—a grandma, I will leave you with sage advice that pretty much covers about any situation: "If it feels icky—don't do it."

What It's All About

Momservation: If you could bottle up the combined energy of kids and puppies, there would be no need for nuclear energy—it's already wiped out my house.

☺   ☺   ☺

If it's not about the remote then it's about what to watch.

If it's not about whose turn it is to set the table, then it's about whose turn it is to clear it.

If it's not about who has to get into the shower first, then it's about who took too long.

If it's not about downloaded apps then it's about downloaded songs.

If it's not about who gets to sit here, then it's about who gets to sit there.

If it's not about who walked the dog last, then it's about who picks up the poop.

If it's not about knock it off, then it's about who started it.

If it's not about that's mine, then it's about not yours.

If it's not about who got more, then it's about who got less.

If it's not about who rides in the front seat, then it's about who chooses the radio station.

If it's not about stay out of my room, then it's about stay out of my stuff.

If it's not about he got to pick last time, then it's about she got to pick last time.

If it's not about that's not fair, then it's about you're being mean.

If it's not about who's first, then it's about who's next.

If it's not about why can't I, then it's about how come you get to?

If it's not about don't touch me, then it's about don't look at me.

If it's not about give that back, then it's about who took it.

If it's not about he won't let me play, then it's about she always has to be included.

If it's not about who was sitting there first, then it's about who got up.

If it's not about he won't leave me alone, then it's about she won't quit bugging me.

If it's about don't do that, then it's about stop it.

If it's about who did it on purpose, then it's about it was just an accident.

...And I'm just scratching the surface of all the things siblings bicker about. These are just the ones I came up with listening to my kids for the last five minutes.

While you think of your own kids' versions of what it's all about to add to the list, I will leave you with my current impersonation of my children:

"Really Whitney? Wooooow."

"Why would you do that Logan?!"

Repeat every five minutes...

Run Down by the Puberty Bus

Momservation: Preteen girls come in like a lamb and go out like a lion.

☺   ☺   ☺

As my mother used to say, I'm in deep kimchi (i.e. deep sh**). I probably shouldn't even be talking to you about this right now and am definitely looking over my shoulder. I'm as jumpy as a cat in a room full of rocking chairs.

Who am I afraid of?

My hormone raging 11 year-old daughter.

What's happened to my baby girl? It's like Poltergeist over here these days. One minute she's squishing me and telling me, "I love you, Mommy!" and then the next minute she's crying and stomping off to her room shouting, "You NEVER let me do anything!"

One day she couldn't care less that she looks like a Goodwill donation and the next she's wearing her long hair down, with a cute Aeropostle shirt and shorts, flipping her hair and walking almost hunched so her hair will stay falling over the front of her shoulders.

One day she's a sweet, perpetual ponytail wearing tomboy and then suddenly you cut two inches of her hair off in a reluctant quick trim and she's screaming at you that you ruined her life.

What is going on here?

I'm guessing I stepped off the curb and got hit by the puberty bus that just picked her up.

I didn't even realize we were an official stop until the Great Haircutting Incident:

She didn't want me to cut her hair. "I'm growing it out," she said.

"Just a trim. It looks unhealthy and natty even when you brush it. Besides, you always wear it in a ponytail anyway," I insisted.

"Fine, but just a little bit and none from the front."

So I proceed to wet her hair, comb it all back and take an inch or so off the bottom in a straight line. As I'm cutting it, I'm trying to kick the hair that's falling, dispersing it because I know she's going to think it's too much.

"Okay, turn around," I tell her ready to check for evenness and fine tuning. Before I can stop her she does the flip all her hair forward over her shoulder thing she's being doing recently.

She looks down to assess the trim and we both notice at the same time that her hair is wildly uneven, one side significantly longer than the other thanks to it falling back to its natural side parting.

"Mom! What did you do?" she screams.

"I'm not done. Here, let me just even it out."

"No! Don't touch it!" she yells horrified. "I don't want it any shorter!" She runs off to the bathroom in a dramatic flourish.

I roll my eyes and call after her, hearing as I say it the Mom-just-doesn't-understand words: "Geez, Whitney. It's just hair. It'll grow back!"

When I reach her in the bathroom she is crying, frantically trying to make her hair somehow look even. She glares at me through the mirror.

"Just let me finish, Whitney. I can fix it," I huff, annoyed she's acting like I'm a puppy kicker.

"No! Then it's going to be even shorter! I told you not to cut it! Why did you make me cut it? It's soooo short," she moans going for Best Dramatic Actress in a Lead Role.

"You're being ridiculous. My God, it's just hair. You're acting like I shaved your head."

"Arggghh!" she yells at me with a look that could kill and stomps out.

In that moment I am mad at her for being mad at me over something so silly in the big scheme of things. But echoing in my ears are my words—that were once my mother's words—and I'm instantly transported back to a time when I felt the frustration of believing my mother just didn't understand.

Taking a deep breath and saying a quick prayer for patience for the duration of this ride I go find Whitney—who is at the computer Googling: *How long does it take for hair to grow?*

Trying to muster sympathy over annoyance I apologize. "I'm sorry, Whitney. I'm sorry I didn't cut your hair the way you wanted it and I'm sorry you don't like it."

Her features soften. The anger drains out of her. She doesn't say, "Thanks, Mom" but I see it in her eyes and with the ever so slight head bob of appreciative acknowledgement.

My baby girl is back.

Until the 2:20 bus arrives.

Why Would You Do That?

Momservation: A lot of emergency room visits could be avoided if someone stopped for a moment and first thought—*just cause I can doesn't mean I should.*

☺   ☺   ☺

I'm going to generalize for a moment here.

If you have males in your household then you've undoubtedly already asked this question: Why do boys see every bad idea as an Everest they need to climb?

This includes big boys too.

I've actually been very fortunate that I have a son, who, like his father, has the voice of reason going off pretty loudly in his head.

Most of the time. A temporary override would explain Hubby's college Pikes on Bikes days when a whole fraternity thought going on a midnight progressive booze pedal was a fantastic idea.

As a general physiological argument, though, I believe there is a constant voice in the male head that grows louder around other males convincing them to think—*That would be so cool to see if I can*...(fill in the blank with various dumb ideas, i.e...)

...smash a soda can on my forehead!
...jump off the roof into the pool!
...swallow a goldfish or whatever else someone dares me!
...see if my athletic cup works by having someone punch me as hard they can in the crotch!
...try to pogo stick onto a skateboard!
...invent parkour!

And success or failure it is worth rolling on the ground hysterically laughing, "That was so awesome!!"

So it comes as no surprise to me that I've been hearing this phrase shouted a lot lately from my 11 year-old daughter to my 12 year-old son:

"Why would you do that?!"

And further proving my theory, his buddy, Anthony, is usually over when I hear it.

Because only two boys would think it was a great idea to:

...push a sister fully clothed into an ice cold pool on a cold day.

...practice parkour flips off a two story play house.

...tell a sister you want to show her something then table-top her (someone secretly kneels below the back of the knees of a victim while a person in front of them pushes them backward).

...engineer a ropes course that has greater chance of strangling them than transporting them.

...want to drag a mattress into the den to practice launching your buddy into a back flip.

This last one I actually gave the green light to since Anthony has been taking gymnastics and they actually did realize practicing it in a cramped bedroom next to a sharp edged dresser, bunk bed, and beneath a ceiling fan was probably a bad idea. (Breakthrough!)

I did, though, make Anthony raise his right hand and pledge: *I, Anthony, promise not to break my neck on my birthday and get Kelli in big trouble for sending me home broken.*

They ended up perfecting launching your friend into a backflip and I was relieved when they moved on to their next *Why would you do that?* event: taping up your face with Scotch tape.

'Cause, you know, it's just so awesome.

Next Stop: Teenage Years

Momservation: The only thing that can make a mother miss changing diapers is standing eye to eye with her teenager.

☺   ☺   ☺

This month I officially become a mother of a teenager. I'm scared.

The first frightening thought: *When did I become old enough to be the mother of a teenager?* Second frightening thought: *Where did the time go—didn't I just have this baby yesterday?* Third scary thought: *Teenager under my roof.* And the scary thoughts just keep coming: *Only two and half years until he can drive; only five more years and he's an adult; only a year and a half and his sister will be a teenager!*

Lord, help us all then.

Okay, let's just deal with this one step at a time—no sense signing up for Survival Training and digging a moat just yet. Like I tell the kids, let's break this up into manageable pieces so it's not so daunting and overwhelming.

First, let's go into this with a positive attitude. Let's give them an opportunity to make positive choices instead of assuming they're going to make wrong decisions.

Teenagers can be fun! There're wider parameters for what they're allowed to do! They're capable of self-sufficiency! They can help you with your electronics—it's like in-house tech support! You can take them to PG-13 movies (in theory)! They can be entrusted with more responsibility (in theory)!

Case in point, I plan on letting my newly minted teenager have an iPhone, allow him to text, and have an Instagram account.

All areas my kids have been restricted from up until this point. Family moto: You are trusted as long as you are trustworthy.

Of course, my preteen daughter is not happy about this at all. As far as she's concerned, I'm playing favorites and further proving to her that life is not fair. The responsibilities attached to these privileges, of course, lost on the girl who currently does not know where her flip phone is, lost two sweatshirts and her history notebook in one week, and in the same week tried to find out if pirating computer apps was illegal.

But like I tell her, someone is always going to be older than you, allowed to do more than you, or have something you want. You can walk around being bitter and angry about it, or you can let it go and live your own life happy with what you do have.

Now that I'm looking at the teenage years with a positive attitude, I might as well be open-minded about it too. Like the Terrible Twos that everyone warned about that never materialized for my children (if you don't count my daughter's refusing to apologize phase). I shouldn't assume I'm about to embark on a nightmare trip. My teenagers just might turn out to be delightful. Like I've always believed—children are works in progress; they may have their moments of unsavoriness, but by giving them room to grow the hope is that they'll mature past that and turn out okay. Although, I do believe teenagers should come with an eye-roll quota.

Even if I can talk myself into being positive and open-minded about entering these teenager years I can't extinguish the fear that this is all going too fast. It's hard not to be frightened that you're losing your babies when your kids wake up one morning and are suddenly able to look you in the eye without a step-stool. I'm not done cuddling them. I'm not done wanting to protect them. I'm not done wanting to sing them silly songs, tickling them until they laugh snot bubbles out their noses, not done tucking them into bed at night with an "I love you" and a kiss.

I can deal with the teenage part of raising my babies, it's what comes at the end of the teenage years that truly scares me: that I have no more children to raise.

But as my son just reassured me: "No matter how big we get, we'll always be your babies, Mom."

Awww, aren't teenagers great?

Now That's Inappropriate

Momservation: Nothing can fully prepare you for the moment your kid drops their first "F-bomb" in front of you.

☺   ☺   ☺

Our word for the day, friends, is "inappropriate." Meaning: Not suitable or proper in circumstances. Used in a sentence: *My kids think I'm no fun because I think PG-13 movies are inappropriate.*

Now, let's talk about some things that are inappropriate since this seems to be a word I use a lot with my teenagers when laying down boundaries.

Using foul language is inappropriate. So, yes, even though I know you hear it all over middle school and your friends use profanity like the word "the," it is still inappropriate. Just because your virgin ears have now become "experienced" doesn't mean cussing like a sailor on shore-leave is "acceptable." If you think you can drop an "F-bomb" in front of your mother and not be in deep kimchi—my kids are not hanging out with you because you are inappropriate.

Sexual references are inappropriate. Those pictures you post on Instagram with your provocative "duck-lips" and aren't-I-sexy poses even though you're still in a training bra: inappropriate. Using sexual innuendo like you really have any clue about competently proceeding in a mature relationship is inappropriate—just because you have some peach fuzz to shave doesn't mean you now know how to command the ship. If my kids "Like" any of your inappropriate photos or comments on Instagram you will no longer be seeing them on Instagram.

Disrespectful behavior is inappropriate—toward adults, toward others, toward yourself. If you think acting like an idiot is an attractive quality—good luck with that. If you think it's cool to disregard people's rules and expectations of you, you are not just inappropriate; there's also another word for you and it starts with "A" and ends in "hole." Conducting yourself in a manner that makes people say, "Man, those parents are really raising an A-hole" means you won't be invited into our home as a guest.

Degrading humor is inappropriate. You're not sure what degrading means? It means humiliating or demeaning. I'm also going to let you in on a secret right now that will help you here: You think you're funny…but you're not. Being funny and being a bully is a thin line to walk at the teenage level. If you are laughing at other people's expense you are inappropriate. If you are using your "friends" or anyone else for your laughs, my kids don't need friends like you because you're inappropriate.

And while we're here, let's go ahead a get this pet-peeve out of the way: PG-13 movies are inappropriate. Now that you are old enough to see PG-13 movies doesn't mean they are no longer inappropriate. It just means your parents have tried their best to shield you from these mature themes, but you're just going to go over to a friend's house and see it anyway. If we're using Hollywood's standards for appropriate, we're all in trouble.

Oh, and one more that should be a no-brainer: Glorifying using drugs or alcohol is inappropriate. Enough said.

I'm glad we had this little talk. I feel much better now that we've clarified things. And if you see my kids being inappropriate, go ahead and whisper "A-hole alert" so I can get my can opener cause someone's going to be in deep kimchi.

Is It Too Late to Throw the Race to Independence?

Momservation: Love may conquer all, but sleep deprivation puts up a mighty fight.

☺   ☺   ☺

My son turns 13 this week. It is a milestone that makes my eyes sting with tears.

Not the kind that burned my eyes nearly 13 years ago when I was a new, sleep-deprived mom with poop on my hands and dodging pee geysers.

This time I'm overwhelmed with emotion because I can see the finish line ahead instead of wondering how I'm ever going to make it there. Is it too late to throw the race to independence?

Gone are the days when I could rain kisses upon his face and he would squeal with delight. It's been about a year since he turned his cheek to me—lip kisses from your mom no longer cool.

Those days when I would wish he would just go watch TV instead of waking me to play Crazy 8's, do puzzles, or play with his rubber snakes in bed have been filed under Careful What You Wish For. Hearing him walk by my room to turn on SportsCenter in the living room makes me want to put the genie back in the bottle.

Just when you think you want to change your name from "Mommy" due to whining overuse, you become "Mom" and it just doesn't have the same ring to it.

"Mommy, watch me! Mommy, help me! Mommy, come here!" will never drive you crazier than being met with a distancing silence.

But the worst part about realizing you only have five years until your first born child officially doesn't need you anymore, is recognizing that it happened long ago:

He doesn't need me to button his coat.
He doesn't need me to tie his shoes.
He doesn't need me to fix his hair.
He doesn't need me to push him on a swing.
He doesn't need me to read him a story.
He doesn't need me to get the soap out of his eyes.
He doesn't need me to give him a boost.
He doesn't need me to blow on his food.
He doesn't need me to hold him until his tears dry.

But now I need him to hold me until mine do.

Uncommon Courage and Charisma

Momservation: Believing in yourself is the best talent of all.

☺ ☺ ☺

It's that time of year again. Time for our elementary school's talent show.

Of course, talent has very little to do with it. But that's what I love about it.

I love hearing each off-pitch song.

I love watching each stiff, unrhythmic dance routine.

I love seeing the kids who thought they were dazzling in front of the mirror at home become muted in their stage fright.

I love the jokes and skits that fall flat even though they were sure it was going to be hilarious in rehearsal.

I love dropped batons, squeaky violins, missed cues, and wrong piano notes.

Why? Because I love that these kids believe in themselves that they have something valuable to offer the masses. I admire their courage to stand before their peers, exposed, and say "Look at me! Look what I can do!"

I think it's absolutely fantastic to see these young children take a risk of flying, only to shake it off with an "oh well, I tried" smile when they fall flat. It brings tears to my eyes to see them soak up the attention of an audience packed with kids, parents, grandparents, teachers and strangers giddy with confirmation that they deserve that spotlight.

I applaud each and every one of them the second they step foot on that stage because their talent is already apparent: They have uncommon courage to be who they are.

Whitney has been in the school talent show every year since first grade when she announced at the dinner table, "I'm going to sing in the talent show."

The fact that she was born of two tone deaf individuals deterred her none.

Each year she sang and danced her way through songs that had the audience cheering her performance, leaving them admiring that she was something special. It wasn't necessarily her abilities, but that she absolutely owned the stage when she was on it.

This year, as a fifth grader, my heart dropped when she told me she wasn't sure if she was going to do the talent show.

"I don't have a talent," she said in a tone of c'mon Mom, you know that.

My biggest fear was coming true. That the day would come when little girls stop believing they are as beautiful, smart, and talented as they believed themselves to be at five years old.

"That's not true," I said.

"Then what's my talent? I can't sing and I can't dance."

My heart constricted at the thought that the person she saw in the mirror wasn't good enough anymore.

I didn't want to prop her up with exaggerated encouragement, giving her a false sense of self. But I knew she was selling herself short.

"You know what your talent is?" I said with absolute conviction. "Charisma." She looked at me perplexed. "You know why people love you on stage? Because they're buying what you're selling. You make whatever you do look fun and effortless with an extra shot of pizazz. You may not be the best singer and dancer, but everyone wants to join you and sing along and dance with you. *That*, is a special talent. That is a gift."

I could see she was thinking about it, giving measure to my words against what she saw in herself.

"Okay," she finally said. "I'll think about it."

I didn't want to push her, make her do it for me. As I left her alone I hoped she would do it for her; for the beautiful, smart, talented person I hoped she always saw in the mirror.

So tonight is the talent show and Whitney is in it. It's her last one before she goes off to the self-esteem gauntlet of middle school.

What did she decide to do?

She's co-Master of Ceremonies. She's using her uncommon courage and charisma to host the show, tell jokes, keep the audience interested, and go out on top of her game.

I can't wait to stand up and applaud each mess-up.

Going at Life with Eyes Wide Open

Momservation: Summer is God's fountain of youth.

☺   ☺   ☺

OMG! This was, like, the BEST summer EVERRRRR!

Okay, sorry about that. I vowed to live this summer with my kids carefree and full-tilt like a 12-year old. Mission, like, so totally accomplished! I'll SnapChat you my selfies!

Wow…harder than I thought to get back in working-mom mode.

School starts in two days, and for the first time ever I'm actually sad that summer's coming to an end. Normally, I'm giddy like a kid on Christmas to get my kids out from underfoot, back to productive days without the background bickering, unleashed from nearly three months of trying to keep kids entertained. I will not confirm nor deny that I may have sent a thank you fruit basket to the school district.

But this summer I had good fortune and a change in perspective collide. I was able to put on hold my major writing commitments and I realized that I only had a few summers left with my kids. At 12 and 13 years old, the majority of the time I have to spend with my kids constantly with me has passed. Not only will they be heading off to college in five years, but as friends become more encompassing, I probably won't be seeing them for much of the summers that are left.

Ouch Hang on a second while my heart gets over its panic attack…

So I recognized time was running out to take advantage of and appreciate the gift that comes with having kids: slowing down and reliving the joy and excitement of summer vacation and the endless possibilities it promises.

Plus, I just really like these kids of mine—they're fun to play with!

So when that last bell rang in June, we hit the ground running on the Summer of Living Like a 12 year-old. We stayed up late and slept in late. We went to restaurants and started with dessert. We woke up without a plan and let the day have its way with us. We went to every 7-Eleven we could think of on 7/11 Free Slurpee Day. We instituted Fun Wednesdays and invited our friends to join us at places like Raging Waters water park, miniature golfing, Sky High indoor trampolines, and the State Fair.

We had endless hours of swimming and playing with friends, camping, and said "yes" to every opportunity. For two months and ten days we lived in the moment and it was glorious.

But now it's back to responsibilities of work and school and like a 12 year-old kid, I just don't want summer to end. However, I did one last magical thing by myself to commemorate a summer well-spent:

I set my alarm and got up at 1:30 a.m. to see the last night of the Perseid meteor shower.

I almost didn't get up for this annual August shooting star show and ritual—I knew it would be hard to top last year's experience of witnessing it over an alpine lake with two dozen of our camping friends, lying on our backs under a brilliant canopy of stars, oohing and ahhing over the exciting flashes of light streaking across the sky every few minutes.

I bundled up and slipped outside, deciding against trying to cajole my sleepy family to join me since I didn't plan on being out long.

Nearly 15 minutes passed as I lay on my back in our backyard scanning the light-polluted sky, beginning to despair that conditions weren't right for me to witness this amazing light show and growing concerned I was more likely to get skunked.

And then I saw one. I brilliant streak of light across the night sky so beautiful and amazing you feel fortunate and breathless to have seen it. Over the next hour I saw nearly a dozen, the city lights affording views of only the most brilliant meteors—but worth the wait for them. And instead of worrying about getting skunked, I suddenly became more aware of the beautiful sonnet of chirping crickets, the quiet rustle of leaves from a gentle breeze, the smell of dewy grass, and the comforting damp warmth of an early morning summer day.

When I climbed back into bed Hubby groggily asked me, "Was it hard to keep your eyes open?"

"No," I told him. "You're afraid to close your eyes because you don't want to miss a thing."

And in that moment, in the after-glow of my wonderful summer with my kids, I realized viewing the Perseid meteors shower was a perfect metaphor for getting the most out of life: With your eyes wide open (perspective), you won't miss a thing.

Perseid Meteor Shower Metaphor for Life

- Once your eyes adjust you see things that take your breath away
- The flashes of brilliance are worth waiting for
- Keep scanning the horizon because you never know where that next opportunity will pop up
- The brightest moments are brilliant, but it's collection of smaller moments that make it why you're out here in the first place
- Don't give up, don't stop believing that something wonderful can happen if you're patient

- The quiet moments in between waiting for something good to happen make you appreciate the things you miss every day
- Slowing down to just look up at the sky keeps things in perspective
- When the world is still your senses come alive and you appreciate the little things
- If you wait for conditions to be right you will miss something wonderful that will happen with or without you
- Making time to experience something fleeting makes you feel fortunate for being a part of something so spectacular
- God's creation is boundless and amazing

You don't have to be able to take a summer off to enjoy your family. You don't have to have the money to spend for extracurricular activities. You don't have to drop everything to make your kids feel special. It's not the quantity of time, but the quality of it.

And if you feel like this summer was a missed opportunity to embrace living in the moment, it's never too late to employ the philosophy.

Just go at life with your eyes wide open.

The Terrible Twos Never Looked So Good

Momservation: Nothing strikes panic in a mother's heart like hearing her preteen ask, "Mom, when can I have a Facebook account?"

☺   ☺   ☺

In two days I'll officially have two kids in middle school. It makes me want to throw up on my shoes with anxiety.

It makes potty training seem like a walk in the park.

It makes teething seem like a minor inconvenience.

It makes midnight feedings seem like a delightful alternative sleeping lifestyle.

I want my babies back.

Suddenly, I've got a kid dousing himself in Axe and another kid who needs to start shopping in the lingerie department.

I want diaper rash and Desitin back!

We're having battles over Twitter accounts, Facebook accounts, Instagram and Kik accounts—two preteens ready and willing to broadcast their perceived monumental lives to the masses, fringe friends and frenemies. Too immature and inexperienced to understand the consequences of bad decisions that go viral at lightning speed.

But what do I know? I have two kids that know everything.

I want my toddler back who says "No!" to everything.

Boys are texting my girl. Girls are texting my boy. They can't tell me what they learned in English, but they can tell me who's going out with who and who just got suspended. Foul and inappropriate talk becomes as normal as ketchup on fries.

How do I go back to the days when "stupid" and "shut up" were bad words?

Girls will be rated as "hot," boys will described as "yummy," and my kids will be existing in a place where the student body morphs into walking hormones in Nike Free Runs.

I want the monotony of hours spent at McDonald's Playland back!

I know in my sixth and seventh graders near future will be dances, overnight field trips, boobies, holding hands, kissing when nobody's looking, make-up, shaving, testing of boundaries and human anatomy exploration.

What just happened? I think I just fainted...

CHAPTER 4

Rule Book for Parenting in the Digital Age

Momservations®
Top 10 Things I Should Be Doing Instead of Updating My Status

1. Buying groceries so my kids don't have to pick fuzzy green spots off their cheese and bread before making their lunches.

2. Starting laundry before everyone in the house has to go commando.

3. Sweeping the kitchen floor because my floor is starting to look more stocked than my fridge with food.

4. Mopping the floors before it's mistaken for a Twister mat.

5. Paying the bills that still haven't disappeared after pretending I didn't see them.

6. Cleaning the bathrooms because shutting the door forever just isn't an option.

7. Vacuuming the house before the dust bunnies and mites join forces and take over.

8. Figuring out what's for dinner so we don't have to have left over left-overs.

9. Putting away everything left on the counters because everyone's pockets, backpacks, bedrooms, closets, and drawers may actually be totally empty now.

10. Pick up toys, shoes, clothes and backpacks I'm tired of tripping over while waiting for a child to actually do what they were supposed to do.

Be Present People

Momservation: Give a toddler a phone and they will be distracted for an hour. Put away your phone and interact with your child and they will be better people for a lifetime.

☺   ☺   ☺

Why would someone do that to a child?

It makes me sad every time I see it. I saw it again today and I had to keep myself from saying something—but really, should I have stopped myself? Because someone needs to give these people a clue that they are missing an opportunity for greatness…

I'm talking about parents/caregivers walking children in strollers yakking on their phones like multi-tasking maniacs, or worse—with their earbuds in, choosing to tune out instead of tune in to a child's basic developmental needs.

It is the equivalent of someone walking up to you and saying, "Hi, what's your name?" and instead of interacting, you pull out your phone and pop in your earbuds, staring past them as if they are invisible. An artificial, digital life more important than human interaction.

Exact same.

So gather round people because I'm standing tall on this soap box and grabbing the microphone to tell you something that grown adults should know better:

Put down the damn phone and be present!

And if you are the caregiver of a child and you are taking them on a walk—for whatever reason: change of scenery, gotta get out of the house before you'll go mad, calming down a fussy child, routine, sense of duty—interact with the child for the love of creating a well-adjusted, intelligent, emotionally stable individual!

My kids are teenagers now and from the MOMENT THEY WERE BORN I never stopped talking to them. People in Target probably thought I was a crazy, sleep-deprived weirdo as I walked down the aisles having a full conversation with my infant, "Should we get some formula today? Do you think it's on sale this week? Oh look! Oreos! If Momma is going to survive this infancy stage that is like the Groundhog Day movie she's gonna need a lot of Oreos…"

When I drove my son to daycare on the way to work, his car seat facing the rear, I would sing songs to him the entire half-hour commute. And when I ran out of material, I made up new material:

♪♫ Mommy loves Logan, Mommy loves Logan, yes she does, yes she does!

Mommy loves Logan, Mommy loves Logan, just because, just because! ♪♫

When my son was at preschool and it was just me and my toddler daughter, did I want to plunk her down in front of a taped PBS loop of "Elmo's World" to complete the break I desperately needed from raising kids 17-months apart? Hell, yes.

But instead, aware of being blessed with the most important job on earth—the nurturing and developing of a quality human being—I put Whitney in a stroller and we sang songs together as we walked. We talked about where to collect acorns that we would throw in the creek (over and over and over again). I would sing "Five Little Pumpkins" in June for the millionth time every time Whitney said, "Punkins again!"

Now this is where I get to brag:

My kids walked early (8 months and 10 months)

My kids talked early (full sentences by 18 months, first
words included perfectly pronounced "helicopter" and
"Afghanistan")

My kids potty trained early (both completely before 2
years old)

My kids rode a bike early (3 years old both)

My son only mispronounced 2 words during language
development (hopgrasser for grasshopper and blacky
webbo for black widow)

My kids could tell you at 3 years-old the names of the
entire Executive branch of office

My kids are honor roll students

My kids are talented

My kids are happy

It is not a coincidence.

I wasn't some tiger-mother pushing them for greatness. I
simply interacted with them. I didn't stick them in front of a TV. I
read to them every night even when I wanted to cry with
exhaustion. I played with them when they wanted to play (and
caught a few winks during Hide-n-Go-Seek). And I **NEVER,
EVER** put on earbuds or chose my phone over an opportunity to
engage with them.

The early development years are just too important to not
be present in your children's lives.

Research supports this! From the National Center for
Infants, Toddlers and Families on why early experiences matter:
"Cognitive learning begins at birth. During the early years,
children develop competency in language and literacy not through
a set curriculum, but through interactions and experiences with the
adults around them."

Research also shows fine motor skills are connected to
language development. Scientist Karen Adolph suggests that a

complex relationship exists between cognitive and motor skills development in infants. To cut through all the scientific mumbo-jumbo she basically concluded motor skills and cognitive skills are connected because infants spend the vast majority of their existence, when they are not sleeping, learning how to learn.

So, trust me. If you put in excellence, you will get excellence in return. And if there are developmental hurdles keeping this from happening, you can still create amazing people from these little sponges just by engaging them.

Because interacting with children shows you love them. And besides food, water, and shelter—this is all any person needs.

Text Me, Text Me Not

Momservation: Thank you technology for inventing another way for kids to feel left out.

☺   ☺   ☺

"I have no friends!" my 17 year-old niece wailed in a moment of self-pity.

Her mother dutifully tried to console her, but the rest of us just chuckled to ourselves. This from the teenager I've never seen alone, has over 1,000 friends on Facebook, and every time I see her has some new friend in her entourage.

We all took her outburst for what it probably was—feeling disconnected because her phone momentarily lay silent without a text.

Woe indeed.

I'm not a big fan of texting. Yes, I do it, but more often than not, people get frustrated with me because I won't notice the message for hours. I'll use it for quick communication or verification, but if we're going to carry on a conversation—call me. I think it can be an important communication tool for adults, but for the demographic that most prizes it, teenagers, I think it is a horrible waste of time and huge distraction.

I didn't allow my ten and eleven year-old children to text, much to the consternation of my daughter. Whitney still bought herself an iTouch (all the bells and whistles of an iPhone without being a phone). Apparently, she had harbored hopes of texting her friends while leading me to believe it was just for the games, apps and camera. Her plan was foiled when she realized it was an ongoing cost someone was going to have to pay for—and it wasn't going to be me.

I told her:

a) I wasn't paying for Wi-Fi or an unlimited texting plan

b) There was no reason for a ten year old to text

c) I wasn't about to send her down the road of not being able to put down a phone for fear of missing something.

As I laid these points out to Whitney I got my first, "But Mom! Everyone's doing it!"

Oh brother, here we go.

"Everyone's shaving their heads too. Let's go do it!" I said with mock excitement. She gave me the look where she cocks her head to the side, tilts her head down and glares at me with the now familiar message of *not very funny, Mom.*

Since then, Whitney's been on a campaign to get me to let her text. She's constantly adding to her list all the friends who are allowed to text and reasons why she should be allowed to also. Some nights when I go to kiss her at bedtime, she'll be sitting up in discussion mode, a carefully crafted argument lurking behind her eyes.

"So, Mom, I was thinking...if you let me get the texting app..." She'll proceed to lay out an articulate justification, making me proud that she will one day make an excellent member of the Debate Team.

But the answer is still no. I explain again, "Whitney, there are so many more things you should be enjoying and worrying about at this age than if someone is texting you. You should be focused on school, not your phone. You should be outside playing, living in the moment, not looking at your phone to see if someone else is having more fun than you somewhere. You should be worried about little things like who you're going to sit with a lunch, not why someone hasn't texted you back. I don't want your value tied to that phone and whether it buzzes with texts or not."

"But I won't be like that Mom!" she confidently assures me, her face lighting up with the hope that her pledge will change my mind.

"Oh, but you will, Whit. Trust me," I say thinking of every phone-absorbed teenager I know.

Whitney still has her iTouch and she still hasn't given up. Unfortunately, her brother isn't helping.

We gave Logan one of our old flip phones for emergencies when they were in grade school. As the pack leader of he and his sister, he used it to call to tell us he and Whitney had arrived at school safely, that he made it to a friend's house okay, or in case a problem arose when he and Whitney were off playing. He had no interest in texting, and unlike his sister, does not see the phone as a social instrument.

No matter, Whitney still sees this as totally unfair that he has an old phone with texting capabilities and doesn't buy the argument that as an older sibling he gets first privileges. We've never specifically told him he couldn't text, because he doesn't feel the need to. Perfect.

However, I got this text recently from him: HOW IS YOUR NEW PHONE?

I reply: GREAT! HOW'S TEXTING IN FRONT OF YOUR SISTER TRYING TO MAKE HER JEALOUS?

Logan: GOOD!

Guess what look I got from Whitney when they got home...

Writing the Rule Book for Parenting in the Digital Age

Momservation: As if we needed the Internet and social media to further convince our children that they know more than us.

☺   ☺   ☺

Can we talk?

Is it just me, or are you parents of teenagers also thinking it's unfair that the rules of parenting teenagers have changed so drastically?

I would gladly take the I-Hope-You-Have-One-Just-Like-You curse and at least get home field advantage and insider knowledge on how to parent an aloof, boy-obsessed, room-bound teenage girl over navigating the shark infested waters of social media.

The sucky thing is there is no Rule Book for parenting in this evolving every nanosecond digital age. As Alison Slater Tate pointed out in her article, "Parenting as a Gen Xer: We're the first generation of parents in the age of iEverything," we're the last of the Mohicans. Our parents can't help us with their experience of raising teens because there was no Internet to contend with. Our children only know a world with information and accessibility at their fingertips. Only we Gen Xers know what it's like to have experienced worlds both with and without Internet.

Our generation of parents is writing the Rule Book for Parenting in the Digital Age.

And I'm sorry, but I'd rather be dealing with the good ol' fashion teen crawling back through a window to their bedroom with alcohol on their breath than to be the forefather on what to do when you find out that teenage boys are constantly asking your daughter for "nudes" and "ass pics" through SnapChat.

Are you with me that it is emotionally, mentally, and physically exhausting trying to convince our children of the dangers of a digital world they think we know nothing about? Having never lived in a world without technology, our preteens and teens are unable to comprehend that it has never been easier to make a life-altering mistake in the unforgiving world of digital footprints that will become the oilfields of the future.

It could be argued that really nothing has changed, only the medium of which teens are communicating has. How can I get mad at the poor relationship etiquette of breaking up via text message—when really, how is it any different from the passed note in the hallway? Or discovering teens under covers talking on their phones past bedtime? They hide under the covers to shield their illuminated screens while texting; I hid under my covers to muffle the sound of my voice. One now has to have her phone charging at night in the kitchen; I got my 20-foot phone cord exchanged for a 3-footer.

But I would argue there is so much more to lose at stake, and thus a new hybrid of sleepless nights with worry. Rumors are now validated with pictures available to anyone with Internet and spread quicker than damage control can be implemented. Instead of a poor choice becoming a private embarrassment, it becomes a public hell. Bad decisions can be learned from, but also resurrected to get you rejected for college, a job, even the military. Humiliation is only a click away. Delete doesn't mean it's gone. Bullies have so many tools for harassment that suicide seems like the only escape.

OMG! Can I please just find a Playboy under my son's mattress instead of making sure he isn't hiding nude pics of girls he knows on his phone that could get him arrested for distributing pornography?

Thanks a lot Vint Cerf, "Father of the Internet," for making the job description of parenting a teenager even more challenging. I-Hope-You-Have-One-Just-Like-You.
#ThisJustGotReal

If I Find Out You Did It You Quit It

Momservation: Social media: where teenagers go to actually become less social.

☺   ☺   ☺

Big day here at the Wheeler house.

Whit gets her cast off…AND…is the last in the family to finally get an iPhone (except for the dog, but who knows where Apple will take us next).

Guess which one is the bigger event?

Better plug your ears around 2 p.m. because the phone is a surprise for after Whit gets her cast off. The scream could be for what her arm looks like under the cast after three weeks (we've done three of these already and it's not pretty), but more likely it will be for the coveted phone and the social world it opens up to her.

"Social" as in sitting alone in the room with the strongest Wi-Fi signal taking "selfies" and posting them on Instagram then checking every few seconds to see how many "Likes" it generates.

Kids these days don't know social. Social when I was in middle school meant the crazy characters you encountered on the bus on the way to the mall where you went with a flock of girls to look for cute boys and cute accessories. It could also mean meeting a bunch of new people at the mall as you tried to bum 20 cents, so you could call your mom on the pay phone to come get you instead of taking the bus home.

So even though Whit finally gets a smart phone, it does come with strings attached so that her world doesn't get smaller even as she thinks it's getting bigger.

Here is my list of **10 Simple Rules for Responsible and Mature Smart Phone Ownership for My Teenager** or

If I Find Out You Did It You Quit It:

1. **The phone is not to be used for inappropriate content.** Yours, theirs, or by association. If you don't know what stands for "inappropriate" use this test: *If Mom was standing over my shoulder right now seeing this would I get my phone taken away?* So before you go "Liking" that raunchy picture or adding your voice to a foul-mouthed commentary or forwarding anything naked, imagine life without an internet connection because you will be living it.

2. **You must answer your phone EVERY time I call or text.** This, contrary to your social media belief, is why you have a phone and why I pay for its services. If you screen me or I can't reach you within a reasonable amount of time, not only do you lose the PRIVILEGE of having a phone, I'll just keep you home where I know where you are and what you're doing.

3. **I take priority over your phone.** If I am talking to you, your phone is away. Let it buzz, ping, vibrate, SportsCenter update, and ring-tone *Radioactive* to your pocket, because no matter what I have to say, it is always more important. I will not compete with your phone. If I do—just like Vegas you'll find out the house always wins and your pockets will become much lighter.

4. **No phones at the table.** Meals are family time. We interact. These days, it's where you actually learn to be social. Your friends are not invited unless they are physically present. If you can't carry on a decent conversation with your family, then there's no need for a phone either.

5. **Manage your time well.** Or I'll manage it for you. If your phone is taking precedence over school work, chores, extra-curricular activities, or anything else more important (which is almost everything) I will remove the temptation until you realize life goes on without it. If I start to see the top of your head more than your face that is non-stop buried in your phone, the management decision will be to make you go cold-turkey on your phone addiction.

6. **Make smart purchases.** Every song, app, and download you purchase will go through my iTunes account and I will see it. You will use your own gift cards and not my credit card on file. If you exceed your limit, you will pay me back and if you can't control excessive and frivolous uploads I will control it for you by changing the password. Consider this a public service for helping you become a smart consumer.

7. **Make smart choices.** The internet is forever. Everyone can see it. What you put out there and what you do on it leaves a footprint that can't be erased. So if you think you're hiding behind SnapChat, erased texts,

and deleted content—trust me, it still leaves a trail.
Don't doubt that someone, somewhere has seen it,
screen captured it, or still has it on their end. Don't
make a bad choice that can haunt you forever. You get
one mistake to learn from with me. Lesson not
learned, phone no longer yours.

8. **I get all-access privileges.** I reserve the right, at any
   time, to go through your phone and all its content. If
   you have nothing to hide, you have nothing to worry
   about. If you are deleting selective content and texts
   I'll think you're hiding something which is a problem.
   If I find something disturbing, we're going to have a
   problem. If you're fighting me on this, it's a problem.
   No phone solves the problem.

9. **Cyber-bullying is zero tolerance.** Using your smart
   phone as a weapon to hurt someone will not be
   tolerated. If I find out you used your phone for evil
   instead of good YOU WILL NEVER OWN A PHONE
   AGAIN UNTIL YOU ARE AN ADULT and YOU WILL
   NEVER AGAIN HAVE UNSUPERVISED INTERNET
   ACCESS.

10. **Using your smart phone while driving is zero
    tolerance.** There is nothing so important on that
    phone that it is worth your life. If you put your life or
    anyone else's at risk because of your phone, you will
    lose the privilege of driving, the privilege of a phone,
    and the privilege of my trust.

Do You Know Where Your Kids are Hanging Out?

Momservation: Checking in on where you're kids hang out on social media is the same thing as sticking your head in the room to make sure everything is still ok.

☺   ☺   ☺

Teenagers are a migrating herd. Like wildebeest following the sustenance they need to survive, young hipsters instinctively gather at the latest social media watering hole like their lives depended on it.

As these social media gathering spots ebb and flow in popularity, with older teenagers abandoning them for the latest over-sharing oasis and preteens rushing in with new-found access, any parent wanting to protect their oblivious migrators from predators (and themselves) needs to know the lay of the land.

As a mother of digital age kids, I've watched (and closely monitored) the migration pattern of my children on social media starting in middle school. Sometimes I blocked access for a little while based on maturity level, but I came to accept that all these social media watering holes are what the modern form of teenage communication looks like.

So the best you can do is educate yourself if you truly want to be the game warden who keeps your kids from wandering off the reserve. (And get a screen name, follow them, and make them follow you back.)

It surprised me recently when some parents of preteens just became aware of sites like Kik and ASKfm. Since my kids had long ago abandoned these sites I assumed all kids had. I realized they never go away—they just attract new visitors stumbling onto the big kid playground eager to join the game.

So I thought I would share what I know about teenage social media migration because there is always a herd right behind the last one—and if your kid isn't careful they can become a casualty of poor choices and bad decisions lurking in the brush. It's always the weak ones who get preyed upon...

Teenage Social Media Migration

Kik Messenger. This is where my kids started in middle school. They liked it because it was a free texting app that you didn't need a smart phone to use. They used it on their iPod Touch. Now kids would use it on their iPads. Like with all social media, it should be monitored because it's the first forum kids (and adults pretending to be kids) will use to ask for nudes. My kids quickly moved on from here for more interactive apps once they got iPhones. **Danger**: KiK does not offer any parental controls and there is no way of authenticating users.

Instagram. The first app I officially ok'd for my kids to use and by far still the most popular photo sharing app with teens. Where we passed notes in class, kids today use photos to tell the stories of their lives (at all hours of the day). Most parents feel safe with this site because of the privacy controls so lots of peers are on it. Giving out your Instagram screen name is the modern day phone number exchange. It is usually kids' first exposure to social currency measured by collecting Followers and Likes. My kids still post to this site but not nearly as much as they did in middle school where they liked to constantly update their bios with latest friends, boyfriends, or girlfriends. **Danger**: Kids will post links to Kik, ASKfm, and other sketch sites in their bio.

ASKfm. I did not allow my kids on this Q&A site where users can ask other users questions anonymously. Straight up it's a forum for cyberbullying. Kids like it because in this age of oversharing they feel popular when people ask them personal questions and cannot resist the opportunity and mystery of someone maybe telling them how "hot" they are. But for every friend who strokes them by telling them they're hot, there will be 10 anonymous users who will say something mean or inappropriate. Users have the opportunity to block these comments/questions, but they usually get sucked into the bad behavior by trying to fight back with equally ugly language. The allure seems to drop off after middle school. **Danger:** ASKfm had been associated with nine documented cases of suicide.

Twitter. I did not originally let my kids download this app even though I had long been on it for work. At the time it caught me by surprise that teens were starting to use this 280-character message system that had primarily been used to network or receive latest news. Obviously now, with its added picture and video sharing capabilities, this collecting Followers, Favorites, and Retweets site is the exact place for instant information and popularity hungry teens to be. I still think middle school kids should not be on it because like with other sharing sites, you will be shocked by the inappropriate things shared by their peers and easier access to finding it than on Instagram. But as long as your mature kids are educated on the dangers of leaving a cyber footprint that can come back to haunt them and always apply the rule to never Tweet, Favorite, or Retweet inappropriate content you have to cut the cord some time and let them hang out where everyone else is. **Danger**: Kids don't like to use the privacy controls because they like the wide potential audience. You don't have to Follow someone to see their posts. And that's the problem—kids don't realize that without privacy controls on ANYONE can see what they post and interact with them.

SnapChat. I fought a losing battle against this app that allows you to send a photo or video from your phone to another user that will "self-destruct" after a certain amount of time set by the sender (a few seconds to 10 seconds). I finally gave in when my kids were in eighth grade because along with Instagram and Twitter these are three of the Big 4 social media communication tools—used not just by teens but by the world (Facebook being number 1). Kids like posting to their SnapChat Story where a compilation of pictures and videos stay for 24 hours and all Friends can see it— and with all the tools SnapChat is constantly adding (stickers and graphics to enhance pictures/videos) it has become teenagers' number one communication app. I've adopted an If-You-Can't-Beat-Them-Join-Them attitude and actually enjoy seeing what my kids and their friends are up to because they post to it constantly. And everyone knows now that the pictures never really go away because SnapChats can be Screenshot-ed (or even saved before sending by the user themselves to their camera roll). SnapChat did add a feature that tells you when someone has Screenshot your picture. **Danger:** Unless they put it on their Snapchat Story or save it to their camera roll you cannot see what your kids are sending or receiving on SnapChat. You better make sure your child is well-versed on boundaries and consequences before letting them on SnapChat because this app is the ultimate form of a Trust Test for parents. The temptation is just too great to send and receive inappropriate pictures and it is the main tool for asking, being asked, and sharing nudes.
#StayInTheGame

Combatting an Epidemic of Artificial Validation

Momservation: 1980's teen girl: Give me big hair and AquaNet or give me death. Millennium teen girl: Give me my smartphone or give me death.

☺   ☺   ☺

My most popular topic when speaking to groups is "Parenting in the Digital Age."

That's because parenting has never been harder in this era of always being "plugged in." Though the basic rules of parenting still apply—you're trying to love, protect, and nurture your kids into likable, functioning, responsible, happy adults—it's the playing field that's changed.

I've talked a lot about how to set parameters in this new age of social media with its unlimited, easy access to information and constant barrage of updates and messages.

But something I haven't addressed is how constant access to the internet and bombardment from so many forms of information technology is really wreaking havoc on our children's self-esteem.

Never has there been a quicker and easier way to feel left out, isolated, unpopular, insecure, unable to measure up, and be constantly comparing yourself to those you know and don't know.

And because everything you read and see on the internet is true (*snark*), the impossible body images, seemingly around-the-clock partying, and celebrity worship have created an atmosphere of chasing the impossible (or should I say the wrong priorities).

Since today's generation of kids seek validation in social media "Likes," "Friends," "Followers," "Retweets," and "Shares" they are chasing artificial friendships and unrealistic or unattainable ideals. All too much, our kids are putting value in superficial validation instead of putting their energy into true achievements that are the foundation of self-worth.

I didn't work this hard to brick by brick try to build a solid foundation of love, support, and security for my child to just to have it torn down by one hateful and cowardly anonymous posting on ASKfm or from a fake Instagram profile.

I'm never going to get my kids off social media—I accept it is how their generation communicates.

Instead, I fight to keep them grounded in the real world with tangible values, friendships, and the reward of true validation found in a worthy effort, achieved goals, charity, kindness, and selflessness.

But I also need to speak their language. So every chance I get, I try to direct my kids to the more positive sites and messages of the Internet.

Like the one for our daughters thanks to singer Colbie Caillat. Her song and video, *Try,* rallying against Photoshop, is an empowering message for girls (and women) to just be yourselves. It's about putting your efforts into building yourself up with what really matters instead of what people think of you.

Thanks @ColbieCailliat for getting this social media message right.

I Know Who Your Kid Is Sleeping With

Momservation: What comes first: That you Liked someone's Instagram photo because they Liked yours, or they Liked your Instagam photo because you Liked theirs?

☺   ☺   ☺

Oooooooh, I'm telling!

So I busted my daughter the other night for being on her phone after bedtime. But the interesting thing is this:

I busted your kids too.

In catching my daughter in the act of posting an Instagram photo at 10:30 at night on a school night (I happened to be checking in on her Instagram when a brand new photo popped up), I also caught ONE HUNDRED of her friends who most likely snuck their phones into bed too.

Our kids are "sleeping" with each other through their phones.

When I went in to take my daughter's phone away (who pretended to be sound asleep despite posting a picture 3.5 seconds earlier), her phone was lighting up like a Rockefeller Square Christmas tree lighting with kids Liking and commenting on her picture.

I watched as notification after notification rolled in from good kids gone bad.

It was so amazing to me how many kids were still trolling Instagram after they should've been long asleep—and wondering if their parents knew (or cared) that their kids were having a late night affair with their phone and thus my child. I couldn't resist staying up myself, curious to see how far into the night these kids would engage with Instagram.

I only made it to midnight. But I'll tell you what—many of your kids made it longer.

This is one of the things I hate about social media and why I was so resistant to letting my kids add Twitter to their list of colossal time sucks that take their attention away from the real and more meaningful world.

These young kids don't have the willpower to affectively monitor themselves—and damnit—I'm too tired at night to try and run interference on a kid that is bent on sneaking their phone into bed for a little make-out session with social media.

But you know what? I care too much about my kid to give up. If she's not going to see the folly in staying up until all-hours, then being unable to rouse herself from bed in the morning, starting her day off sleep-deprived, then her bedtime gets moved back until she gets it.

If she can't resist reaching for a phone charging on her nightstand that is lighting up with notifications, then the phone charges in the kitchen.

If she can't keep time spent on social media in perspective, then social media accounts go away until perspective properly adjusts.

But I need one more thing to happen to help me teach my kid to use her time more wisely.

I need your kid to stop "sleeping" with my kid and put their damn phones away too. If everyone would do this—then there would be no late night texts and notifications, nothing to check out on Instagram, Twitter, SnapChat, Kik, ASKfm, Vine, YouTube…

Because everyone would be asleep. Like they're supposed to be.

#Supervision

Quiz: Is Your Teen Ready for Twitter?

Momservation: And we thought a 20-foot phone cord, Call-Waiting, and an answering machine were the height of modern communication…

☺   ☺   ☺

A few months ago, my then 12 year-old daughter asked me if she could have a Twitter account.

The good news is she asked first. The bad news is she gave me this answer to my question of "Why?":

"Because all my friends are doing it."

That is always the wrong answer. How come kids never realize this is the Do Not Pass Go reason to a parent? Has there ever been a parent who then said, "Oh! *All your friends* are going to sneak out past curfew and meet down at the river with a keg tonight? Oh, okay then. Sure! Go."

Since she did not have a good reason ready for why she so desperately needed to be on Twitter and I think it's just one more colossal time suck for teenagers who already have enough forums to be vapid and self-obsessed, I said, "Okay, let's see what you're friends are saying on Twitter."

I'm on Twitter for business purposes. I do not have a personal account. I am there as Momservations®. (Something I pointed out to my daughter to show that if you have something of value to contribute—Twitter can be an important resource.)

The second thing I pointed out to her as I searched out her friends on Twitter was that I represented ANYONE who can view what her peers are putting out there for public consumption. (Another point: Only a few had a privacy setting.)

I quickly found "friends" who posted vital information like this:

"I'm so stoned right now!"

"If he's going to be such a f**cking a**hole he can go suck someone's d**k"

Retweeted: "How to get a white girl in bed" with a picture of a Starbucks condom.

I looked at my daughter who was perched over my shoulder. "So this is the conversation you're dying to join? Should we see what other quality Tweets your friends have to share?"

"No. You made your point," my daughter grudgingly said before dropping the Twitter issue.

This last weekend my 14 year-old son finally asked for a Twitter account. Exact same good news/bad news scenario.

But this time he pointed out (respectfully): whether I like it or not, Twitter is modern communication for teens. And grudgingly, I had to admit he was right.

So taking into consideration his maturity, trustworthiness, social media usage and online intelligence, his dad and I agreed to these terms for him (and for when his sister is ready) for having a Twitter account:

- Same rules apply to all social media: abuse it, lose it.
- Your account must be private with protected Tweets (only people you allow to Follow you can see them). No strangers allowed.
- I will be one of your Followers so I can see all your Tweets.
- You will pay the $10 a month surcharge for exceeding data usage because you are already regularly going over it just with Instagram.

But for those of you still on the fence about a Twitter account for your child, try taking my handy-dandy quiz:

Is Your Teen Ready for Twitter?

1. **How many hours a day does your child spend outside playing?**
    a. All waking hours
    b. Depends if there's anyone to play with
    c. Outside?

2. **How many social media accounts does your child have?**
    a. None. My kid doesn't have a smart phone
    b. A couple, but mainly they use Instagram
    c. Instagram, SnapChat, Kik, ASKfm, YouTube, Tumblr, TikTok...

3. **What is the first thing your child does when they wake up?**
    a. Go to the bathroom
    b. Gets their phone off the charger to check Instagram
    c. Looks at the phone that they slept with connected to a 10-foot charger to check all their social media accounts

4. **If your child tells you they just talked with a friend, what does this actually mean?**
    a. They saw their friend in person and talked with them
    b. They had a text conversation with a friend
    c. They FaceTimed a friend while both said nothing as they surfed their social media accounts

5. **How many times does your child's phone give an alert at the dinner table?**
   a. Never. They don't have a phone
   b. At least three, but they aren't allowed to check it because phones aren't allowed at the table
   c. Too many to count. Conversation with my child is nonexistent because they are too engrossed in phone interactions

6. **What is the first thing your child does when they climb into a car driven by another adult?**
   a. Gives a polite greeting to the driver and engages in friendly conversation
   b. Greets their friends in the car and takes their social cues from them (either talking and laughing or checking out each other's social media)
   c. Gives a barely discernable head nod before disappearing into an app on their phone

7. **When your child is at an exciting event, what do they do?**
   a. They are fully engaged, not wanting to miss a thing, excited to later share with a friend what a great experience it was
   b. At all the best parts they stop to take a selfie (or if in a group have someone take a picture for them) and post it on Instagram so everyone can see how much fun they're having and then keep having to be reminded to "Be present" instead of checking to see how many Likes they got

c. Not realize they are at an exciting event because they are more interested in the "social life" they have on their phone

8. **What does your child give as a sample Tweet?**
    a. What's a Tweet?
    b. Braces off in 2 weeks!!!
    c. Follow me @2hot2handle

9. **What is the most important thing in your child's life right now?**
    a. Family and friends
    b. Seeing how many Followers and Likes they can get
    c. B. plus video games, LiveStreaming, searching the web, a WiFi signal...

10. **If you took your child's phone away, what would they do?**
    a. Continue on with life because they didn't have a phone to begin with
    b. The Five Stages of Grief: Denial and Isolation, Anger, Bargaining, Depression, Acceptance
    c. Stop talking to you only to tell you they hate you and obsessively seek out other electronic devices either at home or somewhere else like a heroin addict desperate for a fix

If you answered mainly A:

Congratulations! You have a child untainted by modern technology! (You also probably do not have a teenager.) If you are lucky enough to have a child who isn't constantly badgering you for a smart phone or prefers human interaction to virtual relationships—do everything in your power to keep it that way or enjoy it while you can.

If you answered mainly B:

Congratulations! You have a normal teenager! Yes, it's annoying how much they are connected to their phones and social media, but this is the modern age of teenagers. Go ahead and let them have a Twitter, but continue to monitor social media habits so that they have boundaries and balance.

If you answered mainly C:

Uh-oh. It's time for an intervention. Not only does your child not need Twitter (though they've probably already gotten an account without asking), you're child needs to be weaned off of electronics. Start setting stricter ground rules, institute better balance in their lives, and make them put down their phones and be present. (Start by being a good role model and maybe putting down yours too).

Nudes Are the Modern-Day Trading Cards

Momservation: Self-respect means never having to say "I broke the internet."

☺   ☺   ☺

Holy Brazilian wax Batman!

I may be late to the party, but I just saw the cover of the latest Sports Illustrated Swimsuit Edition. It gives new meaning to "How low can you go?"

It also pisses me off.

How am I supposed to reinforce the message that less is more when media outlets keep bombarding our kids with the perception that sharing (nudity) is caring?

How do I teach my son to respect women when Kim Kardashian perpetuates the objectification of women by "blowing up the internet" by posting a full frontal photo?

How do I convince my teenage daughter that sending nude selfies is not acceptable or desirable behavior when her Disney Channel idol continues to bare all on a regular basis to much attention and fanfare?

Is it any surprise then that the latest disturbing trend on social media is the proliferation of "Nudes"—as the kids like to call them?

Yes, kids.

Nudes have become a modern day trading card among the no-need-to-brazilian-wax or manscape yet set. Boys ask girls for them via text and SnapChat like they would ask a favorite band. Once they get them, they share them with their friends trying to start a collection. They hide them from their parents in apps like Keep Safe and Private Photo Vault that require a code and which they bury in Utilities or Games icons on their phones.

As a kid posted on an ASKfm profile of a middle school *child* I know: *"You're not a real man if you don't have Nudes."* (FYI idiot—you can be prosecuted as a real man for possession of child pornography)

And why is this a Disturbing (with a capital D) new trend instead of the sexual harassment offense it should be?

BECAUSE THERE ARE PLENTY OF GIRLS WHO ARE STUPID ENOUGH TO TAKE AND SEND THEM!

Like getting a tattoo (a permanent marker of a temporary feeling), it boggles my mind that young people can't foresee regret and how regrettable taking, sending, and keeping Nudes on their smartphones can be. Beyond ruining a reputation it can deny entry to college or from getting job. It can get you a felony record for possession of child pornography or registered as a sex offender.

Some blame the idiotic decision to take and send Nudes on the underdeveloped front temporal lobe of teens that controls rational decision making. Some blame low self-esteem. Others blame it on poor parenting.

I'm blaming Sports Illustrated, Kim Kardashian, and Miley Cyrus.

Rules of Digital Engagement

Momservation: Unless that electronic device or social media is making you money, it doesn't deserve all the attention you're giving it.

☺   ☺   ☺

As a family columnist and author I get asked to do speaking engagements on parenting. But recently, when I was asked to speak to a local Kiwanis Club where the demographic was grandparents, my first thought was:

Boy how times have changed! Parenting must have been so easy before cell phones, internet, around the clock cable, video games and computers.

However, whether you raised kids in the 1960's, 70's, 80's or now in the twenty-first century, it's the same game: You're trying to love, protect, and nurture your kids into likable, functioning, responsible, happy adults.

Besides the obvious changes in technology—a little more on TV than what ABC, NBC, CBS and PBS have to offer or the need for a twenty-foot phone cord for talking privacy—the basic rules of parenting still apply:

- Supervision
- Boundaries
- Trust=Reward, Defiance=Consequences
- Open communication
- Mutual respect
- Be a good role model
- Love
- Guidance
- Support

It's the playing field that's changed. So with a new playing field, comes new rules of engagement.

When I realized I would only have 20 minutes to speak, I tried to think of the best use of my time for my audience. (BTW, my kids were horrified to learn I would speak for that long—in their digital age six-second attention spans, not only would 20 minutes be an excruciating amount of time to do public speaking, it's an unbearable amount of time to have to listen to someone.)

I boiled it down to these rules we use in my house with my 13 year-old daughter and 14 year-old son when technology comes into play. (Which is pretty much always. We are surrounded—time to mount a defense.)

Momservations®
Rules of Digital Engagement

1. **First respect yourself. Respect others. Always.** If you do this, all other rules are pretty well covered.
2. **Be present.** Life moves too fast to not be a part of it. If you've got your nose in your phone texting, posting a status update, or checking your selfie Likes you are actually missing the moment and the true value of the experience. You can't get it back. Experience life fully not virtually.
3. **Remember the Mom Test.** If you wouldn't say it, do it, or suggest it with Moms standing next to you—think twice before you post or hit send.
4. **Manage your time well.** Everything in moderation. If it starts taking precedence over things worth giving your time to like school, extra-curricular activities, physical

relationships, or getting outdoors and doing physical activities—it's time to re-evaluate priorities.

5. **No phones at the table.** Whether at home or in a restaurant, it's rude to the company you're with. Civilized people make eye contact and interact.

    a. **When someone is talking to you, they take priority over your electronic.** Look away from the computer screen, put the phone down, the controller, the remote, the whatever and quit being rude.

6. **First do no harm.** Social media is to be used for good not evil.

    a. **Be a leader not a follower**. Set the bar high and associate with the people who can compete. Avoid those who just want to see how low they can go.

7. **Be smart.** Make smart choices. Make smart purchases. Watch smart television. Post smart content. Don't be an idiot. A mistake on the internet can haunt you forever and is there for the world to see and judge.

8. **Cool it with the selfies.** Nothing says narcissism, low self-esteem, and fishing for compliments like constantly posting pictures of yourself in search of Likes.

9. **Respect privacy.** Don't read over people's shoulders, don't try to memorize their passwords, don't sneak their phones and change profile info or pretend to be them— you think it's funny but it's not. It's a violation of trust. And so is secretly reading someone else's text or emails— which is just creepy and an obvious personality flaw.

10. **Never. Ever. Text and drive.** There is nothing so important on that phone that is worth your life.

Lethal Weapon in Our Children's Hands

Momservation: If you wouldn't have the courage to say what you're about to post to someone's face, then that should be a clue not to do it.

☺   ☺   ☺

I have a love/hate relationship with many things:

- My Body Pump class on Thursdays that makes me hurt for a straight hour but then afterward makes me feel like I can conquer the world with my Buns of Steel.
- Ranch dressing, Oreos, Ben and Jerry's Chocolate Fudge Brownie ice cream…love them all but hate that it makes me have to go to Body Pump.
- My smart phone.

I love that my iPhone keeps me connected to my kids so I don't have to worry. I love that I'll never be lost again with my map app. I love that no one can ever stump me with a question with my instant access to Google.

I hate that my phone has me addicted to every kind of bubble, gem and jewel game. I hate that if I have a second of down time I mindlessly reach for my phone. I hate that I can't resist constantly checking in to my social apps.

But mainly, I hate what smart phones have done to society. I believe they've become lethal weapons:

- Distracted drivers and their smart phones rule the roads and are raising body counts every year.
- Kids are using their phones to cyber bully others to the point of suicide at an alarming rate.

- People "connecting" more through social media facilitated by phones rather than true interpersonal connections are creating a society that thinks nothing of attacking each other through "anonymous" or insensitive postings without the consequence of facing the pain they've inflicted.

Though both my teenagers have iPhones, I'm doing everything I can to keep these electronic devices from turning into lethal weapons in their hands:

- I'm laying the groundwork now before they get their driver's licenses that distracted driving will be zero tolerance.
- I work on modeling responsible smart phone behavior by keeping my phone in my purse while I drive.
- We put our phones away when we have the opportunity to socialize in person.
- I monitor their social media and electronic communications.
- They aren't allowed to be on sites like Ask.fm where people are allowed to hide behind anonymity and have a tendency to be cruel and incite drama.
- They are discouraged from spending too much time on sites like Instagram, Facebook, and Twitter that fuel teenage anxiety and insecurity by basing their self-worth on "Likes" and "Followers."
- SnapChat is a privilege based on trust and maturity and can be revoked at any time.
- Phones are to be used for good and not evil.

I know I can model, teach, and enforce responsible smart phone usage and my kids can still be "taken out" by the idiots who are inevitably around us. But smart phones are not going to go away. Besides instilling responsible phone ownership and practicing "defensive driving" of these lethal weapons, I only know one other way to keep my kids safe from the dangers that lurk:

Put the dang phone down and go outside and play with an actual person.

Love it.

6-Second Nation

Momservation: Sometimes you have to go with shock and awe to get a good point across.

☺   ☺   ☺

It's come down to this: You have six seconds to make an impression.

I guess I better get straight to the point.

The other day my 13 year-old daughter told me she didn't like watching the videos people posted on Instagram.

Why?

They're too long.

"Wait," I said. "Aren't videos on Instagram only allowed to be like 25 seconds long?"

"No. Fifteen seconds. Vine's are better."

For those of you who had to look up what "twerking" was in the Urban Dictionary after last year's MTV Video Music Awards, Vine is (was) Twitter's video-sharing app—the originators of keeping things brief on social media. You can be the director of your own mini-movie…as long as it's not more than six seconds (which then plays in a continuous loop).

"Vines are ridiculous!" I said clearly showing my age and hecka unurbness. "They're over before they even start! Six seconds isn't enough time to tell a story! And then it just loops around making the same inane point."

Of course, all I got to my commentary was the eye roll that said: *You're so out of touch, Mom. It's time to apply for your AARP card.*

Later, when I tried to regain some street cred with my teens, I tried to show my 14 year-old son a funny video on YouTube.

261

Before he'd even consider looking at it he asked, "How long is it?"

Not "What is it?" Not "Is it funny?" Not, "Is it inappropriate?"(Wait—that's usually my first question.) "Three minutes and forty-seven seconds," I told him already knowing it would be a deal-breaker.

"Geez! What is it? The *Titanic* movie or something?"

Yes. Because to a teenage boy a three and a half minute video is like watching three hours of a water-logged Leonardo DiCaprio.

"It's another NFL Bad Lip Reading," I said clearly hurt that he couldn't spare three minutes of his time to laugh at something I knew he'd enjoy with his mother.

"Fine," he shrugged finally putting down his phone to come over to the computer.

"You know what? No. I don't want to show it to you anymore," I said clearly not acting my age. When my daughter walked in the room I let loose with both petulant barrels.

"You know what? You and your 'hecka urb' friends have become a 6-second nation! You all have the attention span of an amoeba splitting in half because it's already bored with itself! Microwave popcorn ready in two and a half minutes isn't good enough for you anymore—gotta have your Boom Chicka Pop already popped and ready to rip open! Want to watch a sunset? Nope. Takes too long. Lying on your back watching the stars? Who's got time for that?! Let's watch Nicholas Megalis Vines and really have a rip-roaring 6-second time!"

My kids stood frozen in the face of my rant only moving their eyes toward each other to communicate that Mom had lost it. Finally, my daughter said under her breath, "Wow. Who peed in her Cheerios?"

In my ongoing battle with my teenage daughter over who gets to have the last word, I made my last and final point as I shut off the computer and walked out of the room.

"Trust me on this, kids—it will serve you well one day. You're going to want to get over this trend of short attention spans and instant gratification. Because you can't have good sex in six seconds."

#OverTheTopButExcellentPoint

Let's Go Fishing for Compliments

Momservation: You can't spell "selfie" without narcissism.

☺   ☺   ☺

I think this generation of youth should be dubbed "The Trawling Generation." Seriously. In the history of time there has never been such a mass rush of youth eager to take up the profession of fishing.

Fishing for compliments, that is. And their new-age tool of the trade?

Selfies.

Yep, incessantly trawling from their social media vessels: Instagram, SnapChat, and Twitter. Cast into the right crowd and you'll get the compliments you're fishing for:

> *OMG! Why are you so beautiful?!*
> *I hate you! You are perfection!*
> *Hecka urb!*
> *Rate: 10*
> *This is too cute!*
> *TBH: You're cool*
> *So jealous! Why can't I be like you?*
> *Hecka tight bro!*

Heady stuff—instantaneous feedback everyone telling you how wonderful you are—I get that.

But fling your net too far—to followers and "friends" you don't know, those hiding behind anonymity, those who derive their attention from being cruel and crass, or the uncontrollable tide of going viral—and all it takes is one insensitive or profane remark to cut the line of validation. Reeling in instead: shattered ego and devastation.

Sure, on the periphery selfies seem harmless and just another teen trend that will go the way of bellbottoms, big hair, grunge, and skinny jeans. (Or maybe not since "selfie" was just added to the Oxford dictionary.)

Not so harmless though when kids take selfies to a dangerous level like they currently are on Twitter under #Selfie Olympics—posing in front of oncoming trains, dangling from bridges, and on the edge of cliffs.

As a mother I find the selfie trend disturbing. Here I am trying to raise self-assured teenagers, whom I hope will then blossom into trail-blazing young adults, eventually becoming substantive adults—can this be the outcome from a youth society that can't seem to function without constant validation?

A positive self-image should come from within instead of needing to be artificially generated and sustained.

So sure, as the current captains of our children's ships we could go the route of setting limits like: use your selfie allotment sparingly or ask yourself, "What would Kim Kardashian do?" then do the opposite.

But I'd like to take it one step further:

Let's pull in the nets kids. Reel it in. Dock the social media ship and take a little shore leave from habitually checking status updates for some instantaneous validation.

You want to feel good about yourself? Try getting your "Likes" from the one person who really matters: You. #FirstRespectYourself

That's Right. Momma Be Watchin'

Momservation: The Golden Rule: Don't do it if you wouldn't do it with Momma standing right there.

☺　　☺　　☺

My daughter told me the most beautiful words that made my heart sing the other day.

No, it wasn't "I love you." (Touching, but expected.)

No, it wasn't "I cleaned my room without you asking." (Blow me over with a feather, but not monumental.)

No, it wasn't "I appreciate all you do for me." (We throw parades for that one.)

Here's what brought a little tear to my eye that I must be doing something right:

"Every time me and (best friend) see something totally funny but totally inappropriate that we want to retweet, we end up not doing it because we're like 'Can't. Mom's on Twitter and she'll totally see it.'"

See? I'm getting all choked up again! Totally spiritual moment. The Heavens opened and shined a light upon her and the harps of a thousand angels strummed.

She gets it! She gets the Golden Rule: Don't do it if you wouldn't do it with Momma standing right there. Or at least virtual Momma in the form of a Twitter account that follows you and makes you follow them back.

You know all those kids who are Tweeting and Retweeting totally inappropriate, cringe worthy content?

No momma's on Twitter or checking Twitter.

It's the equivalent of letting your kid run across the street during rush hour without looking. Why wouldn't you try to protect them from themselves?

Not only does there need to be more mommas on Twitter getting kids to think twice before posting (until it because common practice), but there needs to be more adults worried that Momma's watchin—because it can be a real idiot parade on Twitter with the adult clowns leading the way.

What Does Your Digital Footprint Look Like?

Momservation: A questionable digital footprint will walk you right out the door of opportunity.

☺   ☺   ☺

Today I volunteered at my son's high school to assist counselors by interviewing sophomores. The goal was to make sure the students are on track to graduate as well as making them aware of how to keep their options open for life after high school.

We did this by:

- Encouraging them to make an appointment to see their counselor for a four-year plan if they hadn't already done so.
- Encouraging them to take the SAT or ACT for college entrance as a junior no matter what their plans—to keep their options open.
- Making them aware of resources to help guide them in plans for life after high school.
- Giving them information and materials to aid in their future success.

Whether the students had no idea where they were headed in life (which, contrast to current societal pressures, is okay for a 15 year-old), or whether they had life after high school well mapped out (and could've been college admissions counselors) the take-away message was the same:

Keep your options open.

- If you make a plan—it keeps your options open because you won't run out of time to complete graduation/college requirements.

- If you take college entrance exams like the SAT or ACT—
it keeps your options open if you change your mind about
community college, military, or trade school or find the
resources for higher education.
- Using free resources to educate yourself on what's out
there, what interests you, and what's a good fit—keeps
your options open to future success and happiness.
- Information is power. When you seek out information—it
keeps your options open by putting the power in your
hands to steer your destiny.

As VICCI (Volunteers In Career and College) members we
had a big binder of resources to guide and educate the students we
met with. It is such a valuable collection of information that we
had to practically sign away our first born child to have it
temporarily in our possession.

And for all the valuable knowledge we gained studying that
binder…and all the information and guidance we provided the
students we met with to keep their options open…

**Something so very, very important was left out of what we
were supposed to communicate to the kids today.**

Something that slams the door shut to keeping your
options open.

No matter the hard work.

No matter the planning.

No matter the information and resources you utilize.

Something that should be the first page of the prized
VICCI binder:

What does your digital footprint look like?

Today's teenagers may live by the sword of social media, but unless they're absolutely careful and diligent, they will die by that sword.

What you post today on social media could haunt you tomorrow.

The first thing a college will do, a job interviewer will do, the military will do, or someone considering you for their program will do:

- **Google you**
- **Check your Facebook**
- **Check your Instagram**
- **Check your Twitter**
- **Check your SnapChat**
- **Check your Tumblr**
- **Check your YouTube channel**
- **Check your TikTok**

...do I need to keep going?

Nothing slams the door shut on keeping your opportunities open than being an idiot on social media. A questionable digital footprint will walk you right out the door of opportunity. #ThinkBeforeYouPost

4 Sad Ways Social Media Has Made High Schoolers Less Social

Momservation: An Instagram picture can be deleted. Remembering when that cute boy said "Yes" to dancing with you every time you hear Justin Beiber is forever.

☺   ☺   ☺

Social media has cannibalized the most fun ways for teens to be social.

Exhibit A: Yearbook signings.

High schoolers aren't interested in getting their yearbooks signed anymore! And why should they? The end of the school year tradition where kids used a yearbook as an excuse to see what friends and that cute guy/girl in 5th period really thought of them (or get a prized phone number with a K.I.T – Keep in Touch!) have become obsolete.

Kids can get constant, instant validation and interaction anytime by posting a pic on Instagram, Twitter, or Facebook and watch the comments pour in: Beautiful! You're so cute! You're such a bae! ILY! You're such a hottie! OMG so hot!

Who needs to actually interact with someone to ask for a yearbook signature when you can just figure out their screen name and troll them on Twitter? Or request to follow them on Instagram without that awkward face to face encounter? Then you can stalk them and have access to way more photos of that cute boy than a yearbook can offer! Or see where they are at that very minute with a Facebook check-in! Or feel like better friends than you are because you always Like each other's pictures! Or never risk rejection because you can do everything from the safety of your phone!

Which brings us back to those coveted yearbook phone numbers...now as casually thrown out as pennies on the ground. But not for calling each other—for texting. I mean, how are kids supposed to communicate with each other if they can't text? Which leads me to...

Exhibit B: Phone Calls.

Teens don't talk on the phone to each other anymore. "It's weird," says my 15 year-old daughter. "What for?" says my 16 year-old son. Because why call when you can text?

It's another social development that has been stifled by the superficial connections of social media.

Like getting the courage up to ask for a yearbook signature, making a phone call to create a social connection with someone you liked was how kids grew outside their comfort zone socially.

Now kids don't have to worry about racing to the phone before their parents answer. They don't have to hide under the covers trying to muffle the sound of a late night phone call stretching into the night. Or have to suffer the awkward leaving of a message with a nosey parent or forgetful sibling.

Texting may be less risky and awkward, but it also has way more room for miscommunication and misinterpretation when people don't respond right away, or tone is unclear, or it's just too much work to type out an answer that would give someone more context (NM – never mind). Plus, a heart eyes emoticon just can't replace the sound of someone telling you how wonderful they think you are and an LOL just can't replace the joy of hearing someone special laugh at your joke.

And when kids do make a phone call—it's a Facetime phone call where they can see each other. And your double chins, and your messy room, and your zit cream on your face, and your little brother thinking he's funny behind you, and your mom telling you to quit leaving panty liners all over the place. Yeah, sometimes a little mystery is good.

Which leads us to the mystery of why kids don't rush out to get their...

Exhibit C: Driver's License

Getting your driver's license was your ticket to freedom. Teens timed their driver's training so the second they turned 16 they could get their license, borrow Mom's car, and go grab friends for any adventure that didn't include a parent picking you up or dropping you off.

A license swung the social door wide open because you could be in charge of your own destiny (if you had access to a car and gas money). You could physically take yourself to where other teenagers were hanging out.

Now kids are like: who needs a car to do that? They feel connected to other teens through all their social media apps. Why drive to the local hangout to see if anyone is there when you can see on SnapChat stories and Facebook check-ins that they are? Why drive to the mall to hang out together when you can just keep SnapChatting selfies back and forth to each other? Who needs a car full of friends when you have nearly 1,000 Instagram and Twitter Followers?

True, new laws prohibit kids from driving with other teens in the car for the first year as well as driving restrictions past 11 p.m. And cars, insurance, and gas are expensive. But settling for connections through a phone just can't replace the thrill of getting behind the wheel and driving down the road of possibilities.

Like say maybe to...

Exhibit D: High School Dances

Like yearbook signings, dances were a way for teens to connect beyond their normal friend group. It gave you an excuse to walk up to that cute girl or guy and interact with them with a "Hey, you want to dance?" or "Hey, will you sign my yearbook?" Sure, you could be rejected but more often than not it was rude to say "No" so there was a built in safety net to take the leap.

Kids don't leap anymore. They'd rather play it safe with their followers and "friends" on Instagram, Twitter, SnapChat, or Facebook—feeling popular with superficial connections. They'd rather get cheap thrills by Liking a cute boy's photo they've never even talked to then the real rush of floating on air as you dance to Justin Beiber's "Sorry" with that cute boy from Chem class, surrounded by friends and classmates, creating a lasting memory that will surge up for decades every time you hear that song.

It still shocks me when teens forgo this opportunity to bond with their classmates in the most memorable way possible— through the music of their times, celebrating youth by dancing and singing with friends and classmates who will all go their separate ways in four years—because "dances are lame" or "nobody goes anymore."

If you ask me, sitting alone in your room posting selfies to see how many Likes you get is lame. And if nobody goes to dances anymore, then what are they doing besides laying the groundwork to look back and realize they have no tangible, memorable social experiences from high school because they mistook 450 Likes on an Instagram photo as really living.

The New Face of Sibling Rivalry

Momservation: World War III will be over a missing 14-ft cord iPhone charger.

☺   ☺   ☺

Think you just scored by calling "Shotgun!"?
Meh.

That is so, *who cares*? If you really want to get under a sibling's skin you gotta do better than that in the 2010's.

Take a sister's iPhone charger (block, chord, any of it) and now Mom's got a fight on her hands.

Fighting over the TV remote?

Who does that? Or more specifically, who needs a TV when you have Hulu streaming on your iPad or Netflix on your phone?

Have too many devices streaming, blocking another user from getting on?

Holy Gossip Girl, Batman! We've got hair pulling and threats of burning favorite Brandy Melville shirts!

Fight over who gets to use the video game console?
Amateur.

Changing the Wi-Fi password to keep your brother from joining your Call of Duty group match? Now some sh*t's going down.

Parents will always have to referee sibling squabbles—that doesn't change. Every parent will forever curse teaching their children to walk and talk while in the middle of another knock-down, drag-out between their kids. It's what causes Family World War III that has changed in the 21st century.

It's all about technology now, baby:

- Someone hogging all the Family Data Plan gigabytes so that the phone stops doing everything except—gasp!—being a phone?
- Someone end up on the short end of phone charger musical chairs (someone lost their chord so they take the bedroom chord, then someone takes the kitchen chord, so someone takes the car chord...)?
- Someone purposely posted an ugly picture or embarrassing Tweet on social media to get someone back for borrowing their favorite jeans?
- Someone won't get off the laptop so they can do their homework?
- Someone thought it was funny to change a password to lock them out of their own phone?
- Someone won't stop making mean comments on all their Instagram pictures?

Same ballgame, different field, Momma. But before you start threatening to shut down the Wi-Fi and confiscate their phones until they get married, just remember: Nothing settles a fight quicker than threatening to go comment on all their social media sites as @MommaBeWatchinICU if they don't knock it off. #DontHateThePlayerHateTheGame

CHAPTER 5

Teenager Tales

A Mother's Garage Sale

Momservation: If a child leaves a house with a jacket, and nobody sees it worn, will still keep someone warm?

☺   ☺   ☺

For Sale:

Warm jacket (rarely used)

Umbrella (never used)

Sunscreen SPF 5-500 (unopened)

Backpack with wheels (apparently for nerds)

Jeans without holes (apparently needs holes)

Cabinet filled with healthy snacks (untouched)

Counter full of zit creams (maybe better luck for you)

Men's dress shoes and tie (used once, free to better home)

Junior's low-cut, short, tight, Homecoming dress (worn once, free to any other home)

Wet towels on the floor (endless supply)

Sage advice (ignored)

Study skills (needs work)

Text books (unopened, mint condition)

Cell phone (doesn't call home)

#MakeBestOffer

BTW, Communication Failure

Momservation: If you're not lecturing your teens in six-second sound bites these days—you're not getting through.

☺   ☺   ☺

Having teenagers means never having to say: "Thanks for listening."

Okay, it hasn't gotten that bad yet, but when one kid is on Instagram and one kid is tuned into YouTube nothing I have to say registers. Unless I'm giving them a "Like" status to their social media of choice, I'm just not speaking their language.

The funny thing is I'm actually pretty fluent in social media. As "Momservations" I've got a Wordpress blog, Twitter account, Facebook page, Pinterest board, YouTube channel, Instagram profile, Kik account, and LinkedIn résumé that I can access from my iPhone. I couldn't be more dialed in than Jay-Z on a new trend. I even know what being "Urb" means. (Although, I did have to have my kids fill me in and show me a sample picture when I didn't initially get it. BTW, it means to post a "candid" of yourself on Instagram looking casually hip. BTW means By The Way, by the way.)

But alas, I am not the target demographic of my teenage children and therefore my voice becomes the equivalent of a dog whistle to them—I am not their frequency. (Especially when I use words like "alas." BTW, when did I suddenly become the mother of teenage children?) Even if I were to preface everything by LOLing, OMGing, and TTYLing, I'd still be tuned out and risk being "blocked"—to be refused access to an online profile—for my lame attempt at teenage communication. (BTW, for the record, I recognize the lameness of adults using Laugh Out Loud, Oh My God, and Talk To You Later as regular lexicon and hearing grown women use the term "Besties" to describe their best friends deserve EER—Exaggerated Eye Roll.)

The straight up truth is that we have officially entered the years when the only thing that matters to these middle school children is their peers. No matter the value, experience, or wisdom of my advice or their father's, our thoughts and opinions have been superseded by what their friends think. These teenage years should be renamed the Can't Save Them From Themselves Years. BTW, the only people who think middle schoolers advice and opinions should be vaulted to gospel truth and sound logic are other middle schoolers.

During these teenage developmental years, as frustrating as it can be to be tuned out by my children just when they need parental guidance the most, I'm trying my best to give them room to discover who they are without my interference. As long as they follow the main rule in the house to respect themselves and respect others, I can deal with being ignored in favor of seeing how many Likes they got to their latest Urb picture to Instagram.

But I'd being lying if I didn't admit that it takes praying to a higher power to give me the strength to sit back and let my kids take the reins of their social lives with just a learner's permit. For all the rest of you parents of teenagers—specifically middle schoolers, I share with you my reworked Serenity Prayer for making it through these trying years of communication failure:

Middle School Parent Prayer

God grant me the serenity
to accept that my teenager won't listen to me;
courage to watch them potentially make fools of themselves;
and wisdom to stay out of the way and let them figure it out on their own.*

*Within reason. Potential mistakes that can result in incarceration or torpedo college acceptance and bar future gainful employment require intervention from a lower power.

BTW, I'm so going to be blocked by my kids for perceived embarrassment because I talked to you all about this. TWI—Totally Worth It.

Coming in for a Landing

Momservation: You just might be a helicopter parent if you're figuring out ways to casually pop-in on your kid three hours away at sleep-away camp cause you "happened to be in the neighborhood."

☺   ☺   ☺

As soon as the doctor announced I was officially a mother to a healthy baby boy, somewhere I heard a voice that I would only later learn was my own:

"Roger that. We are cleared for take-off."

For the next 17 months I hovered, I micro-managed, and I obsessively focused on keeping my baby boy safe and happy. Having never been a mother before, I assumed that my fiercely protective instincts were simply part of motherhood.

Then the doctor held up another vulnerable bundle of delicious babyness that looked suspiciously like my love-filled beating heart and declared I was now the mother to a healthy baby girl. Again the voice:

"Affirmative. Air unit has two, repeat, two units in sight. Maintain altitude."

I had become a helicopter parent.

It's easy to see how you can get lift-off. The second a snot-nosed cousin begs to hold the new baby, or a doctor insists for optimal health you should allow someone to jab a series of needles into your defenseless baby's pristine pudgy little thigh, or you get rear-ended with your kids in their car seats by some idiot not paying attention, or you see your teething infant go for the communal grocery cart handle...

...or you sit your babies in front of the television to watch their favorite Elmo's World and instead you end up watching the

Twin Towers collapse on 9/11 leaving you to worry what kind of world your children will grow up in.

Yeah, that helicopter is never coming down. Send in the refueling plane. It's best if I just stay up here.

It's not that I don't recognize that I hover, trying to shield my child from discomfort, disappointment, hardship, unfairness, or physical, emotional and psychological pain. I am fully aware that these are the experiences that are needed to create admirable qualities like strength, courage, adaptability, perseverance, acceptance, and generally a well-balanced person able to take on life's challenges.

But these are my babies! I don't want them to have to go hungry to remember to grab their lunch off the counter! I don't want them writhing in discomfort from a sunburn just so I can say, "Told you, you should've put on sunscreen." I don't want to watch my daughter fight her own battles when all I really want to do is kick the kid in the shins for making her cry with hurtful words. I don't want to have to stock up on Band-Aids and Neosporin until my son learns to rethink his decisions.

Is it so wrong that I don't want my children to suffer to learn some of life's most important lessons? Can't I just tutor them into an MBA on life instead of having them earn their education through on-the-job training?

Don't answer that. I know the control tower is calling me in. It's become clear that I wouldn't have my wings right now if my parents didn't let me learn to fly on my own.

The truth is if I land this helicopter, their pain is my pain. Their discomfort is my discomfort. The cord might have been officially cut 13 and 14 years ago, but my children will always be connected to me. Their embarrassment, disillusionment, or disappointment equally ache my heart. So who am I really protecting by trying to shield them from the pitfalls of life? Them…or me?

"Copy that. Permission to file a new flight plan. Request clearance for landing."

It's time for me to have courage, strength, and faith that I've given my kids the necessary guidance and skills to begin navigating this world on their own. I need to quit making excuses for grounding them and give them clearance for take-off.

After all, who doesn't want to see their kids fly?

Signs You Might be a Helicopter Parent

1. You run out on a field of play during a time-out to apply sunscreen.

2. You want a syllabus at Back-to-School night to see what projects you'll be working out this year.

3. You think the joke of wanting to wrap your kid in bubble wrap is really not that bad of an idea.

4. You've never thought twice about bringing a forgotten lunch, book, homework assignment, or class project left on the counter to your child at school as soon as you discover it. With a note attached: ♥ u, Mom.

5. When your child complains about their teacher, you volunteer to "help" in the classroom under your policy of "keep your friends close, your enemies closer."

6. You will not let your child have a play-date (side note: you use the term "play-date") with someone whose mom serves unhealthy snacks like trail mix with M&M's.

7. Your kid can't hear what the coach is telling them to do because of your yelling from the stands (actually, that's a sign of an obnoxious parent).

8. If your child is not cool with you seeing them naked and you still put toothpaste on their toothbrush for them.

9. Your child has had a smart phone since kindergarten and checks in with you at snack recess.

10. You've had a doctor tell you the "rash" is just a red Gatorade mustache.

11. You still blow on their food when it's hot even though they are old enough to say, "Please, don't."

12. You frequently "suggest" to the coach where your kid should be in the lineup, how often they should be subbed-in, what play should be run, or which routine is the best.

13. When you tell your child they should talk to their teacher about their problem or concern, by "they" you actually mean "I will."

14. Your child doesn't know how to hold a steak knife because you still cut their meat for them.

15. Your child has never seen a movie that might make them cry.

Didn't See It Coming

Momservation: Only a father holds the answer to the question: *At what point does a boy look at a boob and decide, I think I'd like to give that a squeeze?*

☺   ☺   ☺

Just like the Old Spice "Momsong" commercial sings: I didn't see it coming.

One day you put your little boy to bed with a snuggle and kiss on the lips—playing the game where you see how long you can lock lips and hold your breath ending with a big, smacking "Mmmmah!"—and the next night he turns his head making you settle for a cheek kiss.

Instead of saying, "Don't forget your hug and kissie!" he'll soon start hiding under the covers because he doesn't want a kiss at all. At least, not from his mother.

Shortly after that he will emerge like a butterfly from a very pungent cocoon in a cloud of Axe body spray, bed head tamed with hair product, and underwear changed without being told.

And then the girls start texting and your little baby boy is being referred to as "hot."

It's enough to make a mother want to scream from the highest rooftops: "I did NOT give you permission to grow up!"

Granted, I should consider myself lucky. I was my son's number one Valentine up until his 14th birthday. (Although, it was a close running with our dog, Darby, whom he once lovingly decreed, "You are the air in my soccer ball.") This Valentine's Day I may still retain the title because my son is quickly learning that girls are complicated. It also helps that Dad has counseled him to avoid having a girlfriend around Valentine's Day, Christmas, or any other gift giving holiday for as long as he can.

Now with this young man looming before me I needed reassurance that his father was having more than just yucks with our son over girls.

"Have you had THE TALK with him yet? Tell me you've had THE TALK with him!
You can't let him get to the front lines without a battle plan!"

Okay, so maybe I was being a little overdramatic, but that's what happens when you don't see it coming. It doesn't matter that he now towers over you with muscled hairy man limbs, chubby cheeks replaced with chiseled features, and greets you with a deep baritone that still makes you look around for an adult male. All your mother's eyes can see is a baby boy.

So there I was stunned, feeling sad and blue about this day that had always seemed so far off in the future arriving so quickly. I was feeling isolated in my heartache, the only mother to have ever had to let go of nurture and let nature take over.

And then I saw the Old Spice commercial with the sorrowful mothers singing of their despair to a mournful plinking piano for their little baby boys:

"Oh, I didn't see it coming. But it came in a can. Now my sweet son sprayed into a man.
We know just who to blame...Old Spice! Sprayed a man of my son! He was just my little sweetie, tiny fingers, hands and feet... Old Spice! Sprayed a man of my son! Now he smells like a man...and they treat him like one."

That's exactly what happened! Well, almost exactly. It wasn't Old Spice, but it was a men's body spray—Axe. And it wasn't just me having this problem! It was mothers everywhere! That's when I realized it might be too late for me, but that I could help save other mothers from my heartache.

So here is my warning to mothers of young boys everywhere: Do not buy them men's body spray! No matter how much they want it or beg for it. Convince them it's bad for the ozone and will give them acne. And if your son does get his hands on some, hide it! Destroy it! Convince him it's poisonous! Don't let those baby boys turn into men.

Then, go get those kissies now. While he still calls you Mommy in a squeaky high-pitched voice and smells like outside, dirt, and sweaty hair.

Because you won't see it coming—the day your son decides he's too big for Mommy kisses. It's too late for me...save yourself.

Don't Make Me Talk Nocturnal Emissions!

Momservation: You can't send kids to the frontlines of sexual development without a battle plan.

☺   ☺   ☺

Nothing says "captive audience" like a birds and the bees talk in a moving vehicle.

But the kids left me no choice. When I thought I saw an opportune time to broach the Facts of Life subject, my kids would scatter in all directions like cockroaches when the light flicks on.

Looking for a little outside help, I signed off on permission for my kids to watch the Family Life video at school (which must've been sponsored by Proctor and Gamble because it was essentially an infomercial for deodorant and feminine products).

Afterward I asked them, "How was the video? Do you have any questions? Anything you'd like to discuss?"

My kids, mortified I came within a general question of talking about normal bodily functions—not even the dreaded S-E-X word—would quickly hush me with, "Fine. No. Nothing," before climbing the walls to get away from me and any more questions.

Soon, I began using the S-E-X talk as a threat. "If you don't get in here right now and clean this room I am going to talk to you about the Family Life video!" Instant clean room.

"If you don't quit your bickering we're going to have a serious discussion about where babies come from!" Peace and harmony once again reigned.

I even used it to get chores done without nagging. "Whoever unloads the dishwasher doesn't have to talk to me about nocturnal emissions and menstrual cycles!" Kids fighting over cleaning the kitchen and even desperate offers to vacuum the house.

But the time finally came when I decided I couldn't send them to the front lines without a battle plan. I tried to get my teenagers to come to me on their own by standing hard to my NO PG-13/R-Rated movies stance.

"When you're ready to have a frank discussion about sex with me, that's when I'll think you're mature enough to see movies filled with inappropriate sexual content." No takers, but a great way to avoid Adam Sandler movies.

It was a thirty-minute car ride when I finally seized the chance to educate and inform my daughter without her hope for escape. Interrupting our genial conversation I took a deep breath and said, "I know this is going to be uncomfortable, but I wouldn't be a good mom if I didn't talk to you about sex."

I quickly reviewed all the major points, tried to dispel any misinformation, and threw out the term "something that happens between MATURE, COMMITTED, ADULTS" quite a bit.

When I finally turned my head to make the dreaded eye contact with her she only had one thing to say:

"Now can I see *Bridesmaids*?"

Early Bird Gets Cute Hair

Momservation: Do not underestimate the power of cute hair.

☺   ☺   ☺

Next month my baby girl is officially a teenager. I've agreed to these terms, but it doesn't mean I have to like it.

The winds of change have been gusting through the Wheeler house for well over a year now with Whitney's older brother leading the storm front. Doors are constantly flung shut and search parties sent out gently knocking and asking, "Everything okay in there? What are you doing?" Always to be met with the standard call of the elusive teenager answering back clearly annoyed: "Nothing! I'll be out in a minute, okay?"

So it was no surprise when it was time to confront a foreseeable developing dilemma with my nearly thirteen year-old daughter.

"Whitney, I think we both know you have a serious decision to make," I said looking over at her in the front passenger seat of my car.

She nodded quietly accepting this day she was avoiding was finally here.

"It's time to choose. Do you want to sleep in on school mornings…or do you want cute hair?"

"But it's so hard to choose!" she moaned.

"I know, I know," I said patting her shoulder, remembering back to the day when I gave up an extra half hour of sleep for perfectly curled, spiral-permed, '80's hair cemented in place with AquaNet. "But we all can't take a shower, get ready, and look good in five minutes like Daddy can."

"It's not fair!" said Whitney propping her feet onto the dashboard in a huff.

I snapped my fingers, pointed at her feet and she dropped them. "You're not the only one going through this. Every girl you see at school with cute hair has gotten up early. Sure, we'd all like to sleep in, but if you want cute hair…it takes sacrifice."

I could see she was listening but she wasn't convinced yet. It was time to tell her my story.

"You remember that picture of me you found in the Local Motion sweatshirt with pegged jeans and pink moccasins?"

"The one where your hair was the size of an inflatable bounce house?"

"That was the style, okay?" I defended. "Anyway, I had been taking showers the night before. Not getting up for school until Grampa came in to wake me for the third time. I didn't have my clothes picked out the night before. I'd have to rush to get out the house on time, usually frustrated because I couldn't get my bed-head hair to go the way I wanted it to."

I looked over at Whitney. I didn't even have to say: "Sound familiar?" I could tell she was seeing herself.

"Then one day I decided if I was going to be happy with myself instead of jealous of all the girls at school with cute hair, I had to try something new."

"And a spiral perm was your solution?" teased my just-like-her-father smart aleck daughter.

"No! Well…yes. But it was also getting up earlier and taking a shower that morning because then my hair was more manageable. It was setting out my clothes the night before. It was not leaving the house already in a foul mood because I was mad at my hair. It was realizing I suddenly cared about how I looked—and that was okay. Because I was a teenage girl."

"And…what does that picture have to do with this mother/daughter Hallmark Movie moment?"

"Believe it or not I looked good in that picture!" I said acting offended. But then seriously I told her, "That was the first picture of me where I wasn't dressed like a tomboy…and I thought I looked beautiful."

There was a moment of silence over this statement that is so hard for girls to admit out loud.

"The point is I want you to feel beautiful every time you walk out of the house," I quietly said. "I just want you to do what you need to do to feel that way. Sleep in or have cute hair. Wear your favorite comfy jeans again or put on a little mascara. Whatever it is that makes you feel best in your skin—give yourself time to do it."

Whitney nodded in understanding. "Alright," she said. "I'll get up earlier. But Daddy better look out."

"Why?"

"Because there's gonna be a new sheriff in the town of Good Lookin'."

Mother's Day Hangover

Momservation: The day after Mother's Day is like a hangover. It was a great party, but now back to the real world.

        ☺   ☺   ☺

It was glorious.

I got to sleep in. Someone else fed and walked the dog. I didn't have to take breakfast orders or nag anyone to clean their room.

No one asked me to drive them anywhere. A cease fire had been declared between siblings. My husband was doing the dishes.

I excused myself from a four-course breakfast without a care of who was clearing the table or loading the dishwasher. No one fought about it while I retired to the living room couch, given complete control over the television remote.

No one asked me what I wanted to do that day—I was in charge of nothing except my own happiness.

Hubby took me to a River Cats game with front row seats behind the plate, access to free food in the hospitality suite, and I believe, somehow arranged for my beer and chocolate malt calories to not be admissible.

When I got home my teenagers had done their own laundry for school the next day and no one asked me what was for dinner. I was left alone to binge-watch "Parks and Recreation" until I was called to a simple, yet delicious dinner that I did not have to cook nor clean up after.

The spectacular day finished with lovingly selected cards singing my praises and a group selfie so I would have proof that such an amazing day could exist.

Because the next morning it was all a blur as the pounding headache of reality hit.

There were no spoons because the dishwasher needed to be ran, my daughter forgot to wash her favorite shorts, the dog was trying to eat lunches off the counter, I forgot to submit the school newsletter update, my freelance column was overdue, we had no fruit for lunches, kids couldn't find PE clothes, kids were fighting over the bathroom, my email box was full but I wouldn't be able to get to it until lunch, my son needed money for something at school, I needed to get checks in the mail, I didn't have tortillas for dinner, my husband wanted to know if I would be home for the roofers who were coming any minute as I rushed out the door for school drop-off yelling threats to my daughter not to be late again for carpool pick-up knowing I would again not succeed in trying to be five places at once.

Pass the Advil and water. Mother's Day is officially over.

One Heck of a Dorm Room

Momservation: One person's great idea is another person's mess to clean up.

☺   ☺   ☺

I don't know where my kids are going to end up for college, but it better have ginormous dorm rooms. 'Cause where else are they going to fit a zip line?

Let me explain.

My eighth grade son and seventh grade daughter are constantly coming up with "great ideas."

"We should get a bunny!"

"We so need a zip line!"

"You know what would be great? Our own Hawaiian shaved ice machine!"

"We totally need a hot tub—the kind with all the fiber optic lights and built in stereo!"

"We should get another dog! So Darby has someone to play with—and a kitty too!"

"Mom! We have to build a trampoline course in the back yard!"

"You know what we need? A 108-inch flat screen TV!"

"Mom! You know what would be epic? One of those soda machine in our kitchen that dispenses like 150 different flavors!"

The kids pepper these "great ideas" out at me all the time announcing it like they have just discovered the cure for male pattern baldness.

They expect to hear "no" so throwing out their brilliant ideas is more done for sport. Like a cat that brings a mouse into the house, plays with it until it gets bored, then walks away from the mouse leaving it exhausted and traumatized.

Or in my case finally yelling, "Don't you have some homework to do or a room to clean?"

Logan throws out outlandish ideas like he suffers from Tourette's—he can't help it as a live-in-the-moment guy with an unquenchable thirst for his next fun adventure. Whitney, my stubborn thirteen year-old with a flair for debate, was born with an inability to take "no" for an answer.

With Logan constantly shot-gunning me with ideas and Whitney never letting it drop, I got tired of hearing myself say "no" and getting batted around.

So I started saying "yes."

"Sure! That's a great idea!" I said to the rabbit.

"Really?" they said wide-eyed at their good fortune the first time I changed my answer.

"You bet! As soon as you turn 18 and have moved out of the house, you can have your very own bunny. You can keep it in your dorm room!"

"Very funny, Mom," my crestfallen idea hatchers pouted. There was no more playful cajoling or exhausting debating. Point was made.

When Logan threw out the Hawaiian shaved ice machine idea, I didn't hesitate.

"Great idea! You can have it in your dorm room and sell shaved ice to pay for your iTunes downloads!"

One hundred eight inch flat screen? "You can use the money from your shaved ice sales to buy the flat screen! It'll look great in your dorm room!"

Hot tub with all the bells and whistles? "If you can fit it in your dorm room, that sounds great!"

Another dog for Darby plus a cat? "Darby will have so much fun visiting them in your dorm room. But don't get caught—I'm not paying for an apartment if you get kicked out."

"A soda machine? That's going to make you really popular in the dorms. Are you going to have space in your dorm room with the hot tub?"

These days the mouse is back in charge of the game. My little kiddie-cats have reigned in the onslaught of great ideas and even check themselves:

"I know…It'll be great in my dorm room," they'll chime before I can throw out the phrase that has become code for "Not on my dime, not on my time."

Interesting thought though…You think Mark Zuckerberg's mom told him building a multi-billion dollar social media empire would be a great idea for his dorm room?

I Don't Want Your Participation Ribbon

Momservation: Is there a ribbon for being the first to quit?

☺   ☺   ☺

Never quit in sight of the finish line.

As an athlete there were many grueling races—literally coming down the home stretch, lungs overtaxed, muscles atrophying—where I had to convince my mind to override my body begging me to quit.

As a track coach it is what I tell my track runners: Why would you throw away ¾ of giving all you had, only to coast to a mediocre finish?

Finish strong. Always. Anything worth doing is rarely easy, but the feeling of accomplishment from knowing you couldn't give anymore lasts longer than the pain of your effort.

However, I might have an exception…

I.Am.Done.With.School.

I want to sit down right now in the middle of this last straightaway and be done with this overscheduled, overinvolved, over-long school year.

I don't care if everyone runs right by me and I don't get a participant ribbon. I DON'T WANT TO PLAY ANYMORE!

I don't want to drive to school anymore.

I don't want to pick-up from school anymore.

I don't want to wash anymore PE clothes late Sunday night.

I don't want to do another emergency run to the store for lunch supplies.

I don't want to wake up early so that I can waste a half an hour of good sleep begging my kids to get out of bed.

I don't want to rush to Walgreens for another poster board, flash cards, or binder paper.

I don't want to have to check the Parent Portal again to make sure my kids aren't lying about homework and test grades.

I don't want to pick up from football practice, volleyball practice, track practice, baseball practice or any other practice.

I don't want to sign another permission slip, write another check, or donate another cookie or cupcake.

I don't want to make any more breakfasts that aren't eaten because someone's running out the door late.

I don't want to nag about bedtimes, showers, or getting clothes and backpacks ready the night before.

I don't want to read another newsletter and I don't want to go to another meeting.

I.Am.Done.

We have spent 168 days in school (and, yes, as Academic Support I include myself in the "we.") There are seven more days of school left. The finish line is so close, but yet so far.

I'm exhausted. I'm perpetually grumpy. My brain is overloaded. I want to quit.

But you never quit in sight of the finish line.

Fine. Someone better be waiting with an awfully big watermelon margarita and a great beach book on the other side.

Summer Freedom

Momservation: Summer coming to an end is like getting water up your nose after the perfect cannon ball.

☺   ☺   ☺

I'm officially changing my tune.

School is out and I'm not crying, kvetching, or carrying on about loss of freedom now that the kids are ever-present during summer vacation.

Yep, I actually like having them around 24/7 for two and a half months. I'm even going to go ahead and say it's too bad they have to go back to school before Labor Day.

Go ahead and make the international sign for I'm Going to Strangle You. I know you mothers of newly minted first graders especially want to wash my mouth out for the blasphemy. With school in you finally got a taste of freedom—freedom from worrying about childcare during the day for working moms; freedom to have an uninterrupted train of thought or bathroom break for stay-at-home moms—and now that gravy train has come to a screeching halt.

I know, I know. I was there too. When my son was in kindergarten and my daughter in preschool, between their two schedules I had seven minutes a day by myself; and that was driving to pick one of them up after dropping the other one off. When they were both finally in school full-time I gave praise to the gods of education and left fruit baskets at their altar. I think a cried with joy for a week straight every time I walked back into a quiet house.

But when summer rolled around, I went into a period of mourning for my loss. My productivity! My breakfast I ate sitting down! Going jogging without a bicycle parade circling me! Actually reading the day's paper before the day was over! My house that stayed clean for seven hours...or, actually, didn't get any dirtier for seven hours! My precious silence.

And then I went into a panic. What am I going to do with these kids all summer? I had become acclimated to the serenity of a seven-hour school day! I couldn't go back to hearing Caillou's whiny voice again on the TV. I just couldn't. It would break me. I could envision myself trying to convince CPS that dropping your kids off to do their lemonade stand two zip codes away was just good expansion of your marketing base.

When I finally pulled myself together I decided to go at the perceived problem aggressively. Summer camp! Soccer camp, baseball camp, arts and crafts camp, watersports camp, Camp Have-a-Lot-of-Fun, Camp Winthers, Buzzardball camp...But that was just the weekdays. I had ten weekends to get through. Camping! Donner Lake, Shaver Lake, Lake Tahoe, Lake Berryessa. My strategy with kids on summer vacation was the same as training dogs: A good dog is a tired dog. Gotta work for kids too.

Unfortunately, it also works on parents. By the end of the summer, I couldn't even appreciate that I made it across the finish line to the start of the school year. I would be staggering like that Swiss marathon runner from the 1984 Olympics, the crowd gasping in horror as I lurched forward, torso twisted, left arm limp, right leg mostly seized, waving off anyone who tried to help me for fear of being disqualified for Mother of the Year.

But then a funny thing happened as the summers progressed. My kids grew independent. They matured. Their talents, skills, and abilities came into focus. Their humor and wit sharpened. Their personalities blossomed. It became less about occupying them and became more about playing with them and enjoying each other's company. By the time my kids were preteens I realized spending this summertime together is a fleeting gift. I really like these kids, and soon, they're going to be gone. Lost first to friends, then to the world.

A timely perspective shift: The freedom of enjoying my children for the summer.

Now I can't wait until my kids get out of school so I can turn back the clocks and revel in summer vacation with them. Sleeping in to ridiculous hours. Going to the movies. Walking to get Slurpees or Baskin Robbins. Making chocolate chip cookies for lunch. Backyard cornhole tournaments. Staying in the pool until we're pruney or our lips turn purple. Getting our money's worth from a season pass to the waterpark. Backyard s'mores. Persied meteor shower gazing at midnight. And camping. It wouldn't be summer without camping.

In moderation.

School is Starting Time to Kill a Forest

Momservation: Can I just give a pound of flesh instead of a pound of paperwork for my kid's school schedule?

☺   ☺   ☺

If Back to School shopping is the waterboarding of getting your kids ready for school, then filling out all the paperwork and writing the checks that go with it is bamboo under the fingernails.

Now I know why families have been shrinking in the 21st century. It's the Back to School paperwork!

I have two kids at two different schools and the amount of paper that needs to be read, filled out, signed, or have a check attached to it could wallpaper my house! Could you imagine back in the day when families were big enough to field your own baseball team? Enough Emergency Cards, PTA Membership forms, Band Boosters, Dress Code Policy, Absence Procedures, and TDAP shot notifications to wallpaper Fenway Park!

Actually, no—because back then the only requirement to start school was having a pair of shoes and being able to walk your butt there and back.

I mean, really, for my son to be able to play a sport in high school I have to turn in a 12-page packet that includes three different Conduct Code forms that essentially say:

DON'T BE A MORONIC IDIOT OR YOU'LL BE KICKED OFF THE TEAM

Why is this not a given? There shouldn't be paperwork for this. Simply a "Hope your six seconds of fame on Instagram was worth it. Clean out your locker," will do.

And why, after a collective 19 years of sending my kids to school does the administration not think I'm aware of the attendance policy? That I need to sign something that says I understand that if I don't call an absence in, it's not excused?

Have I not called in over the years enough stomach flus, cold viruses, pink eyes, ear infections, projectile vomiting, high fevers, explosive diarrhea, doctor and dentist appointments to not understand how this system works?

And one more thing: Do I look like the administrator of the Bill and Melinda Gates Foundation? Everyone's got a hand out for my money. The PTA, PTSA, the Boosters, the student body, the arts, the sciences, the academics, the athletics, the photographers, the committees, the administration…

As if Target doesn't have enough of my Back to School dollars for schools supplies, clothes, shoes, and food for lunches!

Christmas ain't got nothin' on my checking account like Back to School. Because Christmas just leaves my bank account empty. Back to School leaves it empty without the warm fuzzy feeling of bringing happiness to the children. Trust me, my children are not happy that they own a packet of #2 pencils, a protractor, and that I support the Science Olympiad so they better dang well participate.

Thank you for this moment to vent. Now excuse me while I go get my kids' medical record number tattooed on my arm because writing it down for the 5,000th time doesn't seem to be making me remember it any better.

Today's Mom Anxiety Level: High

Momservation: The high stakes challenges of the teenage years makes a mother crave the days of guarding against sharp corners, uncovered outlets, and play dates with biters.

☺   ☺   ☺

I'm a wreck. I don't know whether I'm going to cry, throw up, or burst into obscenities. I'm jumpy. I'm tense. I'm emotional. I just want it to be all over...

...the teenage years. With a 14 year-old high school freshmen and 13 year-old eighth grader the combustible danger around here is high.

One minute I'm calling them my little schmoopies, offering to make their favorite lunch, watching their silly TV shows with them, trying to coerce awkward hugs out them, and spend quality time with them. Sometimes they let me and all is right with the world.

But then other times...

...their phones are constantly buzzing, set on vibrate and screens dimmed hoping I won't notice how much they're on it. And all the while I'm wondering: **Who are they texting? Is it a boy or a girl? Is it someone I should be worried about? Are they a good influence? Is someone asking them to do something they shouldn't do? Will they be tempted? Will they make the right choice?**

...they're hunkered down in their rooms with the door shut, headphones on, scanning social media on their phones. And all the while I'm worrying: **Should I give them their privacy? What are they looking at behind closed doors? Are they** taking and posting inappropriate selfies? Are they receiving or commenting on inappropriate selfies? What are they being exposed to on their Instagram and Twitter feeds that I can't see on mine because of privacy settings? Should I be concerned about the amount of time they spend on social media?

...they increasingly interact on SnapChat. And all the while I'm second-guessing myself: **Should I let them have a social media account I can't monitor? Are they trying to hide something by choosing this forum to communicate? Can I still trust them? What are they sending through SnapChat? What are they putting out there that they think is private but can be screen-shotted? What image are they projecting? Will they do something stupid they can't undo?**

...they go off with their friends caring more about their opinions than mine. And all the while I'm hoping: **Can I trust these kids? Will they make good choices? Will they not do something stupid with a pack mentality, egged on by a group? Will they just say no? Will they be the voice that has the courage to speak up for what's right or wrong? Will they set a good example? Do they like who they are when they're with these people?**

...I know they're exposed to sex, smoking, foul language, drugs, drinking, and poor choices in the larger social setting of middle and high school. And all the while I'm panicking: **Have I given them a good enough foundation to rise above the curiosities and temptations? Are they able recognize a bad situation before they step into it? Do they trust that they can talk to me when they're problems seem too overwhelming to handle on their own? Do they understand that I can be a** resource on how to proceed—that I was young once too and probably faced these same issues? Do they believe I won't judge or punish them if they call home in desperate need to leave a bad situation?

Of course, these are the anxieties that reside on the flip side of the coin that are the teenage years—the thoughts that are robbers of sleep, the sand in the sheets that keeps me flipping and flopping. They are the concerns that make me long for the aching sleep-deprivation of infancy, the simple anxieties of keeping a human being alive.

The truth is, I have good kids. They make good choices. They have good friends. They operate in the parameters I have set for them until they are fully formed to fly free. They are likable, lovable, they're fun and funny, and we enjoy each other's company. The coin has landed heads side up and I've called heads.

And therein really lies my anxiety. **Will it stay this way?** *These kids giving me so much joy and pride.* **Do I trust myself?** *That I've done a good job raising my kids.* **Do I believe in myself?** *That I've done all I can to reinforce good values.* **Can I rely on myself to be non-judgmental and understanding when they have failures?** *Because they will have failures. Everyone makes mistakes.*

I am a wreck because my parenting is being put the test that is the teenage years—when a poor decision can be life altering.

So I just need to take a deep breath. Trust that I've put in the work to watch my kids succeed. Believe that they know I'm here for them if they stumble. And now it's time for me to back off and let my kids put my number one rule to the test, the rule that makes all the other rules redundant:

First, respect yourself.

A Halloween Illustration of the Two Types of People in This World

Momservation: If you're taking life messages from Halloween costume stores, we're all just slutty M&M's on the inside.

☺   ☺   ☺

Halloween is on a Friday this year. I have teenagers. One of them is a girl.

Weather report: A perfect storm of parenting anxiety is brewing ready to make landfall in three days.

The winds of change have been howling at my doorstep for a while now, depositing a 15 year-old son who spends more time with his shirt off than on and a 13 year-old daughter who has become keenly aware of the power of Spandex.

The calm, predictable, so-adorable-it-hurts days of zipping your precious little child into a head to toe pink poodle, fuzzy yellow duck, or tubby little bumble bee costume are long gone.

The kids want to pick their own costumes now and I'm no longer controlling the message that Halloween costume stores seem to have hijacked.

In its place: Sexy poodle, sexy duck, and sexy bumble bee. Or as the kids call it: slutty poodle, slutty duck, and slutty bumble bee.

Or as my daughter pointed out on SnapChat as we looked around the Spirit Halloween store trying to find a tutu and a crown that didn't come with fishnet stockings and a garter, it's come down to this:

The two types of people in this world:

"Mom, you're the first one," she said. Though it sounded like a swipe at my hotness factor, I didn't take it as such. I'd like to think I can still rock the second M&M outfit...but I do own, and have been twice, the first M&M. So she was simply stating a fact.

As I'm battening down the hatches trying to keep my kids safe, executing smart decisions, and from doing anything that will haunt them on socials media forever on this Halloween— let's make sure the wine fridge is stocked and ready to raise our glasses in toast Friday night:

May you have done a good enough job raising your kids that they are the doctor, lawyer, or corporate CEO. Not the slutty doctor, slutty lawyer, or slutty corporate CEO.

4 Things Your Teens Want for Christmas

Momservation: The first great gift we can bestow on others is a good example. *~Thomas Morell*

☺   ☺   ☺

Tired of giving gift cards? Money feels too impersonal? Too hard to figure out latest trends, interests, or sizes? Then you've come to the right place for Christmas shopping for that teenager in your life.

Choose from one of the four gifts below and I guarantee your teen will be happier than a kid getting an iPhone for Christmas! (Okay, maybe I don't guarantee that, but I bet it will be right up there with their favorite gifts.)

No judgment. Teens already feel like they're under a microscope with snap judgments from their peers on everything from what they wear, how they do their hair or makeup, what they post on social media, who they hang out with, what they drive, and what they do in class. They don't need nor want their parents' two cents on top of it.

My 13 year-old daughter's favorite words to me right now are "Stop" and "Don't." It is her way of warning me that she feels judged and for me to be back off.

Of course, I don't see it that way at all. I hear myself passing on insight, perspective, or wisdom from life experience. When I try to explain myself—"I just thought you'd want to know…" or "I was just making an observation…" she will swiftly point out that from her perspective it still feels like a judgment.

So this Christmas I will be giving my daughter the gift of biting my tongue. It may bleed from trying not to lambast the need for incessant selfies, harping on never ending SnapChats, clicking my tongue at friends' inappropriate Instagrams or Tweets, and refraining from commenting on all manners of teenage behavior.

These teen years are my children's road to travel not mine. Time to stop being a backseat driver.

Trust. Teens need learning experiences, both good and bad to grow. They need opportunities to confront difficult choices or situations; to learn from mistakes and capitalize on successes. Part of growing up is wanting to be trusted.

In this age of helicopter parenting, we as parents have become accustomed to shielding our children from any little hurt, disappointment, failure, or mis-step. What we've come to see as protecting our kids, our teens see as depriving them of experiences and not trusting they will make good decisions.

When I find myself wavering over letting my teens do something that makes me uncomfortable or nervous my daughter will remind me, "Mom, you need to just trust that I'll make the right choices," or my 15 year-old son will sigh, "Mom, trust me, I'll be fine!"

So this Christmas I will be trusting the decade and a half I have put in to building a strong moral foundation for my children and landing my helicopter. It will be a white-knuckle year, but I'm giving them my trust.

Respect. The teen years are a time of great growth and maturity. It's a time when teens fight to create an identity, try to discover who they are, or seek validation for who they're trying to be. They're becoming individuals with their own set of abilities, qualities and achievements and they're just looking for a little respect for who they've become.

One of the difficulties for teens as they mature toward adulthood is they are still seen as kids. I'm definitely guilty of this. Although I'm a big believer in giving respect if you want respect, I still catch myself talking down to the kids who now tower over me.

It's important to remember that these "babies" of ours are taking on increased adult responsibilities, carrying adult-sized academic and extracurricular workloads, and many times have cars, jobs, and payments like adults. We can become frustrated with their attitude, but they can also be frustrated with our lack of respect for their individuality.

If you're giving respect to your teen this Christmas, make sure they understand it is not a one-way street. It is a gift that should be re-gifted.

Time. Modern teens have very little time to themselves. Between the demands of school (and getting into a good college), extra-curricular activities (sports, music, sciences, and arts), and other expectations (chores, jobs, graduation requirement community service) one of the best things you can give a teen is time.

Time to sleep in. Time to veg on their phones. Time to be with their friends. Time to stay up late. Time to be silly. Time to indulge a passion. Time with no strings attached. Unstructured time. Play time. Down time. Me time. And one more very important one—your time.

Get up from your computer or put down your own phone to take the time to reach out to your room-bound or phone-obsessed teen and do something together. Go mountain biking together. Go shopping together. Go to the movies together. Go to a concert together. Go on a day hike together. Cook together. Do sports together. Play together. Laugh together. Do anything together.

If you have a teenager you have five years or less to spend with these kids before they most likely fly the coop. So enjoy them now before the distancing of living their own life fills you with regret for lost opportunities.

There is no better Christmas gift than time with those you love.

He's Got a Ticket to Drive

Momservation: Why are we surprised when the Potty Training Master Supreme is good at more than just teaching her kids "when it's brown flush it down"?

☺   ☺   ☺

I am an official back seat driver.

Actually, make that an official shotgun seat driver. If I'm sitting in the back seat, although it feels much safer, I can't stomp my phantom brake trying to get my kid not to take a turn at 25 mph.

Yep, it's permit driving time. My 15 ½ year-old son is driving me around like Miss Daisy. Rides to the store. Rides to and from school. Rides to pick up his sister. Rides to go buy more tampons. There is no errand too short, too long, or too never-mind. My kid's got a ticket to drive and he don't care where we go.

To be fair, Logan's a good driver. Don't tell…but I've been letting him drive around the neighborhood since before his 15th birthday. His 14 year-old sister too. (Sorry about the lawn job, Mrs. Smith!)

Logan did everything early as a baby—rolled over, crawled, walked, talked—well before any kids his age. Hubby used to say I put him through Baby Boot Camp so that I would witness all his first milestones before our childcare provider did. Yeah, kinda.

But when he learned to ride a bike at three and was hitting in-the-park home runs in T-ball and scoring at will in Peewee soccer we started to realize that being ahead of the curve is just Logan.

So you could say we were hardly surprised when we got a phone call from our son during his required one hour Beginning Driver Training lesson.

"Hey Dad. The instructor wants to know if he can take me for a two-hour lesson that will take me out of the neighborhood and include freeway driving."

"Um, you aren't driving right now are you?"

"Oh, no. The instructor had me pull over to call you."

"Oh good," Hubby breathed relieved that he hadn't hired a hack to teach his son to drive. "Yeah, that's fine."

"Well, add driving to the long list of things Logan is freakishly good at," Hubby told me when he got off the phone.

"Add driving to the long list of things his mother is excellent at teaching him," I smiled smugly.

"Because it's sink or swim with you! You had him driving and merging during rush hour and trying to park in Loehman's Plaza during the dinner rush!"

"Hey. Don't doubt the methods of the sensei. Walking at 8 months. Second word was "helicopter." Potty trained at a year and a half. Getting kicked up to Advanced Driver Training on his first try—this is what I do."

"Alright then sensei," countered Hubby. "How about the master getting her young grasshopper to keep his room clean then?"

"THAT is not what I do. The cleaning genre is not my level of expertise."

"Explains why the dog is afraid of the mop and vacuum cleaner…"

Mother's Day from Toddler to Teen

Momservation: Diamond earrings can't replace the gift of no more bickering. But they sure help drown out the noise.

☺   ☺   ☺

Boy does Mother's Day look different depending on which side of the diaper bag you're standing.

I'm now in my 16th year of being a mother. Seems like a long time. I feel very seasoned. But just as I sympathetically chuckle at the toddler moms thinking their biggest struggle in life is making it through Target without a meltdown or diaper blowout, my own mother sympathetically pats me on the shoulder with that You-Ain't-Seen-Nothin'-Yet smirk when I vent about raising teens.

And every time I talk to my 88 year-old grandmother about the worries I have for my kids, sure these sleepless nights (now due to anxiety) will pass, she cautions me about putting the Ambien too far out of reach. "No matter how old you get you never stop worrying about your kids, Honey."

So this Mother's Day I thought I'd reflect on what I wanted for my special day at each stage of my children's development.

Pregnant: To be included in Mother's Day because I was finally going to be a mom!

Age 1: Sleep.

Age 2: A break. With two kids under two— a long, quiet, no wiping butts, chopping food, supervising, feeding, entertaining, washing, buckling in and out of seatbelts break.

Age 3: An escape. An escape from fights over toys, Caillou and Elmo, exhaustion, crying, whining, being on constant alert, changing diapers, ear infections, making meals that hit all the major food groups, and constant calls of Mommmmmy!

Age 4: To be left alone. A day of no one needing me for anything.

Age 5: Tag team. When you have to initiate, supervise, and clean up the glittery, gluey, construction paper mess of helping your kids make you Mother's Day cards, all you want is someone to say, "I got this."

Age 6: For school to start. Getting an uninterrupted seven-hour day of productivity and peace and quiet for five days in a row. There is no better gift.

Age 7: A little independence. Kids that will tie their own shoes, wipe their own noses, buckle themselves in and out of a car, wash their own hair, grab their own snacks, and pick up their own toys.

Age 8: No fighting.

Age 9: No fighting.

Age 10: No fighting over the remote.

Age 11: Nowhere I have to be. No carpool, no soccer practice, no baseball game, no all-day swim meet, no guitar lessons, no PTA meeting, no doctor's appointment, no pick-up, no drop-off, no getting in a car to go anywhere.

Age 12: A decent family photo. No fighting about having to dress up. No bunny ears. No whining about why we have to do this. No fake smiles. No are-we-done-yet? pouts. No fights over touching. Look adorable and like you love each other.

Age 13: A head start. So I'll be better prepared for the rapidly approaching puberty bus and all the changes that come with it.

Age 14: No social media. Put your phones away. Engage. Be present. Have a conversation that doesn't involve your thumbs and a selfie.

Age 15: A lot of independence. Kids that get themselves up, wash their own clothes, make their own lunches, do homework without being told, set the table without being asked, brushes teeth without being reminded, make themselves food when they're hungry, clean up after themselves.

Age 16: Be here. I miss my babies. I want my kids home to spend time with me instead of always being gone with friends, school, and sports. I want to hold you and love you and not have a moment of panic that in a few short years I'll have to hope for long distance phone calls and mailed cards from college for Mother's Day. I can't believe I ever wanted time away from you. It's going too fast. Call me Mommy again one more time.

I know my grandma says I'll never get it, but next year I'm going to ask for No Worrying.

Summer of Independence Check List

Momservation: Promise me you will not let the teenage years be the marker for how well you've raised your kids.

☺   ☺   ☺

I've decided this summer will be the **Summer of Independence**. I'm going to resist the temptation to make lunches that hit every major food group, pick up wet towels off the floor, and remind people to brush their teeth.

And in "people" I mean my teenage children who should really be further along on this independence thing.

I blame myself though. I'm a helicopter mom who worries that if I don't feed my children they will starve or if I don't hover over them with sunscreen they will sustain third degree burns.

This summer I've decided to save them from me and a life of never knowing that clean clothes don't just magically appear on your bed folded and ready to put away.

Just to let you know—it's not going well. At least by my standards. The kids think they're ready to move out. I'm ready to abort the mission or flee this hazmat site.

I didn't think I was asking too much on this first test launch of independence. But obviously, putting a new roll of toilet paper on the toilet paper dispenser is setting the bar too high.

Let's look at the checklist of things that would define a successful **Summer of Independence**:

☐ Get up at a reasonable hour and feed yourself breakfast

☑ (If by reasonable, Mom meant after noon and by food she meant Chex Mix for lunch)

☐ Brush your teeth and brush your hair

320

☑ (Jumped in pool and chewed some gum)

☐ Get dressed in something besides what you wore yesterday (and the day before)

☑ (Throw favorite outfit in dryer and spray with Axe or Taylor Swift perfume)

☐ Make sure you put on sunscreen and to reapply

☑ (Try to look like a Coppertone model, complain about burned/blotchy skin, not learn lesson and repeat next day)

☐ Make sure you eat something for lunch

☑ (Skip lunch then come in with friends like a swarm of locusts and eat everything except what would constitute a healthy lunch)

☐ Make sure to pick up after yourself

☑ (Turn the house into a garbage heap)

☐ Pick up the dog poop in the backyard before your friends come over

☑ (Laugh at your friends who step in poop then get mad when you have to clean poop out from between your own toes and bottoms of shoes)

☐ Have you and your friends use same pool towel all day

☑ (Grab a dry towel every time, then leave wet towels all over the yard, house, and in every chair so there are no dry seats to sit in)

☐ Have your friends help you clean up before they leave

☑ (Say you'll do it yourself later and then never do)

☐ Do regular chores like setting and clearing table, unloading dishwasher, and making your bed without being asked

☑ (Must not have to do them because Mom's not nagging me!)

☐ If your clothes you want to wear or need are dirty wash them

☑ (Complain about no underwear and nothing to wear. Continue to be mystified by two square, metal, machines in laundry room)

☐ Help make dinner

☑ (Get invited to a friend's house for dinner or be conspicuously absent and unreachable until food hits table)

☐ Go to bed at a reasonable hour

☑ (If by reasonable hour, Mom meant falling to sleep after midnight with my phone in my hand, headphones on, and nothing interesting on Instagram, Twitter, or SnapChat)

Best Damn Advice for Parents of High Schoolers

Momservation: Sometimes the best advice you can give is no
advice at all.

☺   ☺   ☺

I've been officially banned by daughter from uttering these
words again:

"When I was in high school…"

"How come you have to compare everything to when you
were in high school?" she asked me exasperated, clearly not
remembering my photographic proof that I was once a high-
schooler. (Giant jewelry, giant hair, giant bow in giant crimped
hair, Frosty Pink lip gloss…who can forget these visuals of '80's
high school?)

"Because, believe it or not, I've been there, done that, and
bought the Blue Crew spirit sweatshirt before you! I'm the only
one with four years of high school experience in this little group
here," I said circling my finger between her and me.

Whitney, my high school freshman, the Miss Know It All
with 30 days of high school experience under her belt, gave me
the international teenage look for "Whatever" (something she's
been banned from saying to me) and said, "Fine. But do you
always have to start everything with 'When I was in high
school'?"

Hmmm. That's a tough one.

How else do I commiserate with my 14 year-old daughter
embarking on a four-year journey of ups, downs, angst,
excitement, laughter and tears that are surely coming her way?
How do I prepare her for the social and academic highs and lows
that are the traditional rites of passage of high school? How do I
convey that I understand what she's going through because I, too,
was a teenager who worried about getting asked to Homecomings

and Proms, making the team, fitting in, getting good grades, going to parties, feeling left out, or sad because that boy just wouldn't notice me?

How do I relate to my high school daughter if I can't share my high school stories?

"Just listen, Mom. I don't always want your advice," was my sage daughter's own words of wisdom. "Sometimes, I just need you to listen."

Oh. I can do that.

But when I was in high school…

#JustKidding

I Dare You to Say it to My Face

Momservation: Hate is heavy. The people with the power of positive thinking and forgiveness are a hell of a lot more fun with a lighter load to carry.

☺   ☺   ☺

It starts with you.

If you are parents, of children of any age, your next responsibility after modeling the right thing to do is hold those children of yours accountable for their actions and words.

We used to do this not too long ago: Instill common decency. I am 47 years-old and I still remember when I wouldn't dare say a foul word or something hateful in front of an adult. ANY adult.

Yes, there used to be a time when, as a kid, if you were going to break one of the big No-No's of life—*If you can't say anything nice, don't say it at all*—you would look all around you before you dared say something hurtful. If there wasn't a parent, grandparent, aunt, uncle, neighbor, teacher, crotchety old guy up the street, or a stranger giving you the eye in case you were thinking of saying it…then you might blurt out something that people would consider an everyday Tweet in our "great" new society.

Something like: "Well, you're just an idiot if that's what you think."

Now, if you hadn't looked good enough, or said it quiet enough, suddenly you would hear from an adult looming nearby, "What did you just say?"

Then your blood would run cold, your throat would squeeze shut, and a rock would have just dropped into your stomach…because you knew you were in trouble.

That's what the sprouting roots of common decency feels like.

But if an adult wasn't nearby, and you thought you were almighty enough to pull off bad behavior, there was another check in our society you still had to worry about. You had to be prepared that someone might call you out and say:

"I dare you to say that to my face."

And your blood would run cold, your throat would squeeze shut, and a rock would have just dropped in your stomach…because you knew you were either too chicken to actually say something so nasty to someone's face or you were about to get in a fight over what you just dared to say.

That's called being held accountable. That's also seems long gone in today's society.

We can blame the people at the top, the leaders, social media, video games, toxic pundits, 24-hour news cycle; we can spin all around looking for scapegoats and pointing blame for our societal bad behavior these days—remember that no accountability thing I mentioned?—but all everyone needs to do is just look in the mirror.

It starts with you.

Be a good role model. And then dare to hold yourself and those you are supposed to modeling common decency for, accountable.

Remember my number one rule in *Mom's Top 10 Rules for Kids*?

1. **First respect yourself. If you do, no other rules apply.**

I think it's time to make a new list, because there's an awful lot of people not following Mom's Number One Rule anymore.

So let's go back to the basics of common decency.

The Top 5 Rules of Common Decency

1. **Treat others the way you want to be treated**. This used to be called the Golden Rule. It's time that we all stay golden, Pony Boy.

2. **If you can't say anything nice, don't say anything at all**. If you wouldn't say it to someone's face, with God as your witness...as Momma used to say, "Then keep your damn mouth shut." (And quit hiding behind your toxic keyboard.)

3. **Do no harm**. Not with your words. Not with your hands. Not with your avatar, your phone, your computer, your Finsta. And Lord help us all, not with a gun.

4. **Let it go**. Don't jump into someone's negative energy cesspool with them. Let them stew in their own hateful, disgusting, unimpressive, pathetic swamp of their own making. The people with the power of positive thinking and forgiveness are a hell of a lot more fun with a lighter load to carry. Hate is heavy.

5. **Pretend someone is watching whom you would be devastated if you lost their respect**. Because someone is always watching. Be it your children, your mother or father, a favorite grandmother, your best friend, or God. Pretend they are always standing next to you. Do you want to turn and see admiration and love in their eyes or disgust and disappointment?

The Danger of the Creative Homecoming Ask

Momservation: I'll double check the Urban Dictionary, but I'm pretty sure "No" still means "No."

☺   ☺   ☺

It's Homecoming season and I'll tell you what: It sure is different than when I was in high school. (And saying that out loud officially makes me an old fogey. Saying "old fogey" double confirms it.)

So if you want a date to Homecoming these days there is no more nervously walking up to somebody in the halls and asking, "Will you go to Homecoming with me?"

No, it's a big production now.

First, what I like to call "The Exploratory Committee" gets sent out to make sure the prospective date will be receptive to an invitation by the invitee ("I heard Cory Cutie is going to ask you to Homecoming!" An excited "OMG!" gives the green light. An "Ewww, no!" gets the thumbs down.)

Then, boys are expected to go over the top creatively to ask a girl to the dance—"HC?" spelled out in rose petals on a front lawn; giant posters with a clever play on words with a matching gift (i.e. a box of donuts and a sign saying "I hope you donut say no to going to Homecoming with me."); a dozen roses waiting in lockers; scavenger hunts; or "HC?" spelled out in tea light candles on a driveway (this is what my son did with lots of female coaching and orchestrating).

Of course, it's all posted on social media—another way to make people feel inadequate, left out, unpopular, superior or uber popular. As the pictures roll into Instagram and Twitter the pressure mounts for guys to top each other and expectations rise for girls wanting to get asked.

Sure, it's all cute and exciting, but honestly…I think the scales tip more toward making me feel bad for the shy kids, the kids without resources (mom to drive you all over, dad to pay for all the gear, friends to help orchestrate), the girls that don't get asked, and the guys who would like to go to the dance but opt out because of the expectations and pressure.

I could overlook all this as the sign of the times and just what kids do now except for one thing:

Girls think they have to say "Yes" if asked to the dance this way.

When one of the freshmen girls told me about a girl who was disappointed with her date I said, "Then why didn't she say 'no'? Was she worried no one else would ask her?"

The young lady looked at me horrified and said, "You CAN'T say 'no' after all they did to ask you! You have to say 'yes'!"

Now it was my turn to be horrified. What an awful message to send to young girls!

"Oh, no, no, no!" I told her. "You can ALWAYS say 'no' to anything that doesn't make you feel comfortable. DO NOT believe that if someone does something nice for you that you are indebted to them—that you owe them."

"But saying 'no' would be so rude!"

It was a palm to forehead moment. What a horrible precedent to start these high school girls off on their dating experiences!

Since it wasn't my kid I didn't say what I wanted to say:

"So if a guy takes you to the movies do you owe him a kiss? If a guy buys you a nice meal do you owe him a trip around "the bases"? If a guy tells you you owe him sex for all he's done for you, are you going to say 'yes' because saying 'no' would be rude?"

Instead, I gave her some suggestions for kindly turning down the new style Homecoming date ask:

Say, "I appreciate the gesture, but I'm sorry I can't go."

Or

"I appreciate your kindness, but I don't really know you that well and would feel uncomfortable."

Or

"I appreciate your effort and generosity, but no thank you."

Or

"This is really thoughtful and sweet, but I already have a date." (a white lie if you must)

You want to orchestrate a YouTube million views epic asking of someone to Homecoming? Whatever, I don't get it just the way I don't get obsessive selfie postings. You want to be asked in a way that would be fit for a teen romance movie starring Shailene Woodley? That's fine, but I think you're setting yourself up to be disappointed.

But just remember: **She can always say no. You can always say no.**

And maybe if girls did say no to such a public grand scale peer pressure proposal guys might go back to just asking in the halls between passing periods...

License to Drive the Crash Car

Momservation: In the infant years you are sleepless until you don't hear them crying. In the teenage years you are sleepless until you hear the car pull into the driveway.

☺　　☺　　☺

"Have you bought the Crash Car yet?" my neighbor asked me.

"What's a Crash Car?"

She gave the laugh of jaded experience. She gave the head shake reserved for idealistic mothers who have no clue their carefully laid plans are about to be drop kicked. I half expected her to pat me on the head and say, "You poor, poor dear."

Instead she clarified: "Your son's first car." Before I could protest, pointing out that my soon to be 16 year-old son seemed to be an excellent driver so far, she read my thoughts. "You know he'll crash it, don't you? The first car for a new driver never comes out unscathed."

"Lindsey's?" I asked about her daughter's car.

"Crashed twice in a year."

"Jeff's?" I asked about her son.

"Ran into the neighbor's garage the first day."

As this unsettling theory settled over me, I applied it to my first car: a red 1968 Volkswagen Bug my brother handed down to me when he went into the military.

I gasped in bubble-bursting dismay as I pictured my first car with its bumper tied back on with a rope, a casualty of a 4-way stop collision. (Not my fault. I swear! I won in court!)

Donna laughed and said, "See?" As she walked back to her house after getting the mail she called over her shoulder, "Don't spend a lot of money on the Crash Car!"

Even though the evidence seemed to confirm her theory I decided to conduct an unscientific poll myself.

"Hey, did you ever get in an accident in your first car?" I asked everyone I ran into.

"Hit my mom's car in the driveway."

"Scraped up the side on a light post backing out of a parking space."

"Backed into a dumpster."

"Flipped it on a freeway off-ramp."

With each confirmation the excitement for getting my son his first car and having him relieve my burden of being the family chauffer got gobbled up by a growing pit of anxiety in my stomach.

I started asking my friends who had older children now driving around town if their kids had been in any accidents yet.

"Flipped their first car. Thank God everyone was okay."

"Clipped a car when traffic came to a stop at Watt and Fair Oaks."

"Crashed into a light post in the parking lot."

"They got rear-ended."

"Said they don't know what happened and how that long scratch down the driver's side got there."

The results were in. The first car is indeed the Crash Car. With Logan's 16th birthday this month and him ready to trade in his learner's permit for a driver's license, two things had become evident: it was time to downgrade what we were willing to spend on a car and upgrade our insurance.

It was already bad enough that for the foreseeable future I wouldn't be able to sleep until I heard my son's car pull into the driveway at night; that I would always worry about the temptation to text and drive; that his freedom to drive would also come with the perils of bad drivers, distractions, and bad ideas that seemed like a good idea at the time.

And now I had to live with the knowledge that come Logan's 16th birthday and his license to drive— it is not if, but when, he will crash his first car. All the fun has been sucked out of the excitement of buying my son his first car because it will be a Crash Car.

I guess we'll get him a minivan. Nobody cares if those things get banged up.

Too Precious to Fail

Momservation: I pray every day for God to keep you, my child, healthy, happy and safe. But ultimately, it's in your hands.

☺   ☺   ☺

I am terrible at the trust-fall team building exercise.

If you want me to trust you, just don't take a bite of my Ben & Jerry's when I ask you to hold it for a second. No one has to fall. No one has to tragically over-estimate their ability to catch my lied-about weight. And no one has to profusely apologize for reinforcing trust issues.

So it's no surprise that I have a hard time letting my kids fall. Fall as in fail. Fail as in know disappointment, experience rejection, suffer pain, give in to anger, miss an opportunity.

Do I know these are growth opportunities? Yes. Did I experience all these challenges in life and survive, even thrive because of them? Most definitely. Am I trying to nurture the best possible people to send out into the world? Hell, yeah.

And yet I can't stop myself from throwing my body under theirs at the slightest hint of failure from my children.

They have become too precious to me to fail.

I know I'm not doing my kids any favors because of my own personal demons that cause me to shelter my babies from life's inevitable pain, suffering, and hardships. I can see I'm depriving them of necessary growth, experience, and opportunities to learn how to weather life's storms and become resilient.

And yet, like a hoarder, I just can't stop myself.

Well, guess what? Now that my teenagers are closing in on adulthood it's time. I'm doing my own personal intervention and I'm going to do the trust fall.

- Because there's a critical difference between guiding your kids and doing it for them. I want problem solvers not impotent thinkers.
- Because disappointments are a part of life and I don't want whiners who always complain that everything's unfair.
- Because rejection and pain are the battle wounds of the strong and the capable.
- Because watching a missed opportunity makes you hungry to do and be better.
- Because we aren't getting out of this life alive. I want kids who use this time to seize the moment no matter how daunting, not spend it running from fears and uncertainty.

I'm holding my arms out in support, but I'm letting my kids fall. It may be a scary fall backward for them, but these are lessons they need to learn. It is painful for me to watch them fall—I just want to keep propping them up. But fall and hit the ground they must.

By letting them do it in the safety of a loving, supportive home I will trust that they will be okay. There will be other opportunities and valuable perspective gained that can only arise out of failure.

Then when my kids pick themselves up from their disappointment and hardship, I will watch with pride as they dust themselves off and forge ahead wiser and more determined.

And I will reward us all with Ben & Jerry's that no one has to share.

Activity a Day Holiday

Momservation: No regrets means putting down the dishtowel and dropping the laundry basket to go play with your kids.

☺   ☺   ☺

Yes, there was a time when my young children's needs were so all-consuming that all I wanted for Christmas was for them to take a 3-hour nap every day.

Now, I just want my teenagers to give me three hours of their full-attention—no status updates, Tweets, texts, checking Instagram, or SnapChat selfies that take priority.

But whether you have little ones at home or school kids on a two-week Christmas break, why not make the most of this time together the last weeks of the year? The holidays lend itself to tradition, making memories, and making the most of time with loved ones. You can celebrate these values by having an **Activity a Day Holiday**.

Whether you want to make every day count or your counting until the kids go back to school, here's a list of activities to take you through the two week Christmas Break:

Activity a Day Holiday

1. **Take a holiday light tour.** When it gets dark hop in the car, put on some Christmas music, and drive local neighborhoods to enjoy the festive lights. Or look up online your city's best light shows. If you're hardy and adventurous, decorate bikes in battery powered lights, snuggle in warm clothes, and take a bike riding light tour!

End the night by dropping off a donated toy to a local toy drive.

2. **Get crafty.** Hit up the local Michael's craft store or forage from your own yard and closets to make Christmas table centerpieces and holiday decorations. Check out my Momservations® Christmas with the Kids Pinterest board for some fun holiday projects.

3. **Get cooking.** Nothing says Christmas like cookies! Sugar cookies are fun to make and decorate, plus giving cookie plates to neighbors celebrates the giving season. Kids can help with dinner with something easy like a Jell-O salad or pie for dessert (with premade crust). Depending on patience and attention spans you can increase the level of difficulty. Great pride and sense of accomplishment for kids and ownership of traditions.

4. **Go shopping.** Have the kids learn the value of money while finding gifts for ones they love. Take them to the Dollar Store, Walmart, or other discount store. Have them create a list of people they'd like to buy for, give them a budget, their own basket, and enjoy watching their delight when they find that perfect gift at the right price for Grandma and their brother or sisters.

5. **Start wrapping.** Many hands make light work—turn gift wrapping into a Wrapping Party! Set up a wrapping station, put on festive music, put out yummy snacks and drinks, and encourage creative bows and original packaging.

6. **Scavenger Hunt grocery style**. Turn the shopping for Christmas or Hanukkah dinners with the kids into fun instead of a nightmare. Give everyone a copy of the list and see who can find the correct brand or type of food

first. Points lost for running, bad manners, or things not put back where they were found. Winner gets to pick a favorite dessert with dinner that night.

7. **New toy or game day**. Spend the day playing with whatever new gifts your kids received. Go bike riding, make Lego creations, play a board game, have a video game challenge, throw the new ball for the dog at the park. Just play like a kid.

8. **Go ice skating.** A lot of temporary holiday rinks are open this time of year and it's a fun way to celebrate the change in seasons and feel festive. Even if there's no holiday rink in your town, hit up the local ice rink.

9. **Play a game.** When the weather turns chilly and wet and darkness cuts off outdoor playtime, throw a Duraflame log on the fire, heat up some hot cocoa and pull out some games. If you're tired of your same board games, go buy a new one everyone's been wanting to try. A deck of cards has endless possibilities with this being a great resource for fun card games.

10. **Movie night.** Grab the whole family and take in one of the new release movies for the holidays—for a little extra excitement change it up and go to a late movie that will end past bedtime. Or snuggle in at home with a movie with extra pillows and blankets pulled out, or the hide-a-bed, and a freebie on junk food and soda to go with it.

11. **Pinterest Project Day.** Instead of just pinning things on Pinterest you'd like to make or bake then never getting to them—now's your chance to break the cycle! Spend a day unpinning those projects and doing them. Make the first part of the day collecting resources you'll need and the second part of the day feeling like DIY conquistadors!

12. **Ring in the New Year.** Send the old year out in style by dressing up and toasting with sparkling cider. Make it a free-for-all for dinner—everyone gets to have whatever they desire for the last day of the year. Celebrate with unlimited goodies of choice. See who can stay up the latest. If you have little kids celebrate midnight at midnight East Coast time (9 p.m. for us Californians) and let them bang pots and pans outside. Call Grandma and Grandpa or aunts and uncles to let them wish people Happy New Year.

13. **Recycle/Donation Day.** Go through closets to donate old clothes and toys that have been replaced by new ones to the needy. Take cans or plastic bottles that you've been collecting to the recycler and with the money buy dollar store arts, crafts, books, or toys to bring to a children's hospital or ward.

14. **Watch home movies.** Make some popcorn and pull out all the home videos you've been taking, but never watching. Laugh together, cry together as you watch again your kids grow up right before your very eyes.

Words to Live By

Momservation: A kid would rather learn it the hard way than admit their parents might know a thing or two.

☺   ☺   ☺

We have a number of sayings around our house that we use as guidelines for keeping our family on course. Some have fallen to the wayside as the kids have matured and the positive directive has become habitual. Like:

Remember a "Please" and "Thank you" go a long way.
Nobody likes a biter.
If it's brown flush it down.
Think before you act.

As we were molding respectful, thoughtful, likable young children sayings like these could not be repeated often enough. Especially, "Think before you act," with our son who was building up quite a track record of injuries to his sister while we were waiting for this sage advice to become firmly rooted. (A knocked out front tooth and trip to the emergency room because he hadn't quite thought out the repercussions of swinging a punching bag at your sister or jumping off a teeter-totter mid-flight).

Though the early adages no longer needed daily reinforcement, they continued to be general good rules for life. We added to the collection as the kids grew and took on more responsibility. Moving beyond solidifying good habits and hygiene the family sayings became a roadmap for being a good citizen. Things like:

The number one rule is to first respect yourself. If you do this, all of the other rules are unnecessary.

Nobody likes a bully.

Don't make someone have to ask you twice.

You gotta be a friend to make a friend.

Measure twice, cut once.

Of course, "Measure twice, cut once" was just another way of saying "Think before you act," but when you have a contractor for a dad who also loves a good analogy, he's going to come at you from all angles until you get it. (Hence, "No one likes a biter" segueing to "No one likes a bully.")

Then, with the new era of social media, our parenting mantras became different from that of our parents. New sayings developed trying to steer our media-savvy kids through an all-consuming instant gratification digital world. And because they can't seem to see beyond the moment to how their online habits will affect their future we tried to get through to them by speaking their generation's language:

Think before you send.

Delete doesn't mean delete and the internet is forever.

Today's Likes are tomorrow's regrets.

It's a fine line between putting up a post you think is funny and being a cyber-bully.

(Put down the phone and) Be present.

Now that our kids are teenagers, letting go of our hands to navigate their own waters, we find our family mottos becoming reminders of the groundwork we've laid in instilling good morals and values, and basically—to not be stupid. Rarely do they leave the house without these reminders:

Make good choices.

Nothing good happens after midnight.

You can't un-ring a bell.

You lie down with dogs you're going to get fleas.

You've got our good name on your back. Wear it proud.

Lately, the kids are so quick to leave out the door with their friends that all we have the chance to say is, "Remember..." before our 16 and 14 year-olds and their herd of friends all yell back before taking off, "We know! Make good choices!"

But of all the sayings we've had over the years, we could probably boil it down to just one; one that communicates the meaning of life in a simple sentence. A life philosophy modeled every day by a great man who is no longer with us, but left a legacy of funny sayings, good advice, and lots of love and laughter—my father-in-law Floyd Wheeler. This day and every day the Wheeler Family lives by this saying and urges everyone this New Year to give it a try as well:

Enjoy the journey.

Dating Daddy

Momservation: Locking the bedroom door means never having to explain "naked wrestling."

☺   ☺   ☺

The boy's driven off to go hang out with friends. The girl's been dropped off for a sleep-over. Both were home just long enough to shower, change clothes, and grab supplies for their next adventure. Rinse. Change. Repeat.

Welcome to the pre-empty nest before the Empty Nest.

Don't tell me, "I remember when you couldn't wait for this day come." That is not fair to throw back at me the words of a sleep-deprived, frazzled, repetition weary mother who used the 100 games in a row of Hide-n-Seek to steal a few moments of peace.

Don't tell me, "Careful what you wish for." Let's see what you wish for when you're cleaning up vomit at 3 a.m. right next to the waste can by their bed and the stain of the last missed-toilet hurl while you curse yourself for hydrating them with red Gatorade which now makes your kid's room look like a crime scene.

Don't even tell me, "This is nothing. Wait until they've really left home." Do you also cook bacon and eat warm chocolate chip cookies in front of a Weight Watchers meeting?

Okay, so I'm having a hard time transitioning from my kids needing me all the time to them seeming to need me not at all (except for a stocked fridge, money, and rides). I thought I would be happier than a free-range chicken to be released from car-pool duty, classroom volunteering, and play-date monitoring.

Instead, the silent house haunts me. I get stuck watching the baby pictures of my kids on the computer screen-saver flashing by in a mocking metaphor. I text my son: WHEN ARE YOU GOING

TO BE HOME? debating whether to make up some chores as an excuse for more time with him. I SnapChat my daughter an imploring selfie with the text: WANT TO WATCH A MOVIE TONIGHT? hoping she'll pick plans with me over her friends one night. I tell them both as they rush out the door: "I've got frozen pizzas and drinks if you want to bring your friends by here!"

Pathetic, I know.

So there I was, another night of just me and Hubby at the dinner table, when I stopped focusing on the two empty chairs on either side of me and noticed the handsome hunk sitting across from me. The blue Kyber Construction shirt he wore brought out the blue in his eyes; at 45 still lean and strong from years of physical labor; laugh lines quick to appear with each witty quip; and a full head of hair without any grey (damn him). What was I doing not taking advantage of an empty house with this man?

That's when I realized it was time to change my perspective. While my kids are gone on their own dates, I'm the lucky girl who gets to date their daddy. I wasn't losing time with my children. I was gaining time to date the man I love.

Now when the kids are gone we go to nice restaurants. We walk the dog together. We cook together. We double-date with friends. We go skiing. We go shopping. We go to concerts. We make plans to do fun things together because we are the reason we had kids in the first place—we wanted to share our love with them. If you retain sight of that, it doesn't go away when the kids go away.

And the bonuses? When the kids see us having so much fun with each other, they want to be a part of it. It also just got easier to Netflix and chill.

Still gotta lock the door in case they come home early though.

More Good Than Harm

Momservation: It's inevitable that your little prince or princess is frequently going to be a royal pain.

☺   ☺   ☺

Boy do I miss the days of Time Outs. Not sharing? Sit on the Time Out bench (one minute for each year of age), learn your lesson, go play again. Didn't take? Repeat until they get it. It all seemed so simple.

Ah, the good old days of disciplining your children; when success in course correction meant your kid didn't become known in playgroup circles as The Biter.

With teenagers though…so much more is on the line. At this age, with the choices they're facing—drugs, drinking, driving, sex, and social media—a bad decision could be life altering. It is a scary time to be a parent. You are in constant anxiety that you haven't done enough, that you aren't doing enough to ensure these kids of yours will make good choices.

I find myself second-guessing all my decisions, worrying that maybe I need to be more strict before I find myself a grandma at 45 or maybe more lax so I don't create a master liar.

Now the prison show "Lockup: Raw" tortures me.

When I see all those prisoners I can't help but think: Oh my God! So many mothers crying, "I knew I shouldn't have let Slash go to the drive-ins with those no good bunch of losers!" Or, "If only I had talked to Romeo sooner about safe sex and the dangers of gateway drugs!"

The problem is despite a good 16 years into this parenting thing I still feel like a rookie.

First, I couldn't believe the doctors sent me home with a baby trusting I could keep it alive.

Then during the impressionable toddler years I was paranoid the kids were going to pick up all my bad habits.

During the grade school years I panicked that maybe I was doing it all wrong and it would only become apparent when I had wildly defiant teenagers.

During middle school I was certain that despite my best efforts at any moment my kids were going to go off the rails.

Now in the high school years I'm constantly reminding my kids, "I've never had to parent teenagers before so bear with me as I figure this out!"

And I have always, always prayed every night: "Lord, please let me have done more good than harm."

That's the hard part with parenting—until those kids are solidly in their 20's, holding down a job, showing capabilities of sustaining a mature relationship, and generally being a positive contributing member to society—you won't know if all your hard work to raise mature, responsible, likable adults paid off.

But you have to start somewhere. And raising good kids (like training obedient puppies) essentially comes down to the basics:

Consistency in enforcing boundaries. Reinforce good behavior. Course correct undesired behavior in a way they respond to. And love. Lots and lots of love.

Love when you're so mad at them you scream, "Where's your receipt? I'm sending you back!"

Love when you're so hurt by them you lock yourself in your room and binge watch "Grey's Anatomy."

Love when you're so frustrated by them you fantasize about running away.

Love when you're so disappointed in them you wonder if your perfect child was actually switched at birth.

Love because you know if you didn't love these children with all your soul you wouldn't care what happened to them.

At some point you have to trust that it doesn't matter if you're doing a good job as a parent, just that you're doing your job. You're loving them. You're disciplining them. You're setting boundaries and holding them accountable.

To paraphrase The World's Most Interesting Man: I don't always parent well, but when I do I can watch "Lockup: Raw" without worry.

The Countdown Begins

Momservation: If we didn't look back we wouldn't be able to see how far we've come.

☺   ☺   ☺

It just got real. My son is taking the SAT this month for college admittance. The countdown has begun—I have 19 more months until my first-born baby is no longer living under my roof.

Nineteen months. A little more than a year and a half to soak up what it means to be Logan's mommy on a daily basis.

The feeling of peace and contentment knowing my baby is warm, cozy and safe in his bed, one wall over. The comforting humming of the fan in his room signaling he is home in bed (a Logan white noise necessity since he was four), blowing on him to keep him cool because I won't let him sleep with his window open for fear of someone stealing him.

Hearing all the Loganisms throughout the day that never fail to make me smile:

"Hello, Mommers!" His excited greeting for me every time he arrives back home or even when he just wakes up.

"Scoober-Doober! How come you're so soft and cute?" Every time he goes near our dog, Darby, inevitably unable to resist stopping what he's doing to pet and hug her.

"What's up Wheat?" When he greets Whitney with the latest who-knows-how-or-why nickname he's given his little sister.

"This guy!" His affectionate chuckle for his dad and hero who never fails to make him laugh or feel cherished.

Nineteen months to savor all the things that used to drive me crazy but have recently become signs that my boy is still with me:

-Wet towels on the floor.

-Backpack and shoes dropped right in front of the door.

-Empty Gatorade bottles and Polar Pop Cups wherever he last sat.

-Car keys thrown on the counter and never hung up.

-A stray football, baseball bat, Chubbies swim trunks, camel-pack backpack, In-N-Out gift card, baseball hat, or even stray firecracker left scattered around the house so often that it's created a family inside joke and game: Where Has Logan Been?

Nineteen months to let go of the baby I will always see in this giant, fuzzy man when he flashes his embarrassed smile; His never ceasing excitement to play; His ability to do everything well the very first time he tries it; His constant fidgeting and need to be around people; His easy-going comfort in his own skin (that he seemed to be born with) that allows him to break into song whenever he's happy (almost always) and leave the house unashamed in slippers, short shorts and an oversized, outdated, thrift store Disneyland sweatshirt.

I've already conceded bits of my boy's heart to the new loves of his life: his friends, his girlfriend, his car, his sports, his adventures. I've come to accept the parceling off of the territory that used to be solely mine, because I can see how happy sharing his heart has made him. It makes me proud to witness the growth that can only come from having the courage to leave a safe harbor.

But it doesn't make it any easier preparing to watch my heart take up new residence somewhere with a roommate who will eat his last Hot Pocket and a mini-fridge stocked with Red Bull.

SAT test today—driving off with a car packed with all his favorite possession tomorrow. The hour glass spilling these nineteen months of moments with my son still under my roof has been flipped and I'm desperate to catch every last minute before they all race by me—leaving my home feeling unsettlingly empty and unbalanced.

I hate SAT tests.

Crash Car Challenge

Momservation: It's not bribery—it's reward based encouragement.

☺   ☺   ☺

Well, the "Crash Car" that I wrote about 18 months ago has survived unscathed and will be handed down this month to Teenage Driver #2 in our house. If everyone reading this could just do a collective knock-on-wood right now that would be great.

In case you missed it, a year and a half ago my oldest child entered the distracted driving masses. My neighbor warned me not to spend too much on the first car because it would inevitably end up crashed in some form or another. When I did my own polling, whether it was a knocked off side mirror or complete total, 95 percent of people I asked had, indeed, banged up their first car or had their teenage drivers do the deed.

Not liking the odds of preserving our modest insurance rates, we gladly accepted a hand-me-down 2001 Honda Accord from my sister-in-law for Logan to start with. Saved us a ton of money on insuring a new driver and if Logan fell into that 95 percent—if the worst thing was losing a car valued at less than $1,000, well then, we could live with that. Thanks, Auntie Zann.

As Logan's Class of 2018 began driving, the Crash Cars started piling up. Thank goodness no one has been hurt, but as polls indicated, there were a lot of injured pocket books out there. Since we had another teenage driver waiting in the wings, we built in an added incentive for Logan to keep the Crash Car out of the pileup:

No tickets. No crashes. Maintain a 3.5 GPA the first year of driving and we would allow him to have the Crash Car Upgrade that Nana likes to give all her grandkids. With his eye on a 2012 Mustang prize, the kid pulled it off. Nice work Loganberry.

Next up in the Honda Crash Car: Whitney, age 16.

She is the youngest in her Fab 5 childhood group of friends and last to get her license. Each of the other four has initiated their Crash Car into the 95 percent. On odds alone, it's not looking good that she will join the five-percenters. Judging on permit driving skills...this could be the end of the line for the Crash Car.

However, we've always said that Whitney's stubborn determination, if channeled correctly, would serve her well in life. As president of her class both freshman and sophomore years, Speech and Debate Club high points leader, straight-A student in advanced placement classes, and multi-sport athlete—it's become evident that our youngest child thrives when not backing down from a challenge.

We told Whitney she'd never last as a vegetarian. She's going on year three.

We told her don't be disappointed if you don't make the JV basketball team after not playing since fourth grade when her team was Buzzardball champs. She made the team, averaged 2 points per game, and became their defense specialist.

We told her it's okay if she got her first B in pre-calculous. She landed in the emergency room on Christmas Day because she literally made herself sick studying all hours of the night during finals week to get that A.

So it's a different carrot we'll dangle in front of our strong-willed daughter. It won't be the promise of a nicer car from Nana that motivates her. There's no need to entice her to keep her GPA up. This challenge, and the grace of God, is what will keep her in the five-percenters:

I bet you can't go one month longer than your brother with no tickets and no crashes in the Crash Car.

That should do it. That should keep Whitney and the Crash Car safe. She is her mother's daughter, after all. Tell her she can't do something (especially in comparison to a boy), and she will prove you wrong.

Prove me wrong, Baby Girl. Work your fabulous determination and skills and prove me wrong.

The Better Offer Years

Momservation: Try to act natural if your children still want to be seen with you.

☺   ☺   ☺

We've come up with names for the developmental stages of raising our children: The No-No Years, Terrible Two's, Know-It-All stage, Tweens, and Hormones in Nikes Years.

I've got another one to add: The Better Offer Years.

This is the stage of high school when you and your teenagers have settled into a nice relationship. They've stepped up in maturity and responsibility. There's not as much nagging and yelling. You have intelligent and entertaining conversations together. And the biggie—they're not embarrassed to be seen with you anymore and actually think it's awesome that their friends think you're kinda cool.

Seems great, right? Something to look forward to, even. But here's the down side of the stage where you can finally catch a glimpse of the future Friendship Years with your kids: their car and their friends.

Here's the thing about the Better Offer Years—you're thrilled that your kids are happy to spend time with you…if they don't have a better offer. And they almost always have a better offer when they have the wheels and money to take off on their own and friends to do it with.

I'm going to admit it. It stings a little.

That's because you'll be cruising along, settling into this wonderful feeling of your kids maturing into people who enjoy spending time with you. You're delightfully surprised when you ask if they want to go to lunch with you, or get your toes done together, or go to the movies and they say "Yes." It happens more frequently and you dare to think it isn't an anomaly—your teenagers might actually think you're pretty great!

Now you start making plans that would normally include one of your friends, but since you've been having such a nice time together, you decide to swap it out with one of your kids. You get excited thinking about this great idea for the two of you to do together. You imagine the fun you'll have, the great conversation, the relationship you're cementing.

Then you get this response that's the cold bucket of water on your sizzling excitement: "Ummm, okay, but let me just check to see what Jack's up to."

Translation: I guess I'll hang out with my mom if I don't have a better offer.

That's when you realize all those times you hung out together were because their friends were busy. It's still a lopsided relationship. You want to play with them way more than they want to play with you. You're forced to admit, like the New York Times Best Seller book: *He's Just Not That Into You.*

But you've loved those times when they didn't have a better offer. And you think they did too (ignoring the fact that it's probably because you usually pay for everything). So instead of letting the sting of disappointment keep you from putting yourself out there again for fear of being hurt by their choice, you keep asking if they want to do stuff together. Because you look forward to the times that you are the better offer, you don't take it personally that these are the years when your children's friends, freedom, and independence are everything to them. Sure, you're growing closer to the Friendship Years when both of you look forward to doing things together, but don't be fooled that you're totally there yet.

However, during the Better Offer Years, it sure is nice that you have a day on the books when they can't say "No" to you. We're going to have so much fun on Mother's Day!

Wishing for Time

Momservation: Careful what you wish for. Except for no more laundry. Wish that sh*t away.

☺   ☺   ☺

Boy does Mother's Day look different depending on which side of the diaper bag you're on.

I'm going on year 17 of being a mom but the tears still seem wet from Mother's Day 2001 when I sobbed into my husband's shoulder over how much being a mom sucked.

Granted, the hormones were elevated to Everest proportions because I'd just had my daughter, I was operating on no sleep, in excruciating pain every time I breastfed, and my 17 month-old toddler was a boy in motion who never stopped.

All I wanted for Mother's Day 2001 was to go back in time and slap some sense into the well-rested woman with the still perky boobs before she turned to her husband and said, "I think it's time to start a family."

Now, as I sit in my quiet house that I wished for at least a half-dozen Mother's Days, tripping over the discarded clutter of my children that I requested to escape from for another half-dozen Mother's Days, the tears are falling again.

Three more years. That's all I get with my messy, loud, bickering, forgetful, procrastinating, exasperating, all-consuming kids under my roof.

It's not enough.

Being a mother doesn't suck at all. It's the best thing I've ever done with my life.

From the mornings when my early-rising son would bump the side of my bed hoping to wake me so I would play with him, to my sassy baby girl standing up to bullies twice her age in the sandbox, being the mother of my two children has been the absolute joy of my life.

They make me proud, they make me laugh, they make me feel valuable, they make me keep perspective on what is really important in life. And I love that every morning I have two reasons under my roof to drag my overscheduled and exhausted self out of bed giving me purpose to enjoy the journey.

Every evening and every morning since the day they were born I touch the precious heads or cheeks of my children and thank God that he chose me to be their mother. I will never stop being their doting mother, but the privilege of laying my hands and eyes on them each day for an instant boost to my soul will only last a few more years.

Now all I want for Mother's Day is more time with them.

More time with these amazing individuals whom I somehow, amazingly, didn't mess up but have somehow managed to set on an impressive course.

From our evening ritual where I lovingly plant a kiss on the stubbly cheek of the son who now dwarfs his big-boy bed to the baby soft cheeks of my sophisticated daughter who still takes charge of life, I will never be able to get enough time with my two children.

But I'll take what I can get. I will cherish these last years of having them under my roof each night. Long gone are the Mother's Days when I just wanted to be left alone and for no one to utter the word "Mom." Forever etched on my heart will be the day I turned to my husband and said, "I think it's time to start a family."

What a wonderful wish to come true.

CHAPTER 6

Operation Independence

Momservations® for the Road

- There is a special place in heaven for mothers who still love their teenage children.
- Sometimes it's a shame kids need to be fed regularly.
- It's all fun and games until someone's signing your cast.
- Listening to the constant bickering between my kids makes me regret all the time I spent teaching them how to talk.
- A boy and his Xbox are soon parted when a note from a teacher comes home.
- It's a girl's prerogative to change her mind and her BFF more frequently than underwear.
- Definition of a miracle: Getting everyone in one household to agree on which TV program to watch.
- No matter how many bathrooms you have, there'll still be a fight over the bathroom.
- It's very hard for teenage children to believe that Mom didn't come into this world as a fully developed mother.
- Comedians are born at the dinner table.
- A slumber party for girls requires a completely different survival plan than a slumber party for boys.
- If everyone expressed their love like kids and dogs the world would be a better place.
- Every day is April Fool's Day to a sibling looking to mess with another sibling.
- Too bad nagging your kids doesn't burn more calories.
- It's not summer until you see a kid riding their bike to the local pool with a towel around their neck.
- If Google knows more about you than your best friend—it might be time to revisit your privacy settings.
- Sometimes setting a good example for your kid is no fun at all.

Working Girl (and Boy)

Momservation: You better have a catapult in your arsenal for Operation Independence just in case there is a Failure to Launch.

☺   ☺   ☺

The freeloading is over. It's time for our teenage boy to realize In-N-Out burgers don't grow on trees and our teenage girl to understand that if you have to pay for it yourself, $30 mascara is not a necessity. It's time for a summer job.

Real summer job too. Not working for Dad like last year. No big secret, but Dad is a pushover when it comes to his kids. Let's just say someone was very well paid for zero construction skills and had schedule flexibility that allowed for emergency runs to the river to go skim boarding with buddies.

My 16 year-old daughter has actually worked the last two summers as a junior leader at a kids' camp—albeit for free. The experience earned her a paid position as a camp leader this year, but that didn't stop Dad from giving in to Whitney's exceptional negotiating skills last year and kicking down a cash payout for her community service hours. He held firm until she pointed out she worked harder for free last summer than a certain son did on the payroll.

With college looming for both our kids in the next two years, Hubby and I decided it was time to see the kids flap their wings as part of Operation Independence. It was time for the official First Job; the one with a paystub and that awful FICA person taking their cut. The kind where you might have to tell your buddies you can't go because you can't get off work. The kind where if there's an event you just can't miss, you have to find someone to work for you. Welcome to the real world type of job.

To be honest, we didn't have to encourage Whitney to take this leap. When she first told us she wanted to be a kids' camp junior leader the summer before her freshmen year of high school I was the one who protested thinking of the summer plans already in place. "But you'll have to work every day of the whole summer!"

"Only a half day, Mom," she said. "I'll still have the other half of the day left."

"But you're not getting paid!"

"It's okay. I'm doing it with Katherine. It'll be fun."

Okay, so maybe Dad isn't the only softy around here.

Not to be outdone by his soaring sister who had her summer job secured by March, Logan, 17, worked hard on…thinking about getting a job somewhere. Maybe.

"Where do you think you might want to work this summer, bud?" we asked nudging him toward the edge of the nest.

"I'm not sure."

"What kind of work do you think you'd be interested in doing?"

"I don't know," Logan said stoking our Failure to Launch anxiety.

"Don't you think you should start applying for a summer job here soon?"

"Yeah, probably." Not a flap of the wings to fly.

It wasn't until we polled all his friends where they'd be working this summer that Logan finally let go of his FOMO (Fear Of Missing Out), because all his buddies were working this summer too. With one more nudge toward a great job for him, he followed through and secured his first official job—a kids' camp leader at a local sports club. We thought it was perfect because it matched his skill set: playing outdoors and playing with kids. He was excited for the dress code.

"Mom! I get to wear my Chubbies and Rainbows!"

I doubt he can rock the short shorts and flip flops like I rocked my straw hat from my first job at Straw Hat Pizza though.

Do You Let Your Teen Uber?

Momservation: If I wanted my kids to like me all the time, I wouldn't be their parent.

☺   ☺   ☺

I'm excited! Hubby and I are officially in the You're So Unfair! Everyone Else is Doing It Club!

I know many of you have probably long been inducted into this club by your preteen or teen regarding SnapChat accounts, going to parties with no parents, and riding in cars with a new driver before a year. But, amazingly, it took us until our kids were 16 and 17 to reach this level of contempt.

And why are we such horrible, awful, unfair, out of touch parents? Because we won't let our kids Uber—specifically to parties and with no set plan for the evening. Call us old fashioned, but we're just not keen on paying a total stranger to drive off with our teenage daughter.

Trust me, during more than a few standoffs we've heard all benefits of Uber and how everyone else has no problem letting their kids play Driving Miss Daisy with Mommy and Daddy's credit card. But before we take this to the Court of Public Opinion, let's review some of the arguments that have been debated in the Wheeler house:

Argument:
"We want to Uber because we can't drive past 11 p.m. for the first year of our license."
Counter argument:
"Suddenly you care about what's legal after driving your friend around all day on a provisional license?"

True Translation:

"I'm planning on breaking curfew and don't want to also get a ticket while I'm at it."

Argument:

"We all want to go to the party together and not have to drive by ourselves."

Counter Argument:

"You can't all park and walk into the party together?"

True Translation:

"Nobody wants to drive to the party because there might be a few vodka Gatorades going around."

Argument:

"We have a ride there but we don't have a ride home and we don't want to wake you to come and get us."

Counter Argument:

"Has this ever stopped you before as your personal chauffer for the last 16 years?"

True Translation:

"We don't want any parents to pick us up because then they'll know we've been drinking or smoking pot."

Argument:

"We're not sure what we're doing yet but I do know the group I want to go with is Ubering."

Counter Argument:

"Sounds like you need to make a plan and find a different group."

True Translation:

"We don't want to tell you our real plan because we know you'll say no and Ubering is the best way to get away with it."

Here's the deal: I'm not knocking anyone's parenting if you let your kids use your Uber account or set one up for them. Everyone has their reasons. I know for some of my friends, they're trying to be realistic about the pressures of underage drinking. Don't ask, don't tell, just take Uber and get home safe. Some are tired of being chauffeurs or they don't have enough cars for all the drivers, or because of the expense of car ownership.

Maybe, like accepting social media as the modern form of communication for teens, Uber is a modern convenience for getting around.

But I'm just not there yet. My kids have cars. We even pay for their gas and insurance. So why am I going to pay someone else to drive you around when you have this privilege?

I know, we're just so unfair.

We Were So Fearless. What Happened?

Momservation: How does a generation of fearlessly unsupervised kids turn into a bunch of hyper-vigilant parents anxious to send their kids away to college?

☺   ☺   ☺

We were badass weren't we?

We survived riding in cars without seat belts, riding in backs of trucks with our dogs, riding bicycles without helmets.

We drank from hoses, ate raw cookie dough, and played on swing sets that could've killed us.

We fell out of trees, stacked it being pulled behind bikes on our roller skates, and wore out the bottoms of our shoes using them as brakes down the monster hill on our Big Wheels—because we actually played outside for fun.

But heaven forbid we let our children apply for a college without visiting it first.

What happened to reckless abandon? What happened to ignorance is bliss? What happened to literally flying by the seat of our pants?

Kids are what happened to us.

And in one generation it made us Helicopter Parents who try to shield our kids from failure and disappointment, dutifully smoothing out challenges and adversity, while making sure they want for nothing.

With a start like we had, what made us become so skittish?

Maybe we are so over-protective of our children because we look back and do surprisingly realize we made it out of our childhoods alive—there are damn good reasons for seatbelts, helmets, and safer playgrounds.

Maybe we look back and wonder where the hell our responsible parents were when we were building half-pipes so we could drop-in on a skateboard from the roof. Or who had no clue where the heck we were and what the gall darn we were up to between the hours of breakfast and dinner.

Our generation didn't visit colleges to make sure it would be a good fit. Getting into college at all was a good fit! You picked San Diego State for the beaches you heard were there or you picked Chico State because you heard it was a party school and it's what your parents could afford. And you could do it with a 2.5 GPA, without an essay, and for $350 a semester.

Okay, so those days are gone (in California anyway) along with the wind through your hair in the back of a Chevy Stepside on the freeway.

So, maybe that's what makes us arrange our vacations around college tours and help our kids select a university like an arranged marriage. (She better be a looker and get you out in four years for our $40k a year!) We want to make sure we are the responsible parents that our parents, for all evidential purposes, were not. And that includes making sure our kids get that good college education that sets you up for a much better shot at a heck of a good life (rather than just surviving it).

So as much fun as I had cheating death on merry-go-rounds, walking barefoot in glass filled creek beds, and squeaking into college because I didn't know any better, I'd rather not leave my children's future to ignorance or chance.

I wonder if we have enough frequent flyer miles to go see Arizona State?

A Long Over-Due Apology Letter to My Parents

Momservation: I'm sorry. I get it Mom & Dad. Now will you please lift the I Hope You Have One Just Like You curse?

☺   ☺   ☺

My son just had his last first day of school last week. The senior portraits came in the mail today. His first senior event, the Senior Picnic, is this weekend. The Reality Bus has run me over while I was dragging my feet to the next stop.

The Baby is now the Bearded Wizard and he's filling out college applications.

Good thing I was wearing clean underwear when I got mowed down by a speeding senior year.

As I laid flat on my back breathing into a paper bag, I reflected back to my own senior year of high school. (Only moments ago, right?) I pictured my son doing everything that I had done that last crazy, wonderful, over in a blink-of-an-eye, surreal leap toward adulthood.

And I realized I needed to write my parents a long over-due apology letter. I get it now, Mom and Dad, and I am so so sorry. It only took 28 years for me to realize what a self-absorbed, insensitive, clueless sh** I had been during that time when I was so eagerly getting ready to take flight from home.

Now I desperately hope my own son won't be that way to me; That he'll recognize my fragile state and go easy on me as the thought of my baby growing up and out crushes my lungs, cinches my throat, and causes permanent stinging in my eyes.

So here goes Mom and Dad. I hope this apology letter will convince you to release me from the I Hope You Grow Up And Have A Child Just Like You curse.

Dear Mom and Dad,

I'm sorry.

I'm sorry that when I was a senior in high school I didn't understand how saying things like, "I can't wait to get the hell out of this place!" was a stinging slap to the face and heart of parent who had tried their best to provide a supportive, loving, home for 18 years.

I'm sorry that I applied for schools as far away as possible just to show you I was ready to be independent.

I'm sorry I thought going anywhere other than my hometown had to be so much greener than our grass.

I'm sorry that I never once considered how hard it would be for you to see me leave, possibly forever, after 18 years of working hard and putting your life aside for the sake of my security and happiness.

I'm sorry I never imagined how quiet and lonely and devoid of my cherished presence our house was when I tried to spend every waking minute being with my friends instead.

I'm sorry for all the times I forgot to call you to tell you I arrived safely or changed my plans or thought it wasn't that big of a deal that I forgot.

I'm sorry I used you as a personal ATM machine without even offering a clean room as the simplest return payment.

I'm sorry that I thought I was so much wiser, more knowledgeable, and thought I knew better than you did what was best for my future.

I'm sorry for the risks I took thinking I was invincible and immune to danger and repercussions of poor decisions

I'm sorry I didn't know all the sleepless nights you stayed awake shouldering the burden of my defiance and irresponsibility.

I'm sorry I fought you on boundaries that I couldn't see I needed to keep me from making a mistake that would change the course of my life forever.

I'm sorry I didn't appreciate the room you did give me to find my own way and discover my own path.

I'm sorry I never noticed the toll it took on you to watch me hurt and suffer over life's heartaches and injustices that help us grow as people.

I'm sorry I didn't hug you more and tell you how much I loved you at a time when you could have really used it.

I'm sorry when I left I didn't think to look back.

I'm sorry I only called you when I needed money.

I'm sorry it took me so long to appreciate you and thank you for giving me a reason to want to come back home.

Thank you for everything even though I was such a**hole.

Love, your enlightened and eternally grateful daughter,
Kelli

Last Laughs Club

Momservation: Doesn't matter to your kids what you've achieved in life as long as you're the maker of pancakes, kisser of boo-boos, and player in make-believe.

☺   ☺   ☺

I still remember my first hate mail like it was yesterday. It was only my second column for Inside Arden as their new family columnist. The subject that provoked such angry responses?
Preschool.

'Cause you know, you just can't talk religion, politics, or preschool with friends or family if you want to maintain harmony.

The column, *Preschool Panic* (May, 2004), was a recounting of the panic I felt when I realized my two year-old son was already behind in school because I had neglected to tour any preschools yet or have him on the waiting list for the Big Four preschools in our area. In the apparently hyper-competitive world of preschool my kid was doomed. Now he was never going to Harvard (insert eye-roll here).

Some people took exception to my poking fun of putting babies on preschool waiting lists in utero. You would have thought I was a child abuser by daring to say I believed a child would be fine without formal preschool as long as you provided an enriching environment.

But guess what? As president of the Last Laugh Club I now get to say this to my detractors (which include people who scoffed at only breastfeeding for three months): Despite not going to a traditional preschool my kid turned out just fine. He's healthy. He's happy. He's smart. And with his good grades and test scores he is poised for college next fall.

So why, 15 years later, am I panicking all over again? Because:

A) I swear I just wrote that column yesterday! How can my first born child who didn't go to a Big Four preschool but a neighborhood daycare three days a week, suddenly be a high school senior? It's September and there have already been senior portraits, Senior Sunrise, Senior Picnic, and his very last Back to School Dance. It's going too fast!

B) Once again everyone with kids my age are stopping to ask me, "So where is your son going to go to school next year?" Then they count off all the schools they've already toured, but instead of being local preschools its colleges all over the United States! Instead of preschool waiting lists its SAT/ACT test prep courses. And if I don't have a college advisor on speed dial, my kid is never going to Harvard.

Who knew that preschool and college acceptance could be so similar and so stressful? But to head off another round of hate mail, let me say this before I continue:

A) Yes, early childhood education is important. However, you can achieve it many different ways and you don't need the most popular, most expensive, nor hardest one to get into to have your child succeed.

B) Yes, a college education is important. However, you can achieve in many different ways and you don't need the most popular, most expensive, nor hardest one to get into to have your young adult succeed.

I know I live in a community that has a high population of college educated parents. We all understand the value of a college degree and its correlation to success. It is a fact that getting into and paying for a California university is not nearly as easy nor affordable as when we earned our degrees. But before we all panic and put too much pressure on our kids let's remember this:

A) There are more than the Big Four colleges out there for our kids (Cal, Stanford, USC, and UCLA). There are thousands of colleges out there including community colleges. And like my friend, Jen, likes to say about our Sacramento State degrees, "We ain't doing too bad with our ol' Harvard of the West degrees are we?"

B) Bottom line is we just want our kids to be happy. College degree, skilled trade, military, entrepreneur— you get out of life what you put into it. Pursue your passion and with dedication and hard work success follows. Didn't get into your top choice school? Go get educated at the one that does want you. Enjoy the journey.

And for all you new parents who have just switched to formula and don't have your kid on a preschool waiting list yet— we're accepting new members in the Last Laugh Club.

Little Loganberry

Momservation: If you're going to miss the hell out of your kids when they leave home, then you've done a great job creating good people for this world.

☺   ☺   ☺

You were due the day before Halloween, but I hoped you would come early because I didn't want you to be doomed to Halloween themed birthday parties for the rest of your life. In Lamaze class when we were urged to write down what we hoped our baby would be I put a blue-eyed, brown-haired little boy. I wanted you to have your daddy's eyes but my complexion. I wanted a big brother who would one day protect his little sister. I had to keep a kick-count card to make sure you were still moving around in there. The doctor wanted 10 kicks in a half hour. You would give me 10 kicks in two minutes. I had three dreams you would be a boy so I was certain it was true. When Daddy (who never remembers his dreams) said he dreamed of the perfect name for you—Logan—I wasn't convinced it would suit my first born child. Logan Wheeler just didn't sound…presidential enough to me.

I'd just finished my last parent-teacher conference, held a week sooner than the rest of the fifth grade teachers in case you decided to come early. I swear I had just thought, "Ok, you can come out now," when the first contraction came. I felt like I was giving birth to a little prince because we were the first to use the new birthing suite at Kaiser South Sac and we had the whole maternity floor to ourselves it was so quiet on October 24, 1999. I was pushing to the sound of the Yankees playing the Braves in the World Series. Dr. Udofia said you'd be born when the Braves got a hit. You arrived at 8:30 p.m. just as Chipper Jones finally broke a shut-out in the ninth inning with a lead-off single.

Gammy likes to say your hair was born first because you had a thick head of hair when you were born, and blue eyes like your daddy—who cried tears of joy when he realized he had a healthy son. Your cry was gentle and undemanding and when the nurse floated you in your first warm bath, you quickly quieted into contented repose. Everyone crowded into the spacious birthing suite to welcome you: Nana, Pa, Gammy, Grampa, Auntie Zann, and even Mommy and Daddy's best friends, Brian and Jen (with Jen just months away from giving birth to your very first best friend: Meghan).

Daddy was right. You were a Logan. A precious, sweet Little Loganberry.

During the nine months you grew inside me, Daddy and I imagined often who might be in there and what you would be like. Funny how you and God gave us all these clues, but we were too inexperienced to understand that the Logan we would one day come to know and instantly love telegraphed who you were from the beginning: A very busy boy with beautiful blue eyes like your daddy with your mommy's olive skin. Our sweet, sensitive, little prince who hates to be late, a rule following pleaser and leader who watches over his sister, makes friends easy, and is a great athlete—especially at baseball and football; who still loves soaking in the hot tub.

I can't believe you are already 18, Logan. An adult in the eyes of the law, but forever our Little Loganberry. Where others see a big, strong, bearded man with thick John F. Kennedy hair and looks, Daddy and I will always see our first-born baby. The day I had you my heart began walking outside my body. These years under the same roof have been too fleeting; such an achingly short portion of what I hope will be a wonderful and beautiful life. I will always thank God for choosing me to be your Mommy and

I'll never stop praying for your good health, happiness, and safety. Our door will always be open waiting for my heart to come home. Enjoy the journey, Little Loganberry.

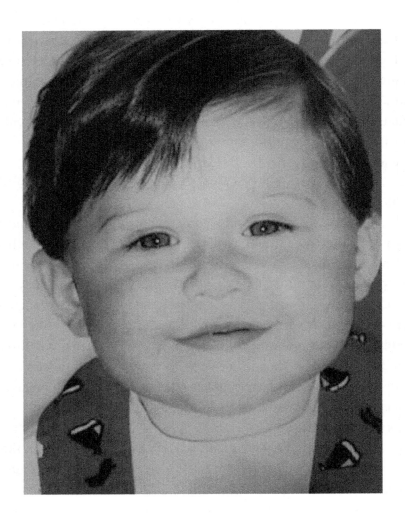

My Little Lady Bird

Momservation: The best way to teach a daughter how to love herself is to be a mirror of loving yourself.

☺   ☺   ☺

Have you seen the Oscar nominated movie *Lady Bird*? You know the opening scene where the mother and daughter start getting under each other's skin and then Lady Bird throws herself out of a moving car? My daughter and I had a good laugh over that because as we both said in unison:

"You'd totally do that."

"I'd totally do that."

Like the mother/daughter characters of *Lady Bird,* Whitney and I just took a college tour trip together. We decided to go down the California coast so that I could share with my beach loving baby a stretch of her home state she'd never seen, but absolutely had to experience while checking out the colleges that met her criteria: Must be on or near the beach.

Unlike the movie mom and daughter, I think Whitney would agree, currently, we have a pretty fantastic relationship. As we've grown closer to the Friend Zone, she has come to respect me as a mother who will always enforce the boundaries and I've come to appreciate her as a daughter who will always test the boundaries. The running joke during our coastal college's tour:

Me: Let me know if you're going to throw yourself out of the car so I can slow down.

Whit: Deal.

It wasn't always like this. There was a lot of work put into taming my wild stallion. There was a lot of resisting the confines of a corral. There were tears. From both of us. There was yelling

379

from both us. There were typical tween accusations of, "You just don't understand," and there was hot button pushed retorts of "Oh, just try me, sister. The House always wins."

When Whitney's apple-doesn't-fall-far-from-the-tree stubbornness showed itself before she was even potty-trained there was a summit meeting between her dad and me:

Me: We need to channel this into good instead of evil before the teenage years hit.

Her dad: Good luck with the mini-me.

When Whitney and I had a prepubescent blow-up (over who knows what anymore) and we both went angrily storming off to our corners, slamming doors behind us, it was up to Dad to negotiate the peace treaty.

Dad: Whitney, I think you owe your mother an apology.

Whit: No. Mom owes *me* and apology.

We worked it out, both apologizing, but let's just say I'm glad we weren't driving in a car when the showdown happened.

And here we are now. Whitney is turning 17 this month. I could not be prouder of the woman she has blossomed into. The stubborn girl who always needed to push the boundaries and would take a lie to the bottom of the ocean like a captain going down with his ship? Three-year president of her student class, points leader in Speech & Debate Club, Camp Kids counselor— two year volunteer, two years paid. Friend to any and all.

Powers used for good instead of evil.

Me? I promised to never write about her again unless she approved it. I made sure to bite my lip instead of saying, "See? I told you so." I learned to be the adult in the room and bury my Hot Button in the backyard so it couldn't be pushed. I gave her room to grow. I gave her room to make mistakes and learn from them. I took Whit's suggestion to check my judgmental self and abide by my early declaration:

"You always say, 'Kids are works in progress,' Mom."

"Yeah, but so are moms too, Whit."

Basically, we learned to cut each other some slack. And in doing so we've put ourselves on the path to mutual respect and friendship. Which we recently celebrated in a fun trip together down the California coast taking selfies along the way in fields of yellow mustard, at a wind-whipped lighthouse, on a Santa Barbara beach at sunset.

Happy birthday Itty Bitty Whitty Little Girl So Pretty. Let's do it again sometime soon. But don't you dare unbuckle that seat belt.

Setting Sail in 86 Days

Momservation: Don't cry that it's over. Be happy it happened.
~Dr. Seuss

☺   ☺   ☺

Eighty-six days. He's still here for 86 days.

Some days, like today, the panic and sadness that it is ending and it will never be the same overwhelms me. But that sorrowful dungeon is too dark a place to reside. So I remind myself that he is still here. And he will, God willing, always be here. It will just be different.

I try to remind myself that different can be good too. The changing seasons and the beauty that comes with each transition is proof of that. But then in these last days of high school when I walk by his empty room, still not cleaned like I asked him, I imagine it different: bed permanently made, sports uniforms retired, no perpetual wet swim trunks on the floor, no fuzzy head poking out from the covers providing me relief that he is safe, a place of vibrant living and laughter turned museum to a past life.

Different then feels unbearable. It is a shot to the heart that makes me shut his door and force myself to say, "Live in this moment. He is still here. Eighty-six more days to cherish this time."

This time. This time of raising my first-born son has been an absolute gift. A series of growth and changes that left sweet memories and hints that the best was yet to come.

I loved when he was born; Making me a mother and bringing with him a realization that love can be so much deeper and stronger than we could ever imagine or describe or promise.

I loved when he was a toddler; Seeing the world again through his eyes of wonder and enthusiasm, sharing with him the joys of this life, being this little person's safe harbor of unconditional love.

I loved when he went off to school; Watching him tentatively venture out into open waters, discovering new joys outside of his family and interests that began to shape him, creating friendships that enriched him, and gaining an education that enlightened him.

I loved when he was a teenager; Feeling pride in his growing positive sense of self, the evidence of his talents and gifts, seeing a maturity, independence, intelligence and kindness to others validating that we did something right with this kid.

I loved it all. Every minute. The trials with the triumphs. The heartache with the hope. The love and laughter.

Now he is leaving in 86 days to go to college; a grown man eager and ready to explore what the open ocean brings.

As his mother, this transition has become a leap of faith. Like a bungee jumper frozen on the edge of the bridge, eager for the experience but fearful of taking that necessary step to launch the adventure, I must trust that the chord will hold.

His father and I have raised the man we had envisioned when we first talked of building a family: Smart, strong, compassionate, loving, kind, confident, adventurous, optimistic, funny, thoughtful, generous...plus all the qualities that make him uniquely himself.

And independent.

We knew and hoped one day he would leave our safe harbor and set sail for his own adventure. And we hoped that the foundation of unconditional love and support and family would inspire him to not only come back home one day, but to expand that love with his own family.

If I look at it that way, this transition seems bearable. I will love this next stage just the way I loved all the others. Yes, it stings a little more now that his growth will no longer be happening under my roof, under my loving and watchful eye, in the safety of my harbor.

But you cannot swim to new horizons if you don't have the courage to lose sight of the shore. For him. For me.

He'll leave in 86 days. But he'll be back. He'll be different. I'll be different. But it will be a beautiful new season.

Boise Bound

Momservation: Are we ever prepared for the next great thing to enter our lives?

♥   ♥   ♥

He (we) did it!

By the time you read this Logan will have graduated high school and committed to going to Boise State University this fall.

You might run into me in the corner of the grocery store produce aisle, looking very emotional over mushrooms, but really, this is a joyous occasion.

It's exciting and exhilarating, a relief and a reward for all that has been done to achieve this goal by all parties invested in my son's success. Proud doesn't have enough letters in it convey the breadth of our emotion.

But there is also anxiety, sadness, and trepidation for what my house, my life, and my family will feel like without my baby boy under my roof each night.

If this is what we've been preparing for my son's whole life—creating a well-rounded, intelligent, kind, independent individual ready to seize the day and explore the world—why do I feel so unprepared for it?

Logan, for the record, is not. He's got his duffle bag packed with some Chubbies shorts, a few tank tops, his flip flops and toe-shoes. He'll be grabbing his hammock, longboard and bike on the way out eager for the adventures that await and the many friends who will be joining him in Boise along with the new ones he'll make. Dad has been reminding him that the purpose of this next chapter is to get a college degree, not just adding to his collection of adventures. Logan assures us he's focused on this next goal, but the packed skim board and skis say otherwise.

In between bouts of crying over Chex Mix in the Costco isle (Logan's favorite snack) and bursting into tears passing the Little League field (He was just playing T-ball!), his Dad and I are trying to live in Logan's excitement. We are trying to be present in his enthusiasm for discovering for himself all the wonderful experiences and opportunities of college life that we still count as some of the best times of our lives. We are constantly reminding ourselves that there is joy to be found in seeing your kid eager to go collect the things that will make them the best versions of themselves.

That is the space I'm trying to live in instead of the sorrowful slide into the quicksand of "Never Again." How do you prepare for never again making the same exact school lunch for 12 years? Never again heading to the ball field on Opening Day? Never again watching your son perform under Friday Night Lights? How do you prepare for never again kissing your son's fluffy head goodnight each night, or having him come in and hug you when he gets home whispering, "Goodnight, Mommer"? Or never again having a reason to enter his messy room that will soon become strangely clean and unlived in?

Never Again is too hard of a place to live in. I'd much rather live in the bright light of Logan's opportunities, the excitement for his possibilities, and the warm glow of a job well-done helping mold this wonderful individual—whom I will always get to call my son. No matter where he goes. No matter what he does. No matter who he brings into his amazing orbit. He will always be my Little Loganberry and I can always hold out hope that one day he'll return. For semester breaks. For holidays. For random visits. To bring his own family one day. To soak up the love that will always reside for him in this home, his first home, his forever home.

I'm not prepared for this chapter to end because it's been so great, but are we ever prepared for the next great thing to enter our lives? New memories will be made, new routines to become the norm, new chapters to write that will be equally cherished.

Do as you've been taught Little Loganberry and go enjoy the journey. Go to Boise and go do fabulous, wonderful you, Logan. And if you don't come back…I hope your new home is somewhere Mommer and Dad will enjoy having a condo!

Class of 2018

Fridge Magnet Mom

Momservation: If you can't beat them, be the first one the hell out of there.

☺   ☺   ☺

Fridge Magnet Mom strikes again! I came up with another good one to add to my growing list of quotables worthy of a refrigerator magnet. Apparently, I do this so often my daughter coined the nickname. I don't even realize I'm doing it until my daughter calls me out.

"If cake mix goes on sale you buy it," I told Whitney excitedly snatching up four boxes of cake mix with no birthdays in sight. "You always gotta be ready to bust out a cake or cupcakes," I told her in earnest like it was ancient wisdom.

"Okay, Fridge Magnet Mom," she laughed rolling her eyes.

After a good giggle we realized I should be writing down all of these quirky bits of family wisdom doled out over the years—especially with Logan going off to college this month. It would be fun to send him off with a playful list of life lessons to help him navigate his way as he takes off into adulthood. My kids already have **MOM'S TOP TEN RULES** that I came up with nearly a decade ago that I think have guided them pretty well. In fact, like Robert Fulghum's popular "All I Really Need to Know I Learned in Kindergarten" my top ten rules can actually be applied by adults to daily life as well.

Like your own family sayings and words of the wise, there's some you say so often it becomes family motto. Others are lost after the moment has passed, but then one day when you realize you always light a match after going to the bathroom you remember Dad once told you, "Always leave it smelling better than when you went in."

So here's a sampling of some Wheeler Wisdom. Feel free to put them on your own refrigerator courtesy of Fridge Magnet Mom:

- Nothing good ever happens after midnight.
- In this family we do extra credit.
- Stay away from U-Haul trucks on the freeway. Any maniac can drive them.
- Never quit in sight of the finish line.
- Always leave it better than when you got it.
- Pet every dog and cat you see.
- Make good choices.
- If one is good, two is better.
- Always buy the good toilet paper.
- Trust that the cream always rises to the top. Be the cream.
- Deodorant can buy you another 12 hours.
- If you ate all the ingredients of a chocolate chip cookie separately it's disgusting. But eat it all together and it's delicious.
- Always sniff it first.
- There is no good reason not to stop for a Slurpee on a 100 degree day.
- Lying by omission is still lying.
- Always stop at lemonade stands.
- Remember everyone is a work in progress.
- If cake mix goes on sale you buy it.

Going Full Golden – Part I and II

Momservation: "Making the decision to have a child is momentous. It is to decide forever to have your heart go walking around outside your body." ~ Elizabeth Stone

☺   ☺   ☺

I left my heart in Boise five days ago. I still have the emotional shits over it. I think today I'm going to go two spoons deep into some raw brownie mix for a shot of happiness. My husband, my dog, and my high school senior daughter would say:

"What about us? Don't we make you happy?"

And to that I'd say:

"Without you, I would be going 'Full Golden'."

"Full Golden" is what my friend, Wendy, has dubbed the complete emotional meltdown of saying goodbye to your kid at college.

I'm going to tell you the "Full Golden" story now because I search out people who make me happy when I am sad. I don't want to read any more commiserating articles about how hard sending your kid off to college is and that we will survive it.

I know I will survive it, but in this moment it sucks. I just need to live it and get through it. There are perfectly functioning adults walking around with grown children, so obviously this stage has a happy ending and solid poops at some point.

In Part I of sharing my story of dropping my first born son off to college, let's share a laugh instead courtesy of Wendy. If you're feeling like a masochist and want a peek at my own going Full Golden moment, feel free to keep reading Part II.

Part I

Hubby and I are almost to Winnemucca, Nevada, half-way into the 8-hour drive home to Sacramento after dropping Logan off for his first year at Boise State University. Amazingly, we haven't touched the tissues we bought when we were leaving town (shortly after Hubby had to use an old, emergency, bottom of the center console Chipotle napkin immediately after the goodbye when the surge of tears caught him by surprise). Maybe the barren, ugly, long-stretching highway through endless sagebrush has lulled us into numb trance. We just want to get through the desolate dessert and get home to the daughter waiting for us.

That's when I get a text from Wendy, who is 2 hours behind us and who has just said her parking lot goodbye to her daughter outside the dorms at Boise.

THAT GOODBYE WAS ROUGH!

Wendy and I like to keep it light so Hubby tells me to text her:

AT LEAST YOU HAVE WINNEMUCCA TO LOOK FORWARD TO.

It gave her the laugh through her tears that she needed before admitting that her husband, Tim, took it especially hard. She then told me about a Golden Retriever they saw have an equally hard time:

WE SAW THIS PUPPER LAY DOWN AND NOT MOVE. I ASKED THE WOMAN IF HE WAS OK AND SHE SAID THIS IS THE LAST PLACE HE SAW HER DAUGHTER AND HE WASN'T GOING TO MOVE. SHE THEN GOT DOWN ON THE GROUND AND GAVE HIM A LOT OF LOVE.

Wendy followed it up with this sad picture with the text caption:

THIS IS WHAT TIM DID WHEN WE GOT BACK TO
THE CAR. DID'T MOVE AND JUST CRIED. SORRY, TRUE
STORY.

Now it was my turn to laugh/cry.

A few hours later Wendy hits Winnemucca (whose welcome sign actually says: "Winnemucca. Proud of it," because they can hear from every passing vehicle, "Who the hell would live here?!"). She reports that they are doing better after some ice cream and good-natured family teasing. Wendy and her youngest daughter have come up with a new phrase for a complete emotional melt-down after leaving your kid at college:

WE NOW CALL THIS GOING "FULL GOLDEN"

I knew my Full Golden moment would probably be as soon as I opened my front door and noticed my son's Labrador-like energy missing. But instead of thinking about that I sent Wendy this picture with this text caption:

HOPE YOU'RE OUT OF NEVADA. DON'T PICK UP HITCHIKERS.

For those of you who would rather laugh through your tears STOP HERE. For those of you who need to bleed to know you're alive...keep reading.

PART II

I don't want my son to read this. It's not fair of me, as he embarks on this awesome journey, to hold him back with worry about how his mom is doing without him.

Because he would worry.

Because he's a good kid.

And that's one of the many reasons why I do miss him so much.

It's Drop Your Kid Off at College Season and there are aching hearts all over this country. Mine is not unique.

I almost didn't even write a blog about it because there already seems to be an oversaturation of sharing words of wisdom to get through it.

At some point you can't prepare for it anymore, you just have to do it and live through it.

But as a family columnist who has guided parents through the joys and pitfalls of raising a family, not writing about the reality of your kid leaving home would be like being left with a cliffhanger ending.

So I'm sorry if you read this, Logan, and it makes you worry about me. Please don't. I'll be fine. We moms and dads are tough. If we can make it through the three delirious sleep-deprived months of you waking up every three hours to be fed, and the time your heart broke over not making the team, and watching you suffer the pain of two knee surgeries relegating an otherwise healthy, active kid to the sidelines of life for six months, we can get through this.

Every night of your entire life, for nearly 19 years I've prayed to God to please bless you with good health, happiness, and safety.

And as I left you in Boise, you indeed were healthy, extremely happy, and safe. My prayers are being answered. What is there to cry about? So, stop reading. This isn't for you. Go live the life we've dreamed for you since before you took your first breath. Dad and I are truly thrilled you have taken over the writing of your story. We know it will be amazing. We look forward to the roles we will get to play in these next chapters. Thank you for letting us watch you grow up.

♥   ♥   ♥

When people ask me how I am doing I tell them: It's a confusing mix of happy and sad. I'm happy for my son. I am sad for me.

Here's the reality: I'm not ready to get used to my kids not being around; for that to be my new normal—a quiet, empty house with two place settings at the table and no reason to restock the Rec Room fridge and snacks. I loved taking care of my kids. I loved the family chaos that having children brings. I was good at it. Plus, I just really, really like who these kids turned out to be and having a front row seat to where they were going.

Here's the truth: I have been walking around with a vice-grip around my chest since before my first-born left for college. Each thought of my son (and his group of friends) leaving and taking their infectious energy with them, squeezed me tighter until I felt I couldn't breathe.

I started crying over Chex Mix, processed turkey, my placid and empty pool…because these favorites of Logan's would be left behind.

When it actually came time to say goodbye, I was okay. He was so happy already in his new home, my heart was lifted. I think for the 8-hour car ride through the ugly Nevada desert I was numb that it actually happened. My child had flown the nest.

But when we pulled into the driveway and saw his beloved car sitting there where it would not move until Thanksgiving, the uncontrollable tears burst forth again.

I kept checking myself because my husband was trying so protectively to hold it together so only one of us at a time would succumb to the sorrow over his absence. I checked myself because I didn't want my daughter to witness the pain of a child leaving— I didn't want to burden her with worry for me when she leaves this time next year.

But the weight of my sense of loss was crushing me inside. Everywhere I looked in my house was the ghost of my son's childhood that had promised to linger, but instead raced away like a kid playing tag.

I couldn't even escape it in sleep, as I dreamt of hurricanes and huge waves crashing—symbolic for big changes and emotional upheaval.

The first morning without my son, my daughter left to go to breakfast with friends (adding to the theme of my children leaving me), and my husband went to get eggs. Finally alone, like a wounded animal, I looked for a place to curl up and hide until I was better.

I found myself in my son's strangely clean and quiet room, curling up in his comforter that smelled like him.

And that's when I went Full Golden—a complete emotional breakdown caused by my kid leaving for college. I released the ache that had been gnawing away my insides and I sobbed out every bit of the 60% of water that my body is made of. I cried so hard and so loud, that my yellow Lab grew concerned and raced over to try to lick away my tears.

For the sake of my worried dog, I calmed myself. Finally releasing the sorrow for this chapter of my life being over was the watershed I needed. Raising Logan was an amazing story that I had written for him. Like any good story, I'm sad it ended even if it did have a happy ending. I wanted to reread it again and again because it was so good.

But as I looked around Logan's room searching for solace, I realized none was to be found there. I was in his empty cocoon. He was now a butterfly who had taken everything with him that makes him Logan and flew off to his new life. Why was I wallowing in his stripped shell instead of marveling at his beautiful transformation?

I dried my tears and got out of his bed. I resisted the temptation to shut his door to shield me from it's now Museum of Logan status.

It was time to accept that it was Logan's turn to write his story. I am no longer the author; he is. I no longer have a front row seat to his unfolding life. I'm now going to have to wait for excerpts through texts, FaceTime phone calls, and SnapChats.

I'm not going to lie. It hurts. I've been binge drinking up the moments of my children's lives for the last 19 years. Then I drop my son off at college and am forced to go cold-turkey. The withdrawals are rough.

But it's necessary. It would hurt more if after raising my son he didn't leave. I would have felt like I failed him if I had never given him the tools, the security, the craving to go out into the world and write his own story.

It's been five days since I went Full Golden. The vice-grip, as promised by my friends who have survived their own children leaving home, has indeed loosened day by day. The waves of sorrow seem to be gently lapping at my feet now instead of crashing down on me. I still have one more year with my daughter, my last child, and I want to give her the best of me for her last year at home. He had the courage to leave. I need to have the courage to let him.

In the meantime, my son has sent us excerpts from his new chapter of life. His dad and I have been sharing excerpts from ours. These first few pages of are pretty promising. I think we are writing a great new sequel.

Have a wonderful adventure, my heart. Lord, please keep him healthy, happy and safe.

Yo Ho, Yo Ho! A College Life for Me!

Momservation: We have entered the years where your college kid now knows "Studying at the library" was actually code for "$1 Pitcher Night at Key Largo."

☺   ☺   ☺

Crack open the lid of Ben & Jerry's Chocolate Fudge Brownie—Baby Girl is going to college!

Okay, well, she has completed all her applications and submitted them, and we don't know which college she's going to yet…but still a time to rejoice with ice cream!

We've reached the final leg of the Child Rearing Years with applying for college signaling the Bell Lap.

We've got one finisher already celebrating up in Boise who you would think has just won the Olympic Decathlon. Our oldest has literally been waving from a float in a parade (for Homecoming) and we've seen so many women-draped pictures of him at parties that his grandpa has wondered aloud, "Is he majoring in Girls?"

And now I have Baby Girl sprinting to the finish line.

She CANNOT wait to go to college. At his point, I don't think she cares which one, although one with a beach nearby would just be the gold medal around her neck.

About a month ago we took her to a Cal football game at UC Berkeley. She loved the Big Game experience, but the fraternity row with their pre-game parties raging with all types of attractive co-eds had her at "Taco Tuesday." As soon as she got home she wrote not one BUT two UC application essays.

The next weekend we went to Boise for Family Weekend and she stayed in the dorms with her brother. After they dropped us off at the hotel each night to "Tuck the parents into bed" Baby

Girl got the college version of night life. I don't think it included a tour of the library.

She promptly came home and in seemingly two clicks, applied to Boise State and University of Hawaii, Monoa.

Two weekends ago she went and visited friends and her cousin going to colleges in San Diego. There were SnapChats of her on the beach, in the dorms, at apartment "kickbacks," and generally not missing being home with her parents in the least.

Her CSU applications were sent before she had even finished dumping the sand out of her travel bag.

The last leg of the College Application 4x4 was finishing her last two essays and having her college counselor look over the application. When the opening day of UC submission came and went on November 1 without the big finish, I thought maybe Baby Girl had finally hit the wall.

But then her brother, who has no classes on Fridays, texted her last Thursday:

IT'S THE WEEKEND!!

She finished her essays.

Another text on Tuesday:

COLLEGE SURE IS HARD! GOT WINE WEDNESDAYS TOMORROW, A FRATERNITY/SORORITY ICE SKATING SOCIAL ON THURSDAY, AND A FOOTBALL PRE-GAME PARTY, TAILGATER & GAME ON FRIDAY!

The last of her applications were submitted that night.

So Baby Girl is going to college and we can thank (I think?) her brother for giving her the second wind to finish strong.

The dreaded college application process is completed. Now we just wait to see what school is going to officially make me and Hubby Empty Nesters. *Sniff*

But there's no tears from Baby Girl. Uh uh.

She sees that red tape marking the finishing line of a stellar prep performance. And though she has some preferences for which college is holding it, at this point she just wants to break through it and start the celebration.

So now it looks like we need to tell Whitney what we are constantly reminding her brother: "You know you're going to college to get a degree, right?"

Where Is Home Going to Be?

Momservation: I don't care if you're a Bronco, Gaucho, Bear or Bruin. I just need to know where your new home will be and how I can get to you.

☺   ☺   ☺

It's March and to most people that means Spring is a few short weeks away with hopefully the promise of warmer days.

Or maybe it means it's time to stop procrastinating getting your taxes done.

Or for my Irish friends—is there any other reason for March than St. Patrick's Day and its season pass to get really drunk and group-sing loudly?

Ah, but for the parents of high school seniors, March is the month that the obsessive checking of college portals will finally end and reveal its truth to anxious parents and seniors alike.

Either your mantra of "Hard work pays off" will be validated or you'll be discredited as a sage and wise parent while your devastated child sobs, "You lied!" and declares their life officially ruined.

So, yes, March is coming in like a lion in my household and it would save us a lot of drama if it will go out wearing a UC Santa Barbara sweatshirt.

But as the date approaches for California universities to let seniors know if they have done enough to be accepted (or lucky enough, which it must come down to, when over 100,000 freshmen apply to go to your school), I realized my own anxiety for my daughter isn't really about what school she'll get into.

It's about dying to know where she'll end up living, possibly for the rest of her life.

Yes, through the fall application season there was hard focus on what my daughter's next academic chapter would look like. As I proof-read her college essays and reviewed her applications for missed dotted "i's" and crossed "t's" the anxiety over what schools to apply to and who would see my senior for the asset to their community that she would undoubtedly be, was off the charts.

I think we both might have cried in relief that it was done and in angst over the achingly long time to find out where she would land.

Now that we are here in March, with a handful of state and out-of-state schools already throwing their doors open for her (which Dad likes to point out: "See? You're going to college. Now chill."), we apprehensively and excitedly wait to hear from the schools my daughter has had her sights on from the beginning.

But in those quiet moments when I look beyond March, when my daughter knows what her choices are for higher education, I realized it isn't about her being a Gaucho or a Bruin or a Bear.

For me, her mother, I just need to know where her new home will be.

My daughter will be leaving me. She will be going to San Diego or Santa Barbara, or LA or Berkeley. I need to know how long it will take me to get to her. I need to know what I'll need to do to get her home for visits. I need to start checking the cost of airfare.

And I need to start accepting that wherever she lands, there is a great possibility that it will become her new home, possibly forever.

Because that's the truth about going off to college. There are three likely reasons your kid will never come back:

1. They meet a significant other from that area or who wants to stay in that area.

2. They find jobs and make connections in that area.
3. They fall in love with that area and put down roots.

I know. All three happened to me. I never went back to the Bay Area. Sacramento has now been my home since I was 19. And Sac State wasn't my dream school. Honestly, it was pretty low to the bottom.

So, there in itself, is another sage and wise life lesson as we wait through these anxious days of March: Your life isn't over if you don't get into your top choice schools. You get out of it what you put into it, so whatever school wants you, love it back. You might be surprised when you realize that it wasn't sunny, beachy San Diego you thought you would call home, but that dark-horse Sacramento that for nearly 30 years has given you a pretty great life.

And will always be my son and daughter's home away from their new homes.

For My Daughter's 18th Birthday:
Keep Doing Fabulous You

Momservation: The goal is to have our daughters always believe they are as smart, beautiful and talented as they felt at 5 years old.

☺   ☺   ☺

You were **born** with a smile on your face and laughter in your heart.

Before your **first year** you were already trying to keep up with your big brother, walking, talking, and having Pa dub you "Me Too!" after your favorite phrase.

By **two** we already knew we had a fire cracker, refusing to leave "Time Out" because you weren't going to say you were sorry—confident already it wasn't your fault and you were right. You also were a budding comedian just like your daddy. When a toot would slip out, with deadpan delivery you'd inform me: "Put THAT in your baby book!" before looking at Daddy and you both cracking up.

At **three,** just like your brother 17 months older than you, you were riding a bike without training wheels. He couldn't do anything without you, you were his courage to try new things, a little curly-haired blonde girl leading the charge any time he said, "Come on, Whitney, let's go." He taught you how to jump your bike off a driveway ramp and itty-bitty you marched off to show him things like how to pass the swim test to be allowed to go down the water slide at a party.

When you were **four** I thought I was about to witness your first rejection when you asked an older boy at the park sandbox if you could play with him and his friend and he turned his back snarling, "We don't want to play with you." Instead of rushing over to comfort you, I watched you scooch over to them anyway with your bucket and shovel and declare, "Well, I'm going to play with you." Not knowing what to do with such assertive friendliness they gave in, turned back around and all three of you did, indeed, play together.

At **five** I watched you go down with your ship in a lie over spitting out your vitamin in the garbage. Despite irrefutable proof of finding a freshly unchewed chewable vitamin in the bathroom waste basket, you stuck to your story, never wavering in your innocence and flabbergasted as to where that exact same color vitamin I just gave you could have come from. That is when Daddy and I realized we needed to make sure your confident stubbornness was going to be channeled into something productive so you would use it for good instead of evil.

We were sitting at the dinner table when at **six years-old** you announced you would be singing in the school talent show. You wanted to do a Hannah Montana solo, but I made you do it with a friend, worried you had underestimated the power of stage fright. There was no fear in sight when you belted out "If We Were a Movie" with your buddy, Meghan, and everyone gushed not over your singing talent, but your radiant charisma.

At **seven**, you came home and shared that there was a new girl in your class. As you excitedly described your new friend, I started to pick up on her probably being a little Black girl. No matter how I tried to get you to describe her physical characteristics, you never said the color of her skin. You simply didn't see her as any different than you.

In third grade when you were **eight**, you won third place in the school Spelling Bee. I was so impressed you out-spelled sixth graders. You were mad you didn't get first.

At **nine** you and your teammates won the 4th Grade Girls Buzzardball Basketball Championship at Arco Arena where the Sacramento Kings played. Again, the confidence was higher than the ability as a shooter, but you were a white-on-rice smothering defender. Victory was yours again, literally, in another arena.

As a **ten year-old** fifth grader, you decided you could use more friends (though you had plenty) and started doing Lunch With Friends where you ate lunch and played with the kids from the special needs class. When you shared that you had been doing that for some time, on your own, you didn't see it as doing something extraordinary but rather, "Why wouldn't I?"

You came home in sixth grade, **11 years-old**, and announced you signed up for the Science Olympiad. After a few practices you quit, not in defeat but self-awareness. "I'm smart, but I'm not THAT smart," you shrugged without a hint of self-pity.

At **twelve**, middle school finally shook your confidence. Trying to find your place in a pecking order of popularity, wanna-be's and queen bees, you weren't willing to sacrifice your authentic self to be with the "In Crowd." I asked you to trust me, to continue to take the high road, because the cream always rises to the top. "As kids mature, they learn how to sort through the bullsh*t and they begin to value what really matters," I promised, hoping you could survive middle school with your amazing self-worth still intact.

In eighth grade at **age 13**, you joined the social media scene, and I did everything I could to protect you, guide you, and save you from yourself (and predators) as we navigated this Brave New World of being social through phones. It was a delicate dance of confidence being built up with one "hecka urb" post only to be torn down with online hate.

At **fourteen** you entered high school and on legs of shaky confidence, but brave determination, decided to run for Freshmen Class President against stiff competition. Not only did you win, your class, who recognized cream when they saw it, also voted you Homecoming Princess.

You became Sophomore Class President at **fifteen** and as if that, volleyball, basketball, and getting straight-A's in Honors classes wasn't enough…you decided to do Speech and Debate Club where you regularly made it to the final Super Congress rounds—many times as the only female. Dad and I were so proud of you using your powers for good instead of evil.

At **sixteen** you got your driver's license and inherited The Honda from your brother. If only your ability on the road then was as strong as your confidence that you were an awesome driver. No question continuing to do a great job as Junior Class President.

It's senior year and in your **17 years**, all the wonderful things you have put out there as you being you, the rewards have come back to you. You are ASB President. Your peers voted you Homecoming Queen. You have mentored kids your entire high school career as both coach and camp counselor. You will be a Valedictorian. You will be going to your dream school, UC Santa Barbara in the fall. And through it all you have had a smile on your face and a laugh in your heart.

You turned 18 at the beginning of this month. All the early hints of the amazing person you were going to be turned into the promise of a kind, compassionate, smart, talented, beautiful, stubbornly confident young woman ready to take on the world.

Dad and I would like to take some credit, but from the moment you were born you have been doing fabulous you. All we added was unconditional love, support in good times and challenging times, and the promise that we would always be here for you. You took it from there.

So in this month of your birth, and every day before and after, Dad and I would like to say: "Thank you, Lord, for choosing us to be Whitney's parents."

Why Be the Apple When You Can Be the Orchard?

Momservation: I've never been prouder that my little apple is rolling away from her tree.

❤   ❤   ❤

She did it!

Baby Girl didn't just graduate from high school—she graduated with a neck-full of honors including Valedictorian! To celebrate she's thinking of sending the Valedictorian medal to her middle school math teacher, Mr. Friedrich, who gave her the only "B" she's ever gotten (and still thinks she didn't deserve).

That's my girl. The little apple who fell right directly below my tree.

Not the ubber-achiever part—that's all her. The "I'll show you" and "oh, just try to tell me I can't do something" part, I think I passed on to her in the womb. But she has likely been taking notes from this mom who bristles and goes into full fight-back mode at the slightest signs of underestimation.

So the fact that my daughter kicked butt and took names through high school—4-year president of her class and school, Speech & Debate president and high honor seal-bearer, National Honor Society and California Scholarship Federation member, Distinguished Scholar, Scholar Athlete, special needs camp volunteer, and kids camp counselor—landing her in her top-choice college, UC Santa Barbara, wasn't just hard work paying off.

It was likely to show that "Logan's little sister has a name" as she used to sassily tell the kids in middle school who called her by her brother's name rather than her own. They were going to know her name—Whitney Wheeler—alright. But along the way she earned more than their respect for ambitious achievements.

As one of many friends put it in her senior yearbook: "You are the most driven, encouraging, caring, funny, sweet, and beautiful person on this planet. You push me to be a ray of sunshine just like you."

That right there…that's what made me cry and swell up with pride at this finish line of trying to raise good kids. Yeah, my kid graduated high school with honors, but she's a damn good human being first.

Her yearbook is full of friends telling her how sweet and kind and caring and positive she is. She even had her student government teacher write that if he had a daughter, he'd want her to be just like her.

Oh man, where's the tissues? I'm crying again.

Didn't cry one drop at graduation, though. Hearing Whitney's name called for Valedictorian and then as she got her diploma? Just happy dancing and overzealous rejoicing because these are important milestones that will set you up for future success. It is the culmination of raising a child to be a contributing member of society and getting them off to a good start in life. High fives all around. We did it! She did it!

But being a good person? That's what takes you furthest in life. It's ongoing. It's not an honor or achievement, but an instilled value and principle—a personal choice. There is no greater achievement in my book than trying to be a better person today than you were yesterday; forever at the top of your To Do List.

Did she get that from me? I hope so. I've modeled it the best I can. I'd be lying if I didn't admit many days I settled for being a mediocre person and some days I had to apologize to the Big Guy for not taking the higher road.

But that's where my little apple has sprouted legs and has headed off to see what else is beyond the tree line. She will never settle for being mediocre. She has a fire and a passion to discover all the amazing things Whitney Wheeler can do. She has the determination to explore beyond what people say are her limits. And she has an innate ability to see everyone as a friend with a level of tolerance and compassion for others that is awe-inspiring to me.

This is where the tree now learns from the little apple.

We've raised Whitney to be the best person she can be while enjoying the journey, but she has, on her own, made it a priority to make sure that her high tide raises all boats.

You go Baby Girl. Go out and plant your orchard. You are going to grow the most amazing apples.

Epilogue

Designated for Reassignment

Momservation: From what we get, we can make a living; what we give, however, makes a life. ~ Arthur Ashe

♥   ♥   ♥

We call it around here the Mother's Day 2001 T-shirt. It's the one with the mascara stain right about where a supportive shoulder to cry on would be. Through the years when it has been worn by Trey, more as a reminder of my husband's prophecy that it will eventually get easier, it has served as a lingering reminder that these days of raising children do truly fly by.

You will hear it from veteran parents starting in the exhaustive newborn days all the way through to the heart-wrenching last days of senior year: *the days are long but the years are short*. Given stock in Tesla every time someone tried to use those words to cushion the fall, we'll all be flying to Mars here soon.

Yet still, the house is awfully quiet today.

Obviously, now that I'm a mostly work-from-home Empty Nester, a quiet house shouldn't be surprising anymore.

But since I've been going through 16 years of my Momservations® parenting columns for this book, you can imagine how haunting a quiet house can be.

Don't get me wrong—I've been transitioning nicely to it just being me, Hubby and Darby dog now. There are definitely perks:

- My time is my own, not dictated by my kids' needs.

412

- Regular Date Nights and going out with friends.*
- A flexible calendar of fun things to do that are not planned around school activities, fundraisers, or my kids' sports/extracurricular events.*
- My dog never talks back, argues, ditches me for her friends, or wants money from me.
- …and my favorite: My kids' problems are their problems now.**

*At least before Covid-19 and hopefully again soon.
**Until they call home trying to make it my problem.

But as I sifted through nearly 1,000 of my parenting tales, causing me to both laugh out loud and tear up with nostalgia…yeah, I miss my kids. I can't believe the heavy lifting of raising them is over. It still feels strange that I have been designated for reassignment.

My job now is to just listen and support my young adult kids.

After 20 years of actively parenting though, to suddenly be removed from duty feels like a proud little tugboat being sent to the scrap yard.

I've been and still am a pretty darn good mommy. I have invested everything of myself into my family. I have enjoyed all the dividends that come with putting all my stock in parenthood. (Though it turned out my particular stock matured and provided the best residual benefit once my kids could wipe their own butts and noses.)

But of course, my husband was once again right (Did I say that out loud?), as were the wise Confucius-like offerings of well-meaning parents who had been there, done that, and had their own mascara-stained T-shirt.

This phase of raising my children did all happen in the amount of time it takes for a mother to look at her child for the first time and fall in love.

In the end, it's time for the Mother's Day T-shirt of 2001 to be retired. I haven't needed it in a long time as reminder that some days children may cause the bottom to fall out of your market. But choosing to start a family has been the best investment in happiness I've ever made.

#EnjoyTheJourney

Acknowledgements

First and foremost, I need to thank my children, Logan and Whitney, for making me a mother, giving me so many hard to edit down pages to write about, letting me write about (most) of it when you realized what I was up to, and for being the best things that continue to happen to me. Of course, it wouldn't have all happened without my partner in this wonderful adventure, Trey, who has always been my biggest supporter (as long as I "keep it clean"), an amazing bookend to the story of raising our greatest achievements and enjoying the journey, and for kicking off this rewarding chapter of our lives by saying, "I guess it's time we hit the workbench."

I am deeply grateful to Inside Publications for giving me my big break into becoming a professional writer and a platform to "write what you know" and brand Momservations®. Thank you to my publisher, Cecily Hastings, for giving me an unrestricted forum to entertain our community with the adventures of raising my children and recognize the village it took to do it, making us feel like we were all one family in it together. A warm and heartfelt thanks to my editor of nearly 15 years, Marybeth Bizjak, who saw the potential for a family column in an unsolicited submission about a mommy's group. Your belief in me, guidance as a veteran writer, and wise words that no matter how successful you get, "writing for your community is the most fulfilling writing you'll do," have kept me inspired on this journey.

I am beyond grateful to Maria Shriver for elevating my platform by hiring me to write for her. Seeing me as a talented writer, comrade in the trenches of motherhood, and friend gave me the confidence to believe that my gift for writing deserved a wider audience. Thank you for the opportunities you've offered, including all the times you turned to someone and said, "Here's someone you should check out." Your support of fellow writers and mothers is a gift I continue to pay forward.

Thank you to my editing fairies: Jan, Michelle and Shirley for helping me find the right mix for this book from nearly 1,000 columns and blogs. Thank you also to Gerry Ward at I Street Press for being my technical support. Without your help I'd still going in circles.

Thank you to my Queens, Jen, Mel, Michelle, Kim, Mindy, Christy, Julie, Amy, Traci and the two Laura's, my tribe of second-mothers who consider my children one of their own, my wagon-circlers for when the going gets tough, who gave my kids their first best friends, and the women I am lucky enough to call my friends (or just call when it's time to whine with wine).

A super big hug and squish to my mom and dad who were the best examples of leading with love, surviving the unimaginable, and never missing an opportunity to cheer successes and lift up from failures. Thank you for instilling in me the belief that I could achieve any goal I worked toward and that God always has better days ahead. Thank you to my second mom, Shirley, and prophet in enjoying the journey, Floyd, and the bonus family you've given me.

Finally, thank you to the inspiring students in my memoir writing class (who my husband calls "The Kelli Fan Club"), for encouraging me to create a "greatest hits" collection for them to enjoy, pushing me to do what I do for them: Believe that you have a great story to tell that's worth sharing with others.